The European Union's Roles in International Politics

This original book analyses the international roles of the European Union by exploring key elements of role theory.

Utilizing both conceptual and empirical arguments, the collected authors provide an innovative perspective on the analysis of the EU as an international actor, and on the ways in which EU actions are formed and have impact. The book:

- Develops a conceptual framework for considering and evaluating the role(s) played by the EU in international politics, drawing upon the literatures of role analysis, international relations and European integration.
- Pays particular attention to five aspects of role analysis: role conceptions, origins of roles, role institutionalization, role performance and role impact. These form themes running through the volume and are dealt with in individual contributions as appropriate.
- Provides applications and empirical cases supporting the conceptual framework, so as to demonstrate the utility of role analysis in relation to the EU and its international activities, and its capacity to inform investigation from different perspectives and standpoints.

This topical volume will be of particular interest to researchers and scholars of international relations and EU politics.

Ole Elgström is Professor of Political Science at Lund University, Sweden.
Michael Smith is Professor of European Politics and Jean Monnet Chair in the Department of Politics, International Relations and European Studies at Loughborough University.

Routledge/ECPR Studies in European Political Science

Edited by Thomas Poguntke

University of Birmingham, UK

and

Jan W. van Deth

University of Mannheim, Germany, on behalf of the European Consortium for Political Research

The Routledge/ECPR Studies in European Political Science series is published in association with the European Consortium for Political Research – the leading organization concerned with the growth and development of political science in Europe. The series presents high-quality edited volumes on topics at the leading edge of current interest in political science and related fields, with contributions from European scholars and others who have presented work at ECPR workshops or research groups.

1 **Regionalist Parties in Western Europe**
Edited by Lieven de Winter and Huri Türsan

2 **Comparing Party System Change**
Edited by Jan-Erik Lane and Paul Pennings

3 **Political Theory and European Union**
Edited by Albert Weale and Michael Nentwich

4 **Politics of Sexuality**
Edited by Terrell Carver and Véronique Mottier

5 **Autonomous Policy Making by International Organizations**
Edited by Bob Reinalda and Bertjan Verbeek

6 **Social Capital and European Democracy**
Edited by Jan van Deth, Marco Maraffi, Ken Newton and Paul Whiteley

7 **Party Elites in Divided Societies**
Edited by Kurt Richard Luther and Kris Deschouwer

8 **Citizenship and Welfare State Reform in Europe**
Edited by Jet Bussemaker

9 **Democratic Governance and New Technology**
Technologically mediated innovations in political practice in Western Europe
Edited by Ivan Horrocks, Jens Hoff and Pieter Tops

10 **Democracy without Borders**
Transnationalisation and conditionality in new democracies
Edited by Jean Grugel

11 **Cultural Theory as Political Science**
Edited by Michael Thompson, Gunnar Grendstad and Per Selle

12 **The Transformation of Governance in the European Union**
Edited by Beate Kohler-Koch and Rainer Eising

13 **Parliamentary Party Groups in European Democracies**
Political parties behind closed doors
Edited by Knut Heidar and Ruud Koole

14 **Survival of the European Welfare State**
Edited by Stein Kuhnle

15 **Private Organisations in Global Politics**
Edited by Karsten Ronit and Volker Schneider

16 **Federalism and Political Performance**
Edited by Ute Wachendorfer-Schmidt

17 **Democratic Innovation**
Deliberation, representation and association
Edited by Michael Saward

18 **Public Opinion and the International Use of Force**
Edited by Philip Everts and Pierangelo Isernia

19 **Religion and Mass Electoral Behaviour in Europe**
Edited by David Broughton and Hans-Martien ten Napel

20 **Estimating the Policy Position of Political Actors**
Edited by Michael Laver

21 **Democracy and Political Change in the 'Third World'**
Edited by Jeff Haynes

22 **Politicians, Bureaucrats and Administrative Reform**
Edited by B. Guy Peters and Jon Pierre

23 **Social Capital and Participation in Everyday Life**
Edited by Paul Dekker and Eric M. Uslaner

24 **Development and Democracy**
What do we know and how?
Edited by Ole Elgström and Goran Hyden

25 **Do Political Campaigns Matter?**
Campaign effects in elections and referendums
Edited by David M. Farrell and Rüdiger Schmitt-Beck

26 **Political Journalism**
New challenges, new practices
Edited by Raymond Kuhn and Erik Neveu

27 **Economic Voting**
Edited by Han Dorussen and Michaell Taylor

28 **Organized Crime and the Challenge to Democracy**
Edited by Felia Allum and Renate Siebert

29 **Understanding the European Union's External Relations**
Edited by Michèle Knodt and Sebastiaan Princen

30 **Social Democratic Party Policies in Contemporary Europe**
Edited by Giuliano Bonoli and Martin Powell

31 **Decision Making Within International Organisations**
Edited by Bob Reinalda and Bertjan Verbeek

32 **Comparative Biomedical Policy**
Governing assisted reproductive technologies
Edited by Ivar Bleiklie, Malcolm L. Goggin and Christine Rothmayr

33 **Electronic Democracy**
Mobilisation, organisation and participation via new ICTs
Edited by Rachel K. Gibson, Andrea Römmele and Stephen J. Ward

34 **Liberal Democracy and Environmentalism**
The end of environmentalism?
Edited by Marcel Wissenburg and Yoram Levy

35 **Political Theory and the European Constitution**
Edited by Lynn Dobson and Andreas Follesdal

36 **Politics and the European Commission**
Actors, interdependence, legitimacy
Edited by Andy Smith

37 **Metropolitan Governance**
Capacity, democracy and the dynamics of place
Edited by Hubert Heinelt and Daniel Kübler

38 **Democracy and the Role of Associations**
Political, organizational and social contexts
Edited by Sigrid Roßteutscher

39 **The Territorial Politics of Welfare**
Edited by Nicola McEwen and Luis Moreno

40 **Health Governance in Europe**
Issues, challenges and theories
Edited by Monika Steffen

41 **Republicanism in Theory and Practice**
Edited by Iseult Honohan and Jeremy Jennings

42 **Mass Media and Political Communication in New Democracies**
Edited by Katrin Voltmer

43 **Delegation in Contemporary Democracies**
Edited by Dietmar Braun and Fabrizio Gilardi

44 **Governance and Democracy**
Comparing national, European and international experiences
Edited by Yannis Papadopoulos and Arthur Benz

45 **The European Union's Roles in International Politics**
Concepts and analysis
Edited by Ole Elgström and Michael Smith

Also available from Routledge in association with the ECPR:

Sex Equality Policy in Western Europe, *edited by Frances Gardiner*; **Democracy and Green Political Thought**, *edited by Brian Doherty and Marius de Geus*; **The New Politics of Unemployment**, *edited by Hugh Compston*; **Citizenship, Democracy and Justice in the New Europe**, *edited by Percy B. Lehning and Albert Weale*; **Private Groups and Public Life**, *edited by Jan W. van Deth*; **The Political Context of Collective Action**, *edited by Ricca Edmondson*; **Theories of Secession**, *edited by Percy Lehning*; **Regionalism across the North/South Divide**, *edited by Jean Grugel and Wil Hout*

The European Union's Roles in International Politics

Concepts and analysis

Edited by Ole Elgström and Michael Smith

Routledge
Taylor & Francis Group
LONDON AND NEW YORK

ecpr

First published 2006
by Routledge
2 Park Square, Milton Park, Abingdon, Oxon OX14 4RN

Simultaneously published in the USA and Canada
by Routledge
270 Madison Ave, New York, NY 10016

Routledge is an imprint of the Taylor & Francis Group, an informa business

Typeset in Baskerville by Wearset Ltd, Boldon, Tyne and Wear
Printed and bound in Great Britain by TJI Digital, Padstow, Cornwall

British Library Cataloguing in Publication Data
A catalogue record for this book is available from the British Library

Library of Congress Cataloging in Publication Data
A catalog record for this book has been requested

ISBN10: 0-415-39093-1 (hbk)
ISBN10: 0-203-08641-4 (ebk)

ISBN13: 9-780-415-39093-4 (hbk)
ISBN13: 9-780-203-08641-4 (ebk)

Contents

Illustrations

Figures

Tables

Notes on the contributors

Lisbeth Aggestam, PhD, is a research fellow at the Swedish Institute of International Affairs. Her most recent books include *A European Foreign Policy? Role Conceptions and the Politics of Identity in Britain, France, and Germany* (2004) and *Security and Identity in Europe* (co-edited 2000).

Chad Damro is Lecturer in Politics at the University of Edinburgh. He has written a number of journal articles and contributions to edited volumes on the European Union in international affairs and transatlantic trade, competition and environmental relations.

Ole Elgström is Professor of Political Science at Lund University. He has published articles on negotiation and mediation in the EU in several international journals and is the editor of *European Union Council Presidencies* (Routledge, 2003) and the co-editor (with C. Jönsson) of *European Union Negotiations* (Routledge, 2005).

Sébastien Guigner is a PhD student in the Centre for Research on Political Action in Europe (CRAPE) (CNRS–IEP of Rennes–University of Rennes 1) and assistant lecturer in political science at the IEP of Rennes (Institute of Political Studies).

Knud Erik Jørgensen is Associate Professor in the Department of Political Science at the University of Aarhus. He has (co-)edited six books on international relations and EU politics. He has published in several journals and contributed numerous book chapters. He is preparing a *Handbook of EU Politics*.

Bart Kerremans, PhD (Universiteit Antwerpen), is Associate Professor of International Relations and American Government, KU Leuven. He teaches courses on international relations, IPE and American government and conducts research on EU and US decision-making with regard to WTO-related trade policies.

Sonia Lucarelli teaches international relations at the University of Bologna. Her areas of interest include IR theory and European security. She has *inter alia* edited *La polis europea* (2004), *Mobilizing Politics and*

Society (with C. Radaelli, Routledge, 2005), and *Values and Principles in EU Foreign Policy* (with I. Manners, Routledge, 2006).

Ian Manners is a Senior Lecturer in Political Science at Malmö University. His research interests include European integration theory and the EU's external actions. He has edited *Values and Principles in European Union Foreign Policy* (Routledge, 2006) with S. Lucarelli.

Stefania Panebianco, PhD, is Associate Professor of Political Science at the University of Catania where she teaches International Relations and Political Science. She is the editor of *A New Euro-Mediterranean Cultural Identity* (2003), the author of *Il lobbying europeo* (2000) and has published various articles on EU politics.

Ulrich Sedelmeier is Senior Lecturer in International Relations at the London School of Economics and Political Science. He is the author of *Constructing the Path to Eastern Enlargement* (2005) and co-editor (with F. Schimmelfennig) of *The Politics of European Union Enlargement* (Routledge, 2005) and *The Europeanisation of Central and Eastern Europe* (2005).

Helene Sjursen is Senior Researcher at Arena Centre for European Studies, University of Oslo. She has published on European foreign and security policy, EU enlargement and transatlantic relations.

Karen E. Smith is Reader in International Relations and Director of the European Foreign Policy Unit at the London School of Economics. She is the author of *The Making of EU Foreign Policy: The Case of Eastern Europe* (2nd edn, 2004), and *European Union Foreign Policy in a Changing World* (2003).

Michael Smith is Professor of European Politics and Jean Monnet Chair in the Department of Politics, International Relations and European Studies at Loughborough University. He has written widely on the external policies of the EU: his publications include *Europe's Experimental Union* (with B. Laffan and R. O'Donnell, Routledge, 2000), and *International Relations and the European Union* (edited with C. Hill, 2005).

Richard Whitman is Head of the European Programme at Chatham House. He is on secondment from the University of Westminster, where he is Professor of European Studies. He is the author of *From Civilian Power to Superpower?* (1998), and editor (with I. Manners) of *The Foreign Policies of European Union Member States* (2000).

Alasdair R. Young is a Senior Lecturer in International Politics at the University of Glasgow. His research focuses on the interaction between trade and regulatory policies and politics, with particular reference to the EU and the World Trade Organization.

Series editor's preface

In the era after the invasion of Iraq cynics might be tempted to maintain that there is little to write about the European Union's role in international politics. Yet, another way of looking at the same events clearly shows that the EU was an important political actor in the developments leading to the invasion of Iraq – if only because of its inability to agree on a common stance. In any case, the current volume demonstrates that the EU's involvement in international politics is much wider, multifaceted and theoretically challenging. The editors and authors of this volume approach their subject with the methodological tools of role theory in order to get a better grip on the theoretical and empirical problems posed by the EU as an actor in international politics. It is the peculiar tension between similarities to nation-state foreign policies and the uniqueness of the EU which confronts analysts with conceptual difficulties, and the current volume shows how role theory can make a valuable contribution to the analysis of the EU as an international actor. Essentially, roles are conceptualized as 'patterns of expected behaviour' (Introduction) which clearly mould actual political action. Following an explicitly pluralistic approach, the book combines conceptual pieces with analyses of attempts by the EU to act as a norm exporter and the EU's role in multilateral negotiation settings.

Lisbeth Aggestam's chapter on role theory serves as a framework of analysis (Chapter 2) and emphasizes that role conceptions in foreign policy are determined not only by material factors but also by historical, cultural and societal characteristics. Arguably, both sets of factors seem to work in favour of a multilateralist role for the EU but Knud Erik Jørgensen argues that there is substantial variation across policy areas and a more differentiated interpretation captures the reality better. Sonia Lucarelli addresses the importance of shared political values for the political identity of the EU based on the belief in peace through co-operation among former enemies (Chapter 3). The next two chapters focus on the normative role of the EU and adequate conceptualizations (Chapters 4 and 5), while Richard Whitman re-examines the concept of 'civilian-power Europe' and concludes that 'the '*status quo* in the EU's foreign, security and defence policy remained largely unaffected by the war in Iraq' (Chapter 6). The chapters by Ulrich Sedelmaier, Stefania Panebianco and Karen E. Smith look at the actual performance of the EU assuming the role as a norm exporter in the enlargement process (Chapter 7), in the Mediterranean (Chapter 8) and in Burma, Cuba and Zimbabwe (Chapter 9) and show that the EU's record is clearly not unambiguously positive. The last chapters of the book move on to the role of the EU in multilateral settings with Bart Kerremans' principal–agent interpretation of the EU's role in the WTO (Chapter 10) followed by Alasdair R. Young's analysis of the effectiveness of the EU as an actor in the process of WTO dispute resolution (Chapter 11) and Chad Damro's investigation of the multilateral competition policy. Finally, Sébastian Guigner employs Norbert Elias's concepts to understand the EU's international role in health policy which is moulded by the configurations of internal and international roles.

While the overall record of the EU as an international actor is clearly mixed, the editors rightly point out in their Introduction that specific institutional set-ups may make it 'well equipped for handling international processes [that] are increasingly characterized by fluidity, complexity and multi-level games, and as actors cannot always rely on traditional power assets in these arenas, the EU's potential as an international actor may well increase'. The volume convincingly demonstrates that the methodological tools of role theory lead to new and interesting insights into this potentially growing field of EU activity.

Thomas Poguntke

Acknowledgements

All but one of the chapters assembled here were first presented at the ECPR Joint Sessions of Workshops in Uppsala during April 2004; the only exception is that by Lisbeth Aggestam (Chapter 1), which was in fact an ECPR workshop paper in Granada (April 2005). A number of the revised drafts were discussed at a colloquium held at Loughborough University in October 2004, supported by the East Midlands Eurocentre, the Jean Monnet Centre of Excellence based at Loughborough. Thanks are due to all who have contributed to and supported the production of this volume, including Thomas Poguntke, the Editor of the series 'Studies in Political Science', and Heidi Bagtazo, representing Routledge. Ole Elgström would also like to thank Sieps, the Swedish Institute for European Policy Research, for financial support.

Abbreviations

ACP	African, Caribbean and Pacific (group of countries)
ANC	African National Congress (in South Africa)
AoA	(Uruguay Round) Agreement on Agriculture
ASEAN	Association of South East Asian Nations
ASEM	Asia–Europe Meeting
AU	African Union
BSE	Bovine Spongiform Encephalitis ('mad cow disease')
CAP	Common Agricultural Policy
CEECs	Central and East European Countries
CFSP	Common Foreign and Security Policy
CHR	(UN) Commission on Human Rights
CoE	Council of Europe
COPS	Political and Security Committee
CPE	Civilian Power Europe
CTE	(WTO) Committee on Trade and Environment
DCP	Development Co-operation Policy
DDA	Doha Development Agenda
DFA	Department of Foreign Affairs
DG	Directorate General
DG SANCO	Directorate General of Health and Consumer Protection (EU)
DoJ	Department of Justice (US)
DSM	Dispute Settlement Mechanism (WTO)
EA	Europe Agreement
EBA	Everything But Arms
EC	European Community
ECHR	European Convention on Human Rights
ECJ	European Court of Justice
ECPR	European Consortium for Political Research
ECSC	European Coal and Steel Community
EEC	European Economic Community
EFP	European Foreign Policy
EMP	Euro-Mediterranean Partnership

ENP	European Neighbourhood Policy
EPC	European Political Co-operation
ESDP	European Security and Defence Policy
ESS	European Security Strategy (EU)
EU	European Union
EUFOR	EU Force in Bosnia and Herzegovina
EUMM	EU Monitoring Mission
EUPM	EU Police Mission (in Bosnia)
FAO	Food and Agriculture Organization
FCTC	Framework Convention on Tobacco Control (WHO)
FPA	Foreign Policy Analysis
FSCs	Foreign Sales Corporations
FTC	Federal Trade Commission (US)
GATS	General Agreement on Trade in Services
GIs	Geographical Indicators (of origin)
GNP	Gross National Product
GSP	Generalized System of Preferences
HRD	Human Rights and Democracy
IAEAA	International Antitrust Enforcement Assistance Act (US)
ICC	International Criminal Court
IGC	Intergovernmental Conference
IPTF	International Police Task Force (in Bosnia)
IR	International Relations
LDCs	Less Developed Countries
MCR	(EU) Merger Control Regulation
MEAs	Multilateral Environmental Agreements
MEDA	Mediterranean Development Assistance
Mercosur	Mercado de Sur (Common Market of the Southern Cone of Latin America)
MLATs	Mutual Legal Assistance Treaties
MTNs	Multilateral Trade Negotiations
NEPAD	New Partnership for Africa's Development
NGOs	Non-governmental Organizations
NLD	National League for Democracy (in Burma/Myanmar)
NSS	National Security Strategy (US)
OECD	Organization for Economic Co-operation and Development
OSCE	Organization for Security and Co-operation in Europe
PA	Palestinian Authority
PHARE	Pologne et Hongrie: Actions pour la Reconversion Économique (programme of technical and financial assistance to the CEECs)
QMV	Qualified Majority Voting
SADC	Southern African Development Community
SDT	Special and Differential Treatment

SEM	Single European Market
SFOR	Stabilization Force in Bosnia and Herzegovina
TA	Treaty of Amsterdam
TACIS	Technical Assistance to the Commonwealth of Independent States
TBR	(EU) Trade Barriers Regulation
TEC	Treaty establishing the European Community (Treaty of Rome)
TEU	Treaty on European Union
TRIPS	Trade-related Aspects of Intellectual Property Rights
UK	United Kingdom
UN	United Nations
UNICE	Union of Industrial and Employers' Confederations of Europe
US	United States
WHO	World Health Organization
WMD	Weapons of Mass Destruction
WTO	World Trade Organization
WVS	World Values Survey
Zanu-PF	Zimbabwe African National Union-Patriotic Front

Introduction

Ole Elgström and Michael Smith

There has been during the past 20 years an almost continuous debate about the nature of the European Union (EU) as an international actor (Allen and Smith 1990, 1998; Bretherton and Vogler 1999; Carlsnaes *et al.* 2004; Hill 1993, 1998; Hill and Smith 2005; Knodt and Princen 2003; Peterson and Sjursen 1998; H. Smith 2002; K. Smith 2003; Tonra and Christiansen 2004; White 2001; Whitman 1998). At one end of the spectrum are those who see the EU as a potential state, or at least the performer of essential state functions in the international political arena. At the other end are those who see the EU as at best a patchy and fragmented international participant, and as little more than a system of regular diplomatic co-ordination between the member states. In between, there are a host of more or less exotic approaches dealing with notions such as 'presence', with the links and the tensions between institutionalization and the generation of collective identities and understandings, and with the specific characteristics of EU actions and impacts in particular issue areas.

One conclusion to be drawn from this analytical heterogeneity is that (to paraphrase Jacques Delors) the EU remains largely an 'unidentified international object' with a rather mercurial existence and impact. Another conclusion to be drawn might be that the EU exists within some of the 'gaps' within the literature of international political analysis, and that this opens the way for new forms of analysis and understanding. The chapters in this volume are generally based on this latter belief: that there is likely profit and analytical purchase in pursuing new ways of analysing the EU's roles and impact, and that the international impact of the EU itself changes the nature of the international political arena.

This volume focuses on three key questions about the EU's international role(s):

- First, why are the international roles and activities of the EU a source of puzzlement in the analysis of international politics, and what are the key elements in this set of puzzles?
- Second, why is role theory a useful approach to investigation of the

EU's international activities, and what specific aspects of role theory should be emphasized in such investigation?

- Third, how does attention to the EU's international roles help us to think about some key issues in international politics, for example debates about theory and policy, about ontological and epistemological differences and about levels of analysis?

The EU: a source of puzzles in international politics

The distinctiveness of EU participation in international politics is a hotly debated issue. While some scholars underline fundamental similarities between EU and nation-state foreign policies, a large number of observers tend to emphasize the uniqueness of the EU as an actor in international politics. The notions of the Union as a civilian or normative power bear witness to the latter argument (e.g. Duchêne 1972; Hill 1990; Manners 2002; Orbie 2003; Rosecrance 1998; K. Smith 2002). Explicit or implicit comparisons are often made with a traditional great power role, exemplified in today's world by the US. The EU, goes the argument, differs in important respects from its Atlantic partner. It is unique – to summarize this literature – in the set-up and character of goals and values; in the configuration of political instruments used; and in its peculiar institutional construction.

EU goals and values

The most potent argument for a distinct EU external identity and role refers to the overall pattern of its international objectives. Many of the EU's objectives are, it is argued, 'milieu goals', rather than 'possession goals' (K. Smith 2002; M. Smith 2004; the terms are from Wolfers 1962). While possession goals are linked to national interests, primarily security, milieu goals aim to shape the environment in which the actor operates. The normative ambitions of the EU, exemplified by the inclusion of normative conditions in most of its international agreements, demonstrate its conscious efforts to shape its environment. They simultaneously distinguish it from the US, which (it is claimed) is more focused on threats to its security (Daalder 2001). Manners (2002) explains the EU's emphasis on universal norms and principles by pointing to a combination of factors relating to its historical context, its legal foundation and its hybrid forms of governance.

This export of values emanates from what Manners calls the EU's normative basis (Manners 2002). He argues that it is possible to identify five 'core norms' from the *acquis communautaire* and the *acquis politique*: peace, liberty, democracy, the rule of law and human rights. Similarly, Karen Smith (2002, 2003) has analysed why and how the EU specifically pursues the promotion of human rights, the prevention of conflicts and regional co-operation. It is, however, much more difficult to argue that the EU is unique in promoting such individual objectives, as it is eminently clear that the US, and many other states, share and pursue similar goals. So it is rather the vague notion that the EU 'so far has represented something different from states in the international system in that it has not been an actor that only is guided by its self-interest' (Sjursen 2002: 15) that possibly makes the EU special. To specify the reasons for, the nature of and the effects of this overall pattern is a key challenge for this volume, and one that we intend to pursue through the medium of role theory.

EU policy instruments

The case seems to be stronger for arguing that the EU is unique owing to its peculiar configuration of external policy instruments. Whitman (1998: 235) even claims that the international identity and role of the EU may be conceived in terms of the instruments available to the Union. In the literature on the EU as a civilian power, attention has primarily been paid to the use of economic and diplomatic instruments (in contrast to the traditional use of military instruments). In more recent literature, the emphasis is rather on persuasion and positive incentives (rather than coercion) and on constructive engagement (rather than isolation) (Orbie 2003; K. Smith 2002). Efforts to exert social influence in terms of shaming and opprobrium (cf. Johnston 2001) are other tools frequently given attention. Indeed, the EU is sometimes said to be unique due to the wide variety of instruments at the EU's disposal. It can rely on a much wider range of policy instruments than any other actor (cf. Hill 1990; K. Smith 2002), and can use this to its advantage, for example in conflict prevention (Björkdahl 2002).

Civilian powers are commonly assumed to focus more on multilateral co-operation than traditional military powers (Orbie 2003). This is indeed also a feature that has been asserted to distinguish the EU from the US. The EU not only encourages regional co-operation in other parts of the world, it also relies on multilateralism to resolve conflicts, rather than on unilateral measures (Orbie 2003; cf. Rosecrance 1998) and to support global and regional institution-building.

The configuration of policy instruments claimed to define EU uniqueness demonstrate close linkages with some central elements of contemporary international politics. First, social influence is intimately linked to negotiation processes. Second, the EU is heavily involved in institution-building and in establishing rules and norms of multilateral co-operation. Finally, it is engaged in linkage politics to further its normative ambitions. How these forms of action are connected to roles and impact is a central concern of this volume.

The EU's institutional construction

The EU governance system, with its mix of supranational and international elements, is usually seen as a problem for constructing and executing a consistent and coherent external policy (see, e.g., Zielonka 1998; H. Smith 2002: 1–7). 'Euro-paralysis' (Zielonka 1998) is thus linked to diverging and conflicting national interests among member states, to weak institutions with competing objectives and to an unclear division of competence between different actors. But the peculiar institutional set-up of the Union can also be seen as an advantage and as contributing to EU distinctiveness. Whitman (1998: 235) refers to the 'distinctive nature' provided by the EU legal order and by its decision-making structure, and K. Smith (2002, 2003) proposes that the EU has externalized some of the principles and rationales that guide its internal relations, like the rule of law and the domestication of inter-state relations. Manners (2002: 240) underlines the 'particular new and different form of hybridity' as one of the factors that makes the EU normatively different. Laffan *et al.* (2000: 189) suggest that it is the 'experimental and innovative nature of the EU that enables it to respond to multiple agendas and Europe's diversity in a flexible manner'.

EU decision makers are used to handling complex multi-level negotiations and processes of policy formation from their internal arena. Being itself a network organization, the EU is particularly well equipped to grasp and utilize the potential of multilateral network negotiations (Elgström and Strömvik 2004); being itself an expression of multi-level and interconnected political processes, it is well equipped to recognize and respond to opportunities for the pursuit of these processes at the international level. As international political processes are increasingly characterized by fluidity, complexity and multi-level games, and as actors cannot always rely on traditional power assets in these arenas, the EU's potential as an international actor may well increase.

The EU institutional set-up and its relationship to roles and impact in different contexts are thus a third focus of attention of this volume. Does the EU institutional construct encourage proactiveness or passivity? Does it encourage problem-solving or bargaining modes of negotiation? How does the EU's internal complexity relate to the management of international complexity, and to the understanding of the EU's potential impact on processes of international institutional construction?

Role theory and the EU's international involvement

As can be seen from the discussion so far, it is not uncommon to find the concept of 'role' in the literature on the EU's international involvement. It is most often used as a synonym for influence ('the important role of the EU in international politics'), but sometimes also as an umbrella concept for general patterns of EU policy behaviour (see for example Knodt and Princen 2003: introduction and conclusion). There is seldom, however, a specification of what roles the EU is actually engaged in, and never any reference to role theory as deployed in the International Relations literature (Holsti 1970; Walker 1987, 1992; Le Prestre 1997). Those scholars that do utilize the role concept in a more systematic way (Hill 1990; Bretherton and Vogler 1999) tend to refer, in their categorizations, to a power dimension: to traditional great power roles, linked to position and status (balancer, intervener, supervisor, patron, global or regional leader), but also to roles that have previously been mostly associated with small states (mentor, model, bridge-builder, mediator, norm entrepreneur). Once again, the distinction between the EU as a military or civilian power comes to mind.

In this volume we argue for explicitly linking role and identity theories to the analysis of EU external action. Roles, in our opinion, refer to patterns of expected or appropriate behaviour. Roles are determined both by an actor's own conceptions about appropriate behaviour and by the expectations, or role prescriptions, of other actors (cf. Holsti 1970: 238–9). Looking at roles in this way, a direct connection can be made to neo-institutional theory and its emphasis on a 'logic of appropriateness' (March and Olsen 1989). According to this logic, actors behave in the way they believe is expected from them in a particular situation or context. Roles are often associated with certain positions ('great power roles', 'presidency roles') (cf. Holsti 1970: 239–40). 'The sharing of expectations on which role identities depend is facilitated by the fact that many roles are institutionalized in social structures that pre-date particular interactions' (Wendt 1999: 227). Roles may also, however, be connected to the behaviour of an actor in a specified issue area or in a certain organizational forum. Roles are thus to a certain degree contextually determined.

Role-taking is, however, by no means a mechanical process. The roles an actor engages in are in part an effect of learning and socialization in interactive negotiation processes (Aggestam 2004a, b) where self-conceptions are confronted with expectations. In these processes, the individual actor has a certain leeway to choose what role to play and how to play it in a given institutional and broader social context. In brief, there is room for agency in role theory. In fact, it could be argued that it is the complex and dynamic interplay between the actor's own role conception and actor autonomy, on the one hand, and structurally guided role expectations, on the other hand, which constitutes the main advantage of role theory. Role theory in this sense allows both for the development of approaches relating to the ideational basis of policy and for the evaluation of material policy concerns and actions.

A major challenge for this volume is thus to try to further our understanding of the extent to which context and agency, respectively, determine roles, and in what ways. Traditionally, the study of how different contexts contribute to the enactment of roles has been the task of organization theory, while investigation into the initial formation of role conceptions has been the realm of social constructivists (Trondal 2001: 3). In this volume we wish to explore how far it is possible to combine these two endeavours and apply them to the EU's international activity. In doing so, we need to take account of the central conceptual categories that have been developed for investigating and evaluating roles: role conceptions, the origins of roles, role institutionalization, role performance and role impact. In brief, these categories can be summarized as follows (see Chapter 1 for more detailed discussion on some of these themes):

- *Role conceptions.* Role conceptions encompass both actors' self-images and the effects of others' role expectations, and they prompt investigation of the interplay between these two elements. In terms of the EU, they give rise to discussion of the extent to which the EU can be seen as a distinctive actor in international politics, generating innovative roles and capable of transferring or reproducing those roles in a variety of contexts. Discussion of the ways in which (for example) the EU plays a leadership role in certain areas of international life, or the extent to which EU international policies enshrine principles such as multilateralism, is a logical consequence of a focus on role conceptions.
- *Origins of roles.* In deploying this concept, we become interested in the extent to which EU roles are strategically conceived and thus linked to design or choice, or the result of contingency and incrementalism. We also become conscious of the variety of driving forces that may lie behind roles – material interests versus identities, ideas and principles – and of the balance between internal and external forces in the generation of roles.
- *Role institutionalization.* One key question that emerges from a focus on role institutionalization is, who or what is the EU for the purposes of role analysis? We know that the EU is a densely institutionalized policy space, but we need to take into consideration the relative importance of transnational forces and institutional actors as well as member states, in providing resources, momentum and commitment to various types of roles and formalizing these through institutional frameworks.
- *Role performance.* Here we become concerned with how, in what ways, a role is played, and thus with the ways in which the EU plays its international roles. Role performance, defined as the actual behaviour of actors, is also influenced by external perceptions of how a certain role should be, has been, and is enacted. Once a role is defined and has become institutionalized, it will act as a constraint, but also as an instrument of empowerment, for the role player – in this case, the EU.

This is not a purely mechanical process; roles ordinarily allow for a certain freedom of manoeuvre and interpretation, albeit within limits, and thus we are interested in the ways in which this can be discerned in the case of the EU (Wendt 1999: 227).

- *Role impact.* In investigating role impact, we become aware of the EU's (in)ability to achieve desired effects, and thus with such concepts as effectiveness (goal realization), efficiency (gains versus costs) and legitimacy. Clearly, variations in performance (see above) may help to explain variation in impact, and may thus condition the EU's capacity to take on further or more ambitious roles. At a broader level, we become concerned with the EU's impact on the world arena and world order: has the EU been able to embed a 'civilizing' role and to act as an agent of international structural change?

The contributions to this volume

The contributors to this volume were all asked to explore a number of role-related themes. These themes, which centre around the basic elements of role theory identified above – role conceptions, origin of roles, role institutionalization, role performance and role impact – were to inform each chapter in order to render the volume homogeneous and to facilitate comparisons across the various contributions and empirical fields of enquiry. They were also to be considered in light of broader conceptual and methodological issues linked with contemporary international politics – the third of the puzzles identified at the beginning of this introduction.

The contributions differ in many respects, despite their common concern with EU roles and with the themes outlined above. First, their emphasis is on different aspects, empirically and theoretically, of this vast research field. While some authors focus their attention on conceptual issues, some others scrutinize processes and others again have their interest in performance and impact. These kinds of differences have influenced our ordering of the various chapters: we start (Chapters 1–6 by Aggestam, Jørgensen, Lucarelli, Manners, Sjursen and Whitman) with a number of more conceptually inclined contributions that focus on the self-images that are expressed and the expectations that others develop in relation to the Union and on the relationships between phenomena such as roles, identities, values and principles. Next (Chapters 7–9 by Sedelmeier, Panebianco and K. Smith), the attention is turned to concrete attempts at EU norm export and to the limits of such active entrepreneurship. Finally (Chapters 10–13 by Kerremans, Young, Damro and Guigner), the roles the Union plays in a number of multilateral negotiation settings are explored, paving the way for empirically based comparisons across policy areas.

Second, the authors adhere – more or less explicitly – to various ontological and epistemological approaches. Broadly speaking, some contributors are clearly within a rationalist tradition, relying on a logic of consequences (actors weigh different options in terms of their consequences in relation to determined preferences) to explain EU (and others') role development and performance. Others adopt a sociological approach with an emphasis on a logic of appropriateness (actors choose to behave according to how they think they should behave, holding the role they have, in the institutional context at hand). We think that the tensions and question marks created by the juxtaposition of these different approaches – which we believe are in principle reconcilable – lead to fruitful discussions and to novel ideas and insights.

Third, the contributions are located at different levels of analysis. Three distinct but interconnected levels can be discerned, which can be summarized as the 'macroscopic', the 'mesoscopic' and the 'microscopic' levels. At the most general level, EU role performance is situated as part of the international system. At the mesoscopic level, the EU interacts with other actors in clearly demarcated and circumscribed settings. The microscopic level highlights the EU itself and the internal processes of role emergence and identity formation. Participants thus start and finish at different points depending on their choices about levels and the focus of their research. The three levels are obviously not in sealed boxes and many important insights may materialize from the ways in which levels intersect or constitute 'layers' in the development and performance of roles by the EU.

References

Aggestam, L. (2004a) *A European Foreign Policy? Role Conceptions and the Politics of Identity in Britain, France and Germany*, Stockholm: Stockholm University, Department of Political Science.

Aggestam, L. (2004b) 'Role Identity and the Europeanisation of Foreign Policy: A Political–Cultural Approach', in B. Tonra and T. Christiansen (eds) *Rethinking European Union Foreign Policy*, Manchester: Manchester University Press.

Allen, D. and Smith, M. (1990) 'Western Europe's Presence in the Contemporary International Arena', *Review of International Studies*, 16 (1): 19–37.

Allen, D. and Smith, M. (1998) 'The European Union's Presence in the New European Security Order: Barrier, Facilitator or Manager?' in C. Rhodes (ed.) *The European Union in the Global Community*, Boulder, CO: Lynne Rienner.

Björkdahl, A. (2002) *From Idea to Norm: Promoting Conflict Prevention*, Lund: Lund University.

Bretherton, C. and Vogler, J. (1999) *The European Union as a Global Actor*, London: Routledge.

Carlsnaes, W., Sjursen, H. and White, B. (eds) (2004) *Contemporary European Foreign Policy*, London: Sage.

Daalder, I. (2001) 'Are the United States and Europe Heading for a Divorce?', *Survival*, 7 (3).

Duchêne, F. (1972) 'Europe's Role in World Peace', in R. Mayne (ed.) *Europe Tomorrow: Sixteen Europeans Look Ahead*, London: Fontana.

Elgström, O. and Strömvik, M. (2004) 'The EU as an External Actor', in O. Elgström and C. Jönsson (eds) *European Union Negotiations: Processes, Institutions, Networks*, London: Routledge.
Hill, C. (1990) 'European Foreign Policy: Power Bloc, Civilian Model – or Flop?', in R. Rummel (ed.) *The Evolution of an International Actor*, Boulder, CO and London: Westview Press.
Hill, C. (1993) 'The Capability–Expectations Gap, or Conceptualising Europe's International Role', *Journal of Common Market Studies*, 31 (3): 305–28.
Hill, C. (1998) 'Closing the Capabilities–Expectations Gap?', in J. Peterson and H. Sjursen (eds) *A Common Foreign Policy for Europe? Competing Visions of the CFSP*, London: Routledge.
Hill, C. and Smith, M. (eds) (2005) *International Relations and the European Union*, Oxford: Oxford University Press.
Holsti, K. (1970) 'National Role Conceptions in the Study of Foreign Policy', *International Studies Quarterly*, 14: 233–309.
Johnston, A. I. (2001) 'Treating International Institutions as Social Environments', *International Studies Quarterly*, 45 (4): 487–515.
Knodt, M. and Princen, S. (eds) (2003) *Understanding the European Union's External Relations*, London: Routledge/ECPR.
Laffan, B., O'Donnell, R. and Smith, M. (2000) *Europe's Experimental Union. Rethinking Integration*, London: Routledge.
Le Prestre, P. (1997) *Role Quests in the Post-Cold War Era*, Montreal: McGill-Queen's University Press.
Manners, I. (2002) 'Normative Power Europe: A Contradiction in Terms?', *Journal of Common Market Studies*, 40 (2): 235–58.
March, J. and Olsen, J. (1989) *Rediscovering Institutions: The Organizational Basis of Politics*, New York: Free Press.
Orbie, J. (2003) 'The EU as a Civilian Power: The Role of Trade Policy?' Paper presented at the EUSA Eighth Biennial International Conference, Nashville, TN, 27–29 March.
Peterson, J. and Sjursen, H. (eds) (1998) *A Common Foreign Policy for Europe? Competing Visions of the CFSP*, London: Routledge.
Rosecrance, R. (1998) 'The European Union: A New Type of International Actor?', in J. Zielonka (ed.) *Paradoxes of European Foreign Policy*, The Hague: Kluwer Law International.
Sjursen, H. (2002) 'Beyond the State? The Role of Identities, Values and Rights in European Security'. Paper presented at the First Pan-European Conference on European Union Politics, Bordeaux, 26–28 September.
Smith, H. (2002) *European Union Foreign Policy. What It Is and What It Does*, London and Sterling, VA: Pluto Press.
Smith, K. (2002) 'Conceptualising the EU's International Identity: *Sui Generis* or Following the Latest Trends?' Paper presented at the First Pan-European Conference on European Union Politics, Bordeaux, 26–28 September.
Smith, K. (2003) *European Foreign Policy in a Changing World*, Oxford: Polity Press.
Smith, M. (2004) 'Foreign Economic Policy', in W. Carlsnaes, H. Sjursen and B. White (eds) *Contemporary European Foreign Policy*, London: Sage.
Tonra, B. and Christiansen, T. (eds) (2004) *Rethinking European Union Foreign Policy*, Manchester: Manchester University Press.
Trondal, J. (2001) 'Is there any Social Constructivist–Institutionalist Divide?

Unpacking Social Mechanisms affecting Representational Roles among EU Decision-makers', *Journal of European Public Policy*, 8 (1): 1–23.

Walker, S. (ed.) (1987) *Role Theory and Foreign Policy Analysis*, Durham, NC: Duke University Press.

Walker, S. (1992) 'Symbolic Interactionism and International Politics: Role Theory's Contribution to International Organization', in M. Cottam and C. Shih (eds) *Contending Dramas: A Cognitive Approach to International Organizations*, New York: Praeger.

Wendt, A. (1999) *Social Theory of International Politics*, Cambridge: Cambridge University Press.

White, B. (2001) *Understanding European Foreign Policy*, Basingstoke: Palgrave/Macmillan.

Whitman, R. (1998) *From Civilian Power to Superpower? The International Identity of the European Union*, Basingstoke: Macmillan.

Wolfers, A. (1962) *Discord and Collaboration: Essays on International Politics*, Baltimore, MD: Johns Hopkins University Press.

Zielonka, J. (1998) *Explaining Euro-paralysis: Why Europe is Unable to Act in International Politics*, Basingstoke: Macmillan.

1 Role theory and European foreign policy

A framework of analysis

Lisbeth Aggestam

> The EU is not an island, it's a part of a global community. For large parts of the world, the word Europe itself has become associated with a philosophy of humanity, solidarity and integration. Therefore the EU has to play a bigger role to work for the 'global common good.'
>
> (Javier Solana, EU High Representative for the CFSP, 2005a)

A commonly asked question about the European Union (EU) is whether it has a foreign policy that is more than the sum of its parts. Is the EU, in other words, a foreign policy actor in its own right rather than a mere aggregation of the lowest common denominator of EU member states' foreign policies? What meaning is attributed to the EU as an agent of foreign-policy action? This chapter proposes that a role theory analysis will enrich our understanding of how to characterize European foreign policy. A role reflects a claim on the international system, a recognition by international actors, and a conception of identity (Le Prestre 1997: 5–6). The coherence and effectiveness of the EU in international politics are largely contingent on how widely shared and stable European foreign policy norms and rules of action are. European foreign policy is here given a broad definition and is understood as the EU's international action.

This chapter aims to sketch out a framework of analysis based on sociological role theory that will suggest how roles are constructed, sustained and changed in foreign policy. A role analysis of this kind can deepen our understanding of agency and action in European foreign policy. It is important to point out, however, that there does not exist a single general role theory to draw on as to why, when and how certain role phenomena occur (Searing 1991: 1244). Hence, this chapter aims to outline the basic building blocks for how to construct a role analysis applicable to European foreign policy.[1]

The chapter is structured in six parts. The first part provides a brief account of the genealogy of sociological role theory and its inception to Foreign Policy Analysis (FPA). The second part develops a structurationist approach to role theory that incorporates an institutional, interactional and intentional perspective of roles. The third part seeks to clarify the conceptual ambiguity that tends to accompany the role concept by distinguishing four different types. The fourth part elaborates on the sources of roles. Identity, it is argued, is an important socio-cultural source for the way in which roles are conceived. The fifth part considers how role conflict and instability relate to foreign-policy change. The chapter concludes with an analytical model that summarizes the framework of analysis.

Sociological role theory and foreign-policy analysis

Sociological role theory is derived from the theatrical analogy in which an actor is expected to behave in predictable ways according to a script (rule-based action) (Jackson 1972). The word 'role' comes from the theatre, where 'rolls' or 'roles' were originally the parts from which theatrical characters were read (Thomas and Biddle 1966: 6). The social or political actor resembles, therefore, the stage actor. The attraction of this conceptualization is that it highlights the relationship between the individual and social structure. The actor 'operates with a script written for him which he has learnt at some point in the past ... He is motivated to follow the script, to comply with the rules of the game' (Bradbury *et al.* 1972: 43). Indeed, the sociologist Ernest Goffman (1959) used the dramaturgical analogy more literally when describing society as a stage on which individuals enter to play parts and assuming different 'masks'. Importantly, role theory encompasses how human agents and social structures in a fundamental sense are dynamically interrelated.

> It is because the individual plays roles that there is a discipline of sociology at all; roles are an 'emergent' property not understandable in terms of the qualities of individuals alone but developing out of the interaction of individuals in particular environmental settings and which then influence the behaviour of these individuals and possible future generations who are socialized or constrained to employ them. It is because individuals are role-players that their behaviour is neither idiosyncratic nor random.
>
> (Bradbury *et al.* 1972: 43)

In a seminal article first published in 1970, Kalevi Holsti introduced the sociological concept of role into the field of foreign-policy analysis. Based on an extensive cross-national study, he set out to investigate decision-makers' perceptions of their own nation, thereby focusing on the subjective dimension of national foreign policy.

> A *national role conception* includes the policymakers' own definitions of the general kinds of decisions, commitments, rules, and actions suitable to their state, and of the functions, if any, their state should

perform on a continuing basis in the international system or in subordinate regional systems.

(Holsti 1970/1987: 12)

Holsti argued that a state's foreign policy was influenced by its 'national role conception' which could help explain the general direction of foreign-policy choices (Holsti 1970/1987: 40). Importantly, he claimed that different role conceptions in some instances could address differences in foreign-policy behaviour between states; a correspondence that was supported in a later role analysis by Wish (1980, 1987: 95–6). A role conception, Holsti (1987: 38–9) stated, is a product of a nation's socialization process and influenced by its history, culture and societal characteristics. This was a different approach compared to how the role concept had traditionally been used in IR theory. From a realist point of view, the sources of roles are predominantly systemic and based on material factors (Rosenau 1990: 213; Walker 1987: 271). Hence, in this type of analysis a state's general role would be studied deductively in terms of the state's position within a structure (for instance, in balance-of-power theory).

The novelty with Holsti's study was that roles were not unfolded from abstract theoretical discussions, but analysed inductively in terms of the roles policy-makers *themselves* perceived and defined. The great strength of this approach is that it tries to take careful account of political reality as it is experienced by the policy-makers, who construct it in a dynamic interaction between rules and reasons (cf. Searing 1991: 1248). The findings of Holsti's inductive research indicated that the practitioners of foreign policy expressed different and numerous roles than the general role stipulated deductively by academics (Holsti 1970/1987: 28). Significantly, this seems to suggest that roles have multiple sources and are not exclusively generated by the international distribution of power. Foreign policy-makers, in other words, are neither completely free choosing agents, nor is their behaviour entirely determined by external structures.

The view of agency adopted in the analytical framework proposed here rests on the assumption that the actor's mind-set is 'theory-driven', i.e. that foreign policy-makers in general have a need to organize perceptions into a meaningful guide for behaviour (cf. Holsti 1963; Jönsson *et al.* 2000: 10). Role theory, as it has evolved in sociology, captures many of these elements of how human thinking tends to be theory-generated. The role concept can be viewed as a cognitive construct, which evolves in correspondence with concepts of self in social reality. It simplifies, provides guidance and predisposes an actor towards one purposive behaviour rather than another. As Horrocks and Jackson (1972: 94) declare, 'Role behaviour is a cognitive affective process because it is selective, internally organized, and interpreted by relational schema.'

Structuration: institution, interaction and intention

The epistemology informing the role theory framework developed in this chapter seeks to incorporate both the individual and structural nature of behaviour. The agency in foreign policy is conceptualized in terms of a 'situated actor' whose behaviour is guided by both rules and reasons in foreign policy (Adler 1997; Hay 1995: 190; see further Aggestam 2004: 36–8). As March and Olsen (1998: 12) assert:

> Political actors are constituted both by their interests, by which they evaluate their anticipations of consequences, and by the rules embedded in their identities and political institutions. They calculate consequences and follow rules, and the relation between the two is often subtle.

Both of these elements of behaviour are accounted for in a framework provided by role theory. Role concepts can provide an essential link between agent and structure, as they incorporate the manner in which foreign policy is both purposeful and shaped by institutional contexts. As Hollis and Smith (1990: 168) argue, 'Role involves judgement and skill, but at the same time it involves a notion of structure within which roles operate.'

This conceptualization of a dual process of structure and agency can be linked to Giddens's theory of structuration, which seeks to reconcile a focus on structures (the conditions of social and political interaction) with sensitivity to the intentionality, reflexivity, autonomy and agency of actors (Giddens 1979, 1984). Rather than viewing social structures as non-subjective and external to actors, Giddens (1984: 172–4) argues that 'society' is manifestly not external to individual actors in the same way as the material environment. The structures – the continuously reproduced rules and resources – do not have any independent objective existence external to actors, nor are they purely subjective. The process of structuration means that actors and structures are only separable on an abstract, analytical level, since structures are upheld by ongoing processes of structuration. Agency and structure are two sides of the same coin (Hay 1995: 197).

To bring down the level of abstraction and to make structuration theory applicable to empirical analysis, we will develop a role analysis that incorporates three important perspectives – institutional, interactional and intentional – of how roles are constructed, sustained and changed. This, it is argued, produces a richer and more nuanced understanding of roles and represents one way in which we may conceive of the interrelated relationship between structure and agency in foreign policy.

Institution

The predominant approach to role analysis is the one that considers roles as deeply embedded in institutions, structuring the range of roles available and the way in which they are played. In other words, institutions, not the actors themselves, determine roles. In sociology, this type of role theory has been applied to the analysis of how normative constraints of society are represented in a system of roles, within which the individual is socialized (Jackson 1972: 1). Actors are expected to perform certain roles given a particular social order. The sharing of norms and expectations creates networks of rights and obligations (Jackson 1972: 3–4). An institutional perspective is important to integrate in our theoretical framework, as it helps us conceptualize how intersubjective beliefs and political culture influence foreign policy, as well as how different international institutions generate expectations of certain role behaviour.

Institutions can be understood as both 'a general pattern or categorization of activity' and 'a particular human-constructed arrangement, formally or informally organized' (Keohane 1994: 47). Young (1989: 32) defines institutions as 'social practices consisting of easily recognized roles coupled with clusters or rules or conventions governing relations among the occupants of these roles', and argues that the states system can be considered an institution in this sense (Young 1989: 33). Apart from this broad definition, an institution can also be a more specific organizational arrangement, like the EU. Whether it is a broad or more narrow conception of institution, the important criterion for being considered an institution is that 'rules must be durable, and must prescribe behavioural roles for actors, besides constraining activity and shaping expectations' (Keohane 1994: 49).[2]

The reason why this institutional perspective needs to be supplemented is that it does not take enough account of the agency as a 'situated actor' nor does it incorporate the dynamics of structuration. Individuals are only relevant in so far as the roles they occupy within these structures; 'there are significant similarities in the performance of actors taking the same part, no matter who the actors are' (Thomas and Biddle 1966: 4). As Rosenau (1987: 45) states, 'there is no individual apart from the network of systems in which he or she is embedded'. Structure is thus largely seen to constrain and even determine agency. Individuals are presented with roles that are built into an institution's structure and will continue to exist whether or not these individuals choose to play them. This perspective leaves little scope for interpretation and innovation of the agency, and thus runs the risk of making the analysis static and deterministic.

To be sure, the role analysis developed in this chapter acknowledges the institutional argument that a role as a set of norms and expectations constrains behaviour. It is precisely on the basis of such expectations and intersubjectivity that enduring social relationships are possible. Yet we need to qualify this assumption in two regards. First, we need to incorporate the structurationist argument that social structure is unceasingly mediated through agency, and thus exists only as it is expressed in human social activity. Second, we must recognize that the degree of intersubjectivity and consensus regarding a particular role can vary greatly.

Barnett (1993: 275) makes a useful distinction in this regard between so-called 'position' and 'preference roles'; the former providing an actor with well-defined and detailed guides to action, whilst the latter provides greater flexibility of interpretation as to the meaning of a role. If we add the agency's identity to the idea of a 'position role', the process by which a particular role is selected can be referred to as 'role-taking'. This role can be interpreted as a concrete manifestation of an identity in behaviour.

> In behavior an identity is implemented by the taking of a role. A role taken is a concrete behavioural manifestation and implementation of one or more of an individual's identities, presenting the observer a picture of the identity in action.
>
> (Horrocks and Jackson 1972: 115)

However, the extent to which different identity discourses lend value to particular roles varies. 'Role-taking' assumes a high degree of intersubjectivity. As we will find out in the following two perspectives, roles are not as stable and predictable as forecasted in institutional analysis, suggesting a considerable scope for 'role-playing'.

Interaction

In a study that concerns itself with the possibility of new roles emerging on a supranational level, it is crucial to bring dynamism and process into the role analysis. We need to incorporate how roles are learned and socialized in an interaction process of negotiations. In contrast to the emphasis on institution, this perspective brings out agency and its capacity for defining its own roles. The stress on process implies that roles have many variations and are usually undergoing change (Searing 1991: 1246). The interaction with other actors may have innovative social consequences, especially if the actor occupies a position of power or authority (Bradbury *et al.* 1972: 50–1).

The interactional approach is closely associated with symbolic interactionism (Mead 1934). Symbols and meanings emerge from a process of social interaction that shape behaviour. Symbolic interactionism pays particular attention to how informal rules are created and recreated through negotiations. In IR theory we find, for instance, this perspective represented in Wendt's constructivist work, captured in his well-known phrase 'anarchy is what states make of it' (Wendt 1992; see also 1999). His point is that it is in the actual interaction process that the construction of meaning takes place: 'I argue that self-help and power politics do not follow logically or causally from anarchy, and if today we find ourselves in a self-help world this is due to process, not structure' (Wendt 1992: 394–5).

The emphasis on process, change and actors' capacity to construct new rules is important to incorporate in the present framework of analysis as it addresses European levels of foreign policy-making. The attempt by EU member states to construct a European foreign policy may indeed be regarded as a learning process involving intense negotiation and socialization of policy-makers within the institutions of the EU.

Nonetheless, there are two reasons why this perspective does not suffice on its own. First, it could be argued that the interactional perspective does not take sufficient account of the fact that actors arrive at their interaction with pre-existing identities and roles. 'There is never a first encounter', as Smith (2001: 245) points out. Second, the interactional perspective makes it difficult to incorporate interests and objectives that flow outside the interaction within which actors are immersed in at any given time. To incorporate a sense of intentionality and rationality, we need to bring in a third perspective which highlights how actors interpret information, monitor their performance and reassess their goals and roles.

Intention

This final perspective of role shows how roles derive from both intellectual and cultural sources. It brings to our attention how actors themselves are involved in defining roles – and, importantly, that these roles may contain objectives as well as norms. As Rosenau (1987: 61) declares, 'While they are not conceived as game-theoretical products of rational actors, neither are they simple resultants of a culture's logic.' The foreign policy-maker, in other words, is actively involved in the construction of roles on the basis of calculations and reasoning: 'Roles call for judgement, which involves reasoned belief, self-monitoring of aims, and a general shrewdness' (Hollis and Smith 1990). The merit of this perspective is that it recognizes that 'man' is not simply a passive reflection of 'society' but an individual capable of exercising some freedom in the choice of ends and means of action.

Hollis and Smith (1990: 165) point out that the foreign-policy actor's independence, or room for manoeuvre, is possible because of 'role distance'.

> Foreign policy is made, in our view, by persons in various offices, who need to juggle with the imperatives of office, to display skill in negotiation and readiness to concede one point for the sake of another, to ride the horses of role-conflict, and to interpret a changing situation with a mixture of impartiality and commitment. These are talents

which, while being broad requirements of office, demand that roles be played with distance.

The extent to which 'role distance' is experienced may vary for different roles depending on their centrality within the overall 'role-set'. Yet, in most cases, and even when rules explicitly specify a particular type of action, roles are likely to leave the actor with some scope for interpretation and choice. However, this view of the agency in foreign policy does not mean that we consider roles to simply be like hats that you can take on and off. Purposive roles are the result of a dynamic interaction between institutional constraints and the actor's preferences (Searing 1991: 1248). Intention, as Giddens (1984: 3) points out, should not be confused with voluntarism. Human agents are knowledgeable and reflect continuously on the conditions and consequences of their actions, but they are also finite in their capabilities of action and perception (Giddens 1979: 215–16; 1984: 11, 296).

Incorporating the three perspectives of role outlined in this section is therefore crucial in relating reasons to structure and allowing for flexibility and judgement in the playing of the role. As Hollis and Smith (1990: 168) conclude, 'in so doing we bring the individual back in without reducing our explanations of foreign policy to the individual as the unit of analysis'.

Concepts of roles

As the previous section has demonstrated, there are a number of ways in which the idea of role can be analysed and understood. The way we understand the role concept is closely related to whether we focus on the actor's subjective understandings, the script, or the actual performance. In the following, we will be making four distinctions of role: (1) role expectation; (2) role conception; (3) role performance; and (4) role-set. These different notions of role are obviously closely interlinked yet do refer to different phenomena and processes when applied to the analysis of foreign policy.

Role expectation

This role pertains to those expectations that other actors (*alter*) prescribe and expect the role-beholder (*ego*) to enact (Kirste and Maull 1996: 289). This idea of role is frequently found in studies that highlight how institutional structures generate expectations of certain role behaviour. 'Roles are induced through the sharing of *expectations* for role behavior . . . those who exhibit the role are stimulated to do so because they learn what behaviours are expected of them' (Biddle 1979: 5). For instance, political culture and the institutionalization of identity generate broad expectations, which tend to set limits to the range of roles that policy-makers perceive.

International role expectations can also be studied as the normative expectations that membership in different institutions generate. The constitutional treaties of the EU and the various EPC/CFSP declarations may, for instance, be viewed as role prescriptions inducing expectations of certain role behaviour (Hill 1993). More specifically, role expectations can be examined in terms of how international actors (*alter*) perceive the appropriate foreign policy behaviour of a specific role actor (see for instance, Edström 1988; Rosenau 1987: 48). Hill (1998: 30–3) lists four categories of actors with high role expectations of the EU: (1) developing countries; (2) applicants for membership; (3) the states of East Asia; and (4) states interested in political dialogue. Furthermore, although ambiguous to some extent, the role expectations articulated by the sole remaining superpower undoubtedly exert influence on how a European role in foreign policy is conceived.

> It is our view that a strong and united Europe that is able to act as a global partner with the United States, given its democratic values and our long history together, will only serve to multiply the forces that are fighting for democracy and freedom and for prosperity across the globe.
>
> (US Secretary of State Condoleezza Rice, 2005)

It could be argued that this role expectation (repeated by the US government over a number of years) was acknowledged and responded to in the European Security Strategy of 2003.

> Acting together, the European Union and the United States can be a formidable force for good in the world. Our aim should be an effective and balanced partnership with the USA. This is an additional reason for the EU to build up further its capabilities and increase its coherence.
>
> (European Security Strategy 2003: 14)

Role conception

This idea of role refers to the normative expectations that the role-beholder expresses towards itself, i.e. the ego-part's own definition. It thus pertains to the subjective dimension of foreign policy. A role conception defines responsibilities and obligations in foreign policy. It tends to reveal the intention and motives of the foreign-policy actor, in other words, the meaning of action. In the present framework, a role conception thus refers to images that foreign policy-makers hold concerning the general long-term function and performance of the EU in the international system.

> Our world is changing fast. It contains new dangers but also many opportunities. The EU has a major contribution to make, in at least two respects. Both through what it is: a highly successful example of building peace through integration; and through what it does – by promoting global security through co-operation.
>
> (High Representative for the CFSP, Javier Solana, 2005a)

A role conception embodies a mixture of norms, intentions and descriptions of reality which vary in degree of specificity and manifestation. It is important to note that actors tend to conceive of multiple roles. The EU, it has been suggested, is conceived to be playing a number of different roles, such as a balancer of power, a regional pacifier, a global intervenor, a mediator of conflicts, a bridge between the rich and poor, and a joint supervisor of the world economy (Hill 1998: 34–6).[3] These roles vary in overall importance and according to the situation and institutional context.[4] Hence, there is always an element of role-playing involved, providing the foreign-policy actor with room for manoeuvre.

Whilst role conceptions concern the actor's subjective understandings of what its behaviour should be, these are assumed to be more or less intersubjective if we are to understand roles as characteristic patterns of behaviour in foreign policy. The emphasis on convergent expectations as the constitutive basis of roles gives them this intersubjective quality. The greater the extent to which policy-makers are socialized into and internalize these role conceptions the more stable a role will be.

Role performance

The actual foreign-policy behaviour in terms of characteristic patterns of decisions and actions undertaken in specific situational contexts can be characterized in terms of role performance. Holsti (1970/1987: 7–8) suggests that foreign policy behaviour is to a great extent characterized by role performance, which in turn can be explained by the role conceptions held by decision-makers. This correlation was explored and supported in a study by Wish (1987: 95). However, I would argue that this correlation between role conception and role performance may be applicable only to more general roles. As pointed out earlier, policy-makers generally conceive of multiple roles and it is difficult to forecast more precisely which role is selected and which particular objectives are attached to it. We should keep in mind that role conceptions do not necessarily determine outcomes directly, but merely define the potential range of options and strategies. Role conceptions are broad categories that allow some flexibility of interpretation, depending on the extent to which they have become formally institutionalized with a specific guide to action. Nonetheless, in terms of foreign policy at the strategic level, role conceptions may indeed provide a clearer view of why the EU adopts a particular orientation and approach in international relations.

Role-set

In sociology, the conceptualization of a 'role-set' has been conceived in terms of one general role: 'Every individual has a series of roles deriving from the various patterns in which he participates and at the same time *a role*, general, which represents the sum total of these roles and determines what he does for his society and what he can expect from it' (R. Linton, quoted in Thomas and Biddle 1966: 7). The term 'role-set' is used in the role analysis proposed here as a comprehensive term that pertains to the predominant school of thought in foreign policy given a number of roles. A role-set illuminates different images of the nature of international relations, perceptions of power and security and, not least, approaches to European integration in foreign policy. The concept of civilian power Europe (Duchêne 1972) could, for instance, be interpreted as such a general role.

Sources of roles

A role conception, according to Holsti (1970/1987), is largely a product of a nation's socialization process and the influence of its history, culture and societal characteristics. As Holsti (1970/1987: 38–9) asserted, 'As these national role conceptions become a more pervasive part of the political culture of a nation, they are more likely to set limits on perceived or politically feasible policy alternatives, and less likely to allow idiosyncratic variables to play a crucial part in decision making.' Given that the EU is a recent political construct and not a state, it is of course debatable the extent to which a European identity can be seen as an important source of EU foreign policy roles. However, few people would dispute that 'the vision of the European Union has been constructed on the ashes of the past' (Solana 2003), and that this vision serves as an important ideational foundation on which EU foreign-policy roles are conceived.

Despite the fact that Holsti indicated the importance of the cultural sources of roles, few studies have explicitly linked the role concept with political culture and identity in foreign policy.[5] Identity and role are, however, closely interconnected. In sociology, the role concept has been central to the development of knowledge about, and measure of, the normative context which mediates between the individual and society (Jackson 1972). Similarly, Hudson and Vore (1995: 226) note that in FPA:

> National role conception is one of the few conceptual tools we have for the study of how society and culture serve as a context for a

> nation's foreign policy. It allows one to bridge the conceptual gap between the general beliefs held in a society and the beliefs of foreign policy decision makers.

A basic idea in role theory is that 'roles provide meaning of the world from the individual's ability to place himself into contexts. Roles provide location and definition of the individual in relation to the world around him' (Horrocks and Jackson 1972: 94).

Although there is not the space in this chapter to elaborate on the socio-cultural component of role (see further Aggestam 2004: 39–55), this is essential to account for if we wish to understand how different European roles are conceived and sustained. Changes in foreign policy may be detected by paying attention to how different identity discourses lend value to or withdraw them from particular roles. This emphasis on the ideational structures of foreign policy does not mean, however, that materialist structures are unimportant. Material attributes and capabilities are important parameters within which foreign policy is conceived.

> As a union of 25 states with over 450 million people producing a quarter of the world's Gross National Product (GNP), and with a wide range of instruments at its disposal, the European Union is inevitably a global player.
>
> (European Security Strategy 2003: 2)

Ideational structures are not conceived to exist apart from material structures in political life. Whilst not denying the existence of a material reality, its importance, however, is crucially related to how material factors are perceived and mediated by the actors themselves.

Role conflict and foreign-policy change

Stability is an inherent characteristic of role as patterned behaviour. If role conceptions were constantly fluctuating and changing, they would fail to provide policy-makers with the consistency they seek. At the same time, roles are sensitive to situational context and time. The potential for a role conflict to erupt within a role-set is always present, i.e. when dominant role conceptions are incompatible or contradictory to one another.

To capture both continuity and change, it has been argued in this chapter, the role concept needs to integrate the structure and dynamics of institution, interaction and intention. The interactional perspective suggests that roles are not static but liable to change, yet not randomly so. The intentional perspective, assuming that the actor in foreign policy is knowledgeable and rational in a bounded sense, illuminates how foreign policy-makers participate in defining their own roles. In this section, we will be discussing when role conceptions are likely to change, as this constitutes an important determinant of foreign-policy change.

One of the most obvious stimuli for foreign policy change is when an actor experiences role conflict. A manifest role conflict would presumably initiate a search for change, given the actor's inherent desire for consistency and cognitive stability. A role conflict exists when dominant role conceptions in the role-set are incompatible with one another. Two caveats should be remembered, however, when we talk of role conflict and foreign-policy change. First, roles have multiple sources and any attempt at explaining change will have to take this into account. Second, roles are sensitive to situational context and time. As Horrocks and Jackson (1972: 102) point out, 'Although a social role may be a means for manifesting an identity it is bound to the context in which it is exercised. Social situations have their own demand character in the sense that they set expectancies for those individuals who participate in the situation.'

There are a number of reasons why role conflicts may arise. First, a 'role-set' normally consists of a number of different roles, several of which are generated from different institutional contexts, both domestic and international. As Rosenau (1987: 46) points out, 'individuals who make foreign policy occupy a number of roles in a number of systems and, accordingly, they are simultaneously subjective to a number of conflicting role expectations'. Combining a range of role conceptions inevitably entails compromises and ambiguities in order to manage competing expectations. Second, role conflicts are more likely when the conditions and context within which they were originally formulated change. Clearly, the end of the Cold War constitutes a 'critical juncture' of this type, but changing context may also apply to unexpected behaviour from another role-player.

In his study of *Change and Stability in Foreign Policy* Goldmann (1988: 25) proposes that policy (in)stability is related to whether cognitive beliefs are (1) central, (2) inconsistent and (3) testable. One way in which we can explore potential role conflicts and foreign-policy change is by focusing on these three issues relating to the (in)stability of role conceptions. Three propositions can be made in this regard.

First, a role conception tends to be stable when it is central and compatible with other roles within the role-set. Role conceptions evolve and dissolve within a particular setting and they derive power from the cultural and cognitive functions they serve within that setting. A role's centrality is indicative of the extent to which it has become broadly shared among policy-makers. A high level of intersubjectivity suggests that the role is closely linked to the EU's international identity. As Rosenau (1987: 59–60) concludes, 'integrated and consensual role scenarios are the glue that holds collectivities together; just as discrepant and competitive scenarios are the acid that paralyze or tear them apart'. The closer the interconnection between identity and role, the more resistant a role conception will be to change. The reason for this is that when states, or an international actor like the EU, develop their roles, they also develop myths and institutions to protect them (Chafetz 1996/97: 666). In contrast, when the centrality or salience of a given role conception is unclear, it is more prone to change.

Second, the role will be unstable if the contents, in terms of norms and objectives, are inconsistent. Given that the actor's mind-set is assumed to be 'theory-driven', there is an aspiration to maintain consistency. This may lead either to information being manipulated to avoid any inconsistency or to an increasingly contradictory foreign policy. Inconsistency may be caused by lack of consensus about the meaning of a particular role. This may in turn be linked to the fact that identity is increasingly contested, generating conflicting normative ideas about appropriate foreign-policy behaviour. It should, however, be pointed out that it is not uncommon to find what appear to be contradictory role conceptions within a 'role-set' (Aggestam 2004: 245–8). As Bradbury *et al.* (1972: 49) note, 'many individuals do not succeed in being consistent and may compartmentalize effective if the conflicting situation can be kept separate in time, place and role-partners, and if awareness of the contradictions does not produce schizophrenia'.

Third, the more questioned and testable a role conception, the less stable it is. As the belief system literature suggests, the extent to which dissenting voices can be heard is related to whether a belief system is open or closed (Holsti 1963). A high degree of intersubjectivity tends to suppress dissent and provide attitudinal conformity. However, as we have pointed out already, this consensus is likely to be challenged when major changes in the environment take place, which may lead to 'cognitive dissonance' (Festinger 1957). Hence, competing discourses, some of which may have been latent for some time, become more pervasive. The search for normative ideas to express a new role legitimizes dissent and debate beyond the bounds of previously acceptable frameworks. 'Those who violate older norms are not automatically sanctioned, which opens considerably the range of positions that can be put forward in the policy debate' (Flynn 1995: 239).

In conclusion, it should be pointed out that whether role conflicts become manifest can be dependent on the skill of the foreign-policy maker. The extent to which roles are socialized and provide detailed normative guidance varies, allowing in some cases considerable scope for interpretation and choice to the individual policy-maker. Policy-makers may indeed find themselves in a situation where a role conception provides little normative guidance and are therefore forced to make their own decisions. As Hollis and Smith (1990: 155) observe:

> No role could possibly be specified in enough detail to make all decisions automatic ... There are some specific duties of a role, some

> dos and don'ts which set limits to what may be attempted. But there is also an area of indeterminacy, governed only by a broad duty to act so as to be able to justify oneself afterwards.

A certain amount of discretion in interpreting roles appears indispensable to accommodate potentially conflicting roles that different institutional contexts generate. The room for manoeuvre and potential for innovation by individual policy-makers, particularly those found in authoritative positions, is most likely when there is a role conflict; when there is no generally accepted means of overcoming a role conflict; or when conflicting roles are so finely balanced that no particular action is favoured (cf. Bradbury *et al.* 1972: 52). This may induce a learning process, giving rise to new definitions and understandings of a role.

Conclusion

This chapter has sought to develop a distinctive framework for how we may analyse and understand common rules of action emerging in European foreign policy. Focusing on role allows one to go beyond traditional explanations of foreign policy as the prudent search for power. In fact, the concept of role helps us understand obligations and commitments that an actor perceives beyond mere considerations to maximize its material interests. A European role conception thus reflects norms about the purpose and orientation of the EU as an actor in the international system.

The main features of the analytical framework outlined in this chapter are summarized in Figure 1.1. The analytical model rests on a meta-theoretical assumption about structuration that incorporates three role perspectives – institution, interaction and intention – which constitute the basic building blocks of the framework. Role theory applied to foreign-policy analysis stresses how foreign policy is both purposeful and shaped by institutions and structures. The situated actor is considered to be embedded in various institutional structures that generate expectations of certain role behaviour, yet is also envisaged to be reflexive vis-à-vis these institutional rules of action. In the interaction process with other actors, role-playing involves an element of experimentation of how to perform roles more adequately. It thus involves a process of learning that may induce the adoption of new roles. Hence, depending on the extent to which role-playing or role-taking (a non-reflective form of action) takes place, the role performance may either reproduce or change the structures of foreign policy.

Since its inception in the 1970s, role analysis has primarily been used in the study of national foreign policy. But as this chapter has argued, role theory is potentially a very productive tool with which to analyse the evolving common foreign and security policy of the EU. In particular, it can help elucidate the shift in the EU's general role as a 'civilian power' to a

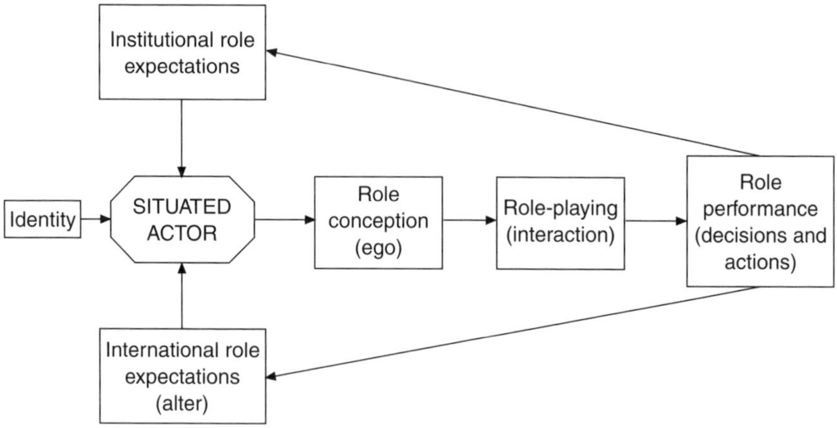

Figure 1.1 Analytical framework for role analysis.

conception of itself as an 'ethical power', willing and able to use military force in support of an ethical foreign policy – in short, its role conception as a 'force for good' striving to make the world a 'better place' (European Security Strategy 2003).[6]

Notes

1 For a more detailed elaboration on role analysis, see Aggestam 2004.

2 A further distinction – between 'status' and 'role' – can be added to this definition of institution. Role is the behavioural repertoire characteristic of a positional arrangement within the structure. The sociologist Ralph Linton used 'status' (position) to define an ideal pattern of conduct, and 'role' to define actual behaviour: 'A status, as distinct from the individual who may occupy it, is simply a collection of rights and duties... A *role* represents the dynamic aspects of status.' However, as Linton went on to argue, 'Role and status are quite inseparable, and the distinction between it of only academic interest. There are no roles without statuses or statuses without roles' (quoted in Thomas and Biddle 1966: 7). This type of analysis, focusing on the relationship between status (capability and rank) and foreign-policy roles was, for instance, conducted during the Cold War of the two superpowers (Jönsson 1984; Westerlund 1987).

3 Hill (1998: 34) prefers to talk of 'functions' rather than roles.

4 A method by which to explore the multiplicity of roles and their relevance within the role-set is to construct a role typology – see further Aggestam 2004: 77–8.

5 For exceptions, see Barnett (1993); Chafetz (1996/7); Hyde-Price (2000); Goldmann (2001); Le Prestre (1997).

6 This convergence on a common role of Europe as an ethical power was found in a comparative role analysis of British, French and German foreign policy (Aggestam 2004: 241–5).

References

Adler, E. (1997) 'Seizing the Middle Ground: Constructivism in World Politics', *European Journal of International Relations*, 3 (3).

Aggestam, L. (2004) 'A European Foreign Policy? Role Conceptions and the Politics of Identity in Britain, France and Germany', Stockholm Studies in Politics 106, doctoral dissertation, Stockholm University: Department of Political Science.

Barnett, M. (1993) 'Institutions, Roles, and Disorder: The Case of the Arab States System', *International Studies Quarterly*, 37 (3).

Biddle, B. J. (1979) *Role Theory: Expectations, Identities, and Behaviors*, New York: Academic Press.

Bradbury, M., Heading, B. and Hollis, M. (1972) 'The Man and the Mask: A Discussion of Role-Theory', in J. A. Jackson (ed.) *Role*, Cambridge: Cambridge University Press.

Chafetz, G. (1996/97) 'The Struggle for a National Identity in Post-Soviet Russia', *Political Science Quarterly*, 111 (4).

Duchêne, F. (1972) 'Europe's role in world peace', in R. Mayne (ed.) *Europe Tomorrow*, London: Fontana.

Edström, B. (1988) 'Japan's Quest for a Role in the World: Roles Ascribed to Japan Nationally and Internationally 1969–1982', doctoral dissertation, Stockholm University: Institute of Oriental Languages.

European Security Strategy (2003) 'A Secure Europe in a Better World', Brussels, 12 December.

Festinger, L. (1957) *A Theory of Cognitive Dissonance*, Stanford, CA: Stanford University Press.

Flynn, G. (1995) 'French Identity and Post-Cold War Europe', in G. Flynn (ed.) *Remaking the Hexagon: The New France in the New Europe*, Boulder, CO: Westview Press.

Giddens, A. (1979) *Central Problems in Social Theory: Action, Structure and Contradictions in Social Analysis*, London: Macmillan.

Giddens, A. (1983) 'Comments on the Theory of Structuration', *Journal for the Theory of Social Behaviour*, 13.

Giddens, A. (1984) *The Constitution of Society*, Cambridge: Polity Press.

Goffman, E. (1959) *The Presentation of Self in Everyday Life*, Harmondsworth: Penguin.

Goldmann, K. (1988) *Change and Stability in Foreign Policy: The Problems and Possibilities of Détente*, Princeton, NJ: Princeton University Press.

Hay, C. (1995) 'Structure and Agency', in D. Marsh and G. Stoker (eds) *Theory and Methods in Political Science*, Basingstoke: Macmillan.

Hill, C. (1993) 'The Capability–Expectations Gap, or Conceptualizing Europe's International Role', *Journal of Common Market Studies*, 31 (3).

Hill, C. (1998) 'Closing the Capabilities–Expectations Gap?', in J. Peterson and H. Sjursen (eds) *A Common Foreign Policy for Europe? Competing Visions of the CFSP*, London: Routledge.

Hollis, M. and Smith, S. (1990) *Explaining and Understanding International Relations*, Oxford: Clarendon Press.

Holsti, K. (1970) 'National Role Conceptions in the Study of Foreign Policy', *International Studies Quarterly*, 14 (3).

Holsti, K. (1970/1987) 'National Role Conceptions in the Study of Foreign Policy', in S. Walker (ed.) *Role Theory and Foreign Policy Analysis*, Durham, NC: Duke University Press.

Holsti, O. (1963) 'The Belief System and National Images: A Case Study', *Conflict Resolution*, 6 (3).

Horrocks, J. E. and Jackson, D. W. (1972) *Self and Role: A Theory of Self-process and Role Behavior*, Boston, MA: Houghton Mifflin.

Hudson, V. and Vore, C. (1995) 'Foreign Policy Analysis Yesterday, Today, and Tomorrow', *Mershon International Studies Review*, 39.

Hyde-Price, A. (2000) *Germany and European Order: Enlarging NATO and the EU*, Manchester: Manchester University Press.

Jackson, J. A. (1972) 'Role – Editorial Introduction', in J. A. Jackson (ed.) *Role*, Cambridge: Cambridge University Press.

Jönsson, C., Tägil, S. and Törnqvist, G. (2000) *Organizing European Space*, London: Sage Publications.

Keohane, R. (1994) 'International Institutions: Two Approaches', in F. Kratochwil and E. D. Mansfield (eds) *International Organization: A Reader*, New York: HarperCollins College Publishers.

Kirste, K. and Maull, H. W. (1996) 'Zivilmacht und Rollentheorie', *Zeitschrift für Internationale Beziehungen*, 3 (2).

Le Prestre, P. G. (1997) 'Author! Author! Defining Foreign Policy Roles after the Cold War', in P. G. Le Prestre (ed.) *Role Quests in the Post-Cold War Era: Foreign Policies in Transition*, Montreal: McGill-Queen's University Press.

March, J. and Olsen, J. P. (1998) 'The Institutional Dynamics of International Political Orders', Arena Working Paper 5, Oslo: Centre of European Studies, University of Oslo.

Mead, G. (1934) *Mind, Self, and Society*, Chicago: University of Chicago Press.

Rosenau, J. (1987) 'Roles and Role Scenarios in Foreign Policy', in S. Walker (ed.) *Role Theory and Foreign Policy Analysis*, Durham, NC: Duke University Press.

Rosenau, J. (1990) *Turbulence in World Politics: a Theory of Change and Continuity*, New York: Harvester Wheatsheaf.

Searing, D. D. (1991) 'Roles, Rules, and Rationality in the New Institutionalism', *American Political Science Review*, 85 (4).

Smith, S. (2001) 'Reflectivist and Constructivist Approaches to International Theory', in J. Baylis and S. Smith (eds) *The Globalization of World Politics: An Introduction to International Relations*, Oxford: Oxford University Press.

Solana, Javier (2003) 'Europe and America: Partners of Choice', speech to the Foreign Policy Association, New York, 7 May.

Solana, Javier (2005a) 'Shaping an Effective EU Foreign Policy', speech at Konrad Adenauer Foundation, Brussels, 24 January.

Solana, Javier (2005b) 'The Future of the European Union as an International Actor', article published by YES (Young Europeans for Security), 23 March.

Thomas, E. J. and Biddle, B. J. (1966) 'The Nature and History of Role Theory', in B. J. Biddle and E. J. Thomas (eds) *Role Theory: Concepts and Research*, New York: John Wiley.

Walker, S. G. (1987) 'Role Theory and Foreign Policy Analysis: An Evaluation', in S. Walker (ed.) *Role Theory and Foreign Policy Analysis*, Durham, NC: Duke University Press.

Wendt, A. (1992) 'Anarchy is What States Make of It: The Social Construction of Power Politics', *International Organization*, 46.

Wendt, A. (1999) *Social Theory of International Politics*, Cambridge: Cambridge University Press.

Westerlund, U. (1987) 'Superpower Roles: A Comparative Analysis of United States and Soviet Foreign Policy', doctoral dissertation, Lund University: Department of Political Science.

Wish, N. B. (1980) 'Foreign Policy Makers and their National Role Conceptions', *International Studies Quarterly*, 24.

Wish, N. B. (1987) 'National Attributes as Sources of National Role Conceptions: A Capability–Motivation Model', in S. Walker (ed.) *Role Theory and Foreign Policy Analysis*, Durham, NC: Duke University Press.

Young, O. (1989) *International Cooperation: Building Regimes for Natural Resources and the Environment*, Ithaca, NY: Cornell University Press.

2 A multilateralist role for the EU?

Knud Erik Jørgensen

Nowadays multilateralism comes with adjectives attached. While the Bush administration talks about 'selective' or 'à la carte' multilateralism (Nye 2002: 154), the European Union (EU) has opted for the notion of 'effective' multilateralism. The concept entered the official vocabulary in *A Secure Europe* (2003), and the objective of supporting multilateralism has been described in more detail in documents such as *The European Union and the United Nations: the Choice of Multilateralism* (2003) and *The Enlarging European Union at the United Nations: Making Multilateralism Matter* (2004). No matter which adjective these powers prefer, the adjectives suggest that multilateralism is in a profound defensive position. Seemingly, multilateralism has been given a bad name and not everything is like it used to be. 'The present situation has a different feel about it' . . . 'this crisis of multilateralism is different', declares John Ruggie (2003). This is significant, because he has traditionally been among the first to downplay crises of multilateralism.

If the present crisis of multilateralism is different, i.e. more profound than previous crises, then the EU's grand initiative to support 'effective multilateralism' has been launched at a very special conjuncture in world politics, perhaps as a kind of rescue mission. For the EU, saving and reforming as well as extending the multilateral system would constitute a significant new role in international politics. Indeed, to take on such a global responsibility would add an important new dimension to the EU's international identity. The initiative comes at a time when key policy areas of EU external relations such as trade, development and 'classic' foreign policy (CFSP) have been reconsidered, and defence policy has been added to the Union's portfolio of external policies. Indeed, the events of 11 September 2001 and 11 March 2004 have prompted a thorough reconsideration of means and ends in international affairs. These increased engagements in foreign affairs are bound to have an impact on the Union's international role. None the less, or for that reason, the precise nature of the Union's foreign policy remains highly contested, ranging from 'existence denied', via widespread scepticism (based for instance on the absence of an EU policy on Iraq) to evidence of significant influence on international affairs.[1] Hence, there are eminently good reasons to focus on the EU's international identity, new international roles and policies.

It is common to argue that the EU has a multilateral 'soul', i.e. that the Union has been built on a multilateral edifice and is aiming at projecting this 'domestic' quality worldwide. In other words, experience with multilateralism 'at home' prompts a preference for multilateralism globally. This school of thought includes some strange bedfellows. Thus, the Italian foreign minister, Franco Frattini, claims that 'the multilateral perspective is written into the genetic code of the European Union' (2003). Former Development Commissioner Paul Nielsson has pointed out that 'The European Union knows better than most that multilateral processes tend to be slow and difficult, and rarely do their results satisfy every participant' (2000). In the view of Robert Cooper:

> Multilateralism and the rule of law have an intrinsic value . . . Multilateralism – for which the European Union stands and which is in some way inherent in its construction – is more than the refuge of the weak. It embodies at a global level the ideas of democracy and community that all civilised states stand for on the domestic level.
>
> (2003: 164, 168)

European policy-makers are not alone in such reasoning. Robert Kagan has made a similar argument. 'The transmission of the European miracle to the rest of the world has become Europe's new *mission civilisatrice*' (2003: 61; see also 2002). Furthermore, he claims that the objective of supporting multilateralism is caused by European weakness. 'Their tactics, like their goal, are the tactics of the weak.' In short, Kagan explains the transatlantic divide by a combination of material and ideational factors. Similarly, Charles Krauthammer (2004) argues that 'the European conceit that relations with all nations – regardless of ideology, regardless of culture, regardless even of open hostility – should be transacted on the EU model of suasion and norms and negotiations and solemn contractual agreements is an illusion' (2004: 9–10). In this fashion, and somewhat paradoxically, the school of thought is represented both by 'liberal' European policy-makers, regarding multilateralism as a virtue, and by American neo-conservatives, believing it is a vice.

Is the EU on a rescue mission? If so, does 'the weak' have the power it takes to save the multilateral system? Has Europe found a new *mission civilisatrice*? I make three arguments in this chapter. First, while it is beyond doubt that the EU has significant multilateral experiences 'domestically', and that it has invested heavily in sponsoring multilateralism internationally, I question whether the shared analysis presented above reflects the Union's foreign-policy practice. I argue that there is significant variation across time and policies; that within the EU there are several currents of thinking about multilateralism, and that processes of collective identity formation and policy-making are intertwined in ways that sometimes produce less than synergetic outcomes. Second, the idea of actors aiming at projecting domestic institutions internationally is in principle applicable to the EU. However, there seem to be serious obstacles to achieving the strategic objective of 'effective multilateralism'. Third, given that the Union also makes use of bilateral and unilateral strategies, the multilateral strategy is only part of the Union's foreign-policy instruments and objectives. Hence, I explore the so-called differentiated approach, i.e. the option of pragmatically choosing among foreign-policy means and ends, arguing that the Union need not be a 'heroic' multilateralist. Indeed, in foreign-policy practice, the Union has never subscribed to such an option but prudently or imprudently aimed at a range of objectives by employing a range of means. In the conclusion, I summarize my findings.

Being multilateral: variations, currents and identity

Terms like 'genetic code', 'intrinsic value', 'edifice' and 'inherently multilateral' connote timelessness and features etched in stone. Concerning the international role of the EU, nothing could be more misleading. It is rather the case that the EU's international role shows considerable variation across time and across policies. Thus, the aspiration to play a major role in the multilateral system, if not to save it, is fairly recent. Furthermore, within the EU there are several currents of thinking about multilateralism. These currents can be defined in a traditional fashion, i.e. within the matrix of member states. Such an approach has its advantages but also some disadvantages. In order to highlight other important aspects, I define the currents along thematic issues associated with multilateral strategies. Finally, there are some complex linkages between international identity, interest and policy. The EU's objective of supporting effective multilateralism provides an excellent case of illustrating these linkages. In the following three sections I explore these issues in further detail.

Varying implications of a multilateral nature

Kagan rightly points out that the EU's contemporary multilateral vocation is far from being based on some timeless national character (2003: 7–8). In a historical perspective, the EU's international role has changed markedly. In the late 1950s, the notion of a 'colonial power Europe' would have made some sense. Half of the founding six European states were colonial powers, and the EC's relations with colonies of member states were from the very beginning institutionalized (Ravenhill 1985; Grilli 1993). When EPC was launched around 1970, one observer contemplated whether we were witnessing a return of the classic Concert of Europe (Berger 1971). Classic debates on the EU's international role go back to the 1970s. Contending perspectives include Francois Duchêne's (1972) conceptualization of the EC as 'a civilian power', whereas Johan Galtung (1973) imagined 'a super-power in the making'. At the same time, Gunnar Sjöstedt (1977) systematically explored what it takes to be an international actor, and the degree to which it makes sense to regard the EC as such an actor. In the early 1980s, Hedley Bull (1982) pleaded for 'a military power Europe', claiming that 'civilian power Europe' is a contradiction in terms. More recently, Ian Manners (2002) has proposed the notion of 'a normative power Europe', thereby closely mirroring one of the self-images of the Union (see Richardson 2002). All these notions of power – civilian, 'super', 'military' and 'normative' – are more normative than empirical and should consequently be analysed as such, i.e. by means of normative theorizing or political theory.

The EU's international role also varies considerably across policies. In some policy fields the EU plays a major role whereas it is negligible in other issue areas of international politics. When explaining variation among policies in terms of power and influence, a suitable starting point could be the former Trade Commissioner, Pascal Lamy, who has put forward some propositions about the influence of the EU. Thus, he identifies connections between European unity and degree of influence in world politics, pointing out that the EU's role is considerable within (1) trade and environmental policy; (2) catching up concerning development; (3) insignificant concerning global financial governance and traditional foreign policy, including security and defence. Lamy's intriguing proposition invites further analysis. Why is it that the EU has so much difficulty in making a coherent policy on the Iraq war, while it is able to promote international environmental policies and to enjoy an entrepreneurial role during the process of setting up institutions like the WTO? These issues will not be addressed in the present context. None the less, it is important to point out that the 'weak' EU, with its inherently multilateral self, produces such gross variations across time and policies.

Currents of thinking about multilateralism

Joachim Krause's 'Multilateralism: Behind European Views' is particularly welcome in two respects. First, it addresses important topical issues on international order and, by extension, the international role of the EU. Second, it will presumably trigger a debate about contemporary relations between the EU and its (key) member states. According to Joachim Krause, there is no single European approach but many different forms and rationales behind the general European preference for multilateralism. 'For purposes of simplification, the greater European perception of multilateralism is better understood when broken down into three schools of thought: the German, the French and British' (2004: 48).

When examining the foundations of European multilateralism, Krause's claim is a suitable point of departure. For purposes of understanding the European approach to multilateralism, it is important to explore its genesis. In a comprehensive study, Lisbeth Aggestam (2004) has shown how a consensus view has developed among the EU 'Big Three' (France, Germany and the UK), and how this consensus position has been elevated to the EU level, to become the EU's sponsorship of effective multilateralism. So, whereas it is misleading to assume a common EU approach to multilateralism and denigrate the influence of key member states, it is equally misleading to claim that behind European views there are national conceptions only and no commonality. Furthermore, national conceptions need not be the only available parameters when analysing the many different forms and rationales behind European views. The EU has adopted an official policy on multilateralism, spelled out by key officials. However, within the Union there are at least three currents of thinking and each current has its subscribers. Each current also carries specific implications for finding solutions to the crisis of multilateralism, including the chances of making 'effective multilateralism' a success. In the following, I examine each current of thinking.

Some hope that a return of 'old time' multilateralism is possible, i.e. an option that perhaps amounts to a return of the 'good old days'. In a splash of double wishful thinking, some EU policy-makers look forward to the end of the Bush administration and to the dawn of a Democratic administration. The outcome of the American presidential election in November 2004 triggered deep disappointment because it would mean another four years before the US would have a chance to find its multilateral instincts – its good old self – defining the national interest as fully compatible with multilateralism. Generally, the assumption is that we are in a Bush (extended) situation and not in a unipolar era. Or, alternatively, that the unipolar era is not as determinate for US foreign policy as both Robert Kagan and Charles Krauthammer believe. Once the Bush situation is over, the benign American hegemon will begin, again, to facilitate, orchestrate and pay for solutions to global problems. This option would allow EU policy-makers to continue to be schizophrenic about the balance between national and EU foreign-policy action; continue to pretend that, individually, member states make a difference in world politics; continue to outsource the provision of European security to the US; agree in principle to multilateral principles, yet feel free to defect when deemed necessary. The option hardly makes it necessary to develop new lasting international roles for the EU. Old roles are more than sufficient, and the function of 'effective multilateralism' would be to keep the multilateral system afloat. It would only be a temporary objective, i.e. it should be in place as long as we are in a Bush situation.

A second current of thought assumes further decline of multilateralism and expects the future to bring more of the same (of the present). The US will increasingly project its domestic institutions to the international arena, indeed it will become increasingly difficult to make a distinction between one and the other. International order will become a function of fear, and investment in the cement of international society will be kept at a minimal level. Global law enforcement will be sought and accomplished by means of zero-tolerance standards. Nationalism and protectionism will be key parameters in the US's international strategies. In other words, a situation characterized by naked unipolarity. Most likely the UN, as we know it, will be dissolved and replaced by a new world organization of democratic states. It is significant that scholars are engaged in reconsidering the usefulness of terms like international hierarchy (Lake 2003) and empire (Ikenberry 2002; Hassner 2003). According to David Lake, we have somehow forgotten that power relations in the international system *de facto* are hierarchical, i.e. some are more equal, than others. It is only *de jure* that all sovereign states are equal and that the system is anarchical. We are reminded of a classic IR rule of thumb: legal rules have their limits. According to Hassner (2003), the US has become an empire, and the global arena is characterized by hierarchical authority structures. Some states are sovereign and some are suzerain. By contrast, Ruggie has ridiculed the employment of the notion of empire, arguing that an (American) empire would not have allowed three of the world's poorest countries to bring the US into a minority situation in the UN Security Council on the Iraq issue in the spring of 2003. In any case, it is possible to further specify consequences for the EU and multilateralism. John Ikenberry argues that the US 'has systematically used multilateral agreements as tools of grand strategy and world order building' (2002: 122). In other words, it is impossible or at least misleading to separate issues of grand strategy from issues related to multilateral institutions. Furthermore, he emphasizes that the US has always been ambivalent about multilateral institutions, exactly because multilateralism for a leading state, is about losing something and winning something else. Yet different actors assess the precise balance between losing and winning differently, implying that the value of multilateralism has been hotly contested most of the time. Finally, Ikenberry argues that 'today one of the United States' central policy problems is its own predominance'. He goes on to ask, 'Why did the United States seek to establish order after World War II in Western Europe through multilateral commitments while pursuing a series of bilateral security agreements in Asia?' The essence of his answer is that power relations between the leading state (the US) and the subordinate states differ:

> The basic difference between Asia and Europe, however, was that the United States was both more dominant in Asia and wanted less out of Asia. In Europe, the US came up with an elaborate agenda for uniting the European states, creating an institutional bulwark against communism, and supporting centrist democratic regimes.
>
> (Ibid.)

During the 1990s all three US rationales for Cold War transatlantic relations have disappeared: communism is gone, democratic regimes have been consolidated in Western Europe (and they have been introduced in Central and Eastern Europe). Furthermore, if Europe becomes politically more united, Europe will constitute not only a partner but also a potential rival to the US. By contrast, in Asia 'extreme hegemony' originally led to a system of bilateral relations. Hence, there are few reasons to change the state of affairs over there. In short, given the present era of unprecedented American predominance, it is tempting to suggest that in the future the US will handle the world more equally, that is, US–Asia relations in the past (and present) provide a model of the future world order. From an American perspective, Europe has become Asia-like. In this perspective, the promotion of 'effective multilateralism' seems to be based on a fatal misreading of opportunities. The role of the EU will be minimal and inter-state bilateralism will characterize transatlantic relations. Such developments will constitute a disastrous blow to the EU's international policies, designed to be conducted in a multilateral environment. Because bilateralism has always co-existed with multilateralism, we will witness a new balance between one and the other institutional form.

Third, others make the plea that the EU should pick up the multilateral torch, arguing that the multilateral system is too valuable to leave behind. The background is that the US's declining interest in multilateral institutions is regarded as an inevitable and regrettable fact. Realizing the unlikelihood of launching global 'multilateralism minus one' by means of collective action, the search for alternative champions of multilateralism begins. The EU emerges as a potential, perhaps the most obvious and willing, candidate. After all, the EU has insisted that effective multilateralism is among its strategic objectives (A Secure Europe 2003). This option would allow the EU to become a truly global player, playing at centre court. Because the EU is not a state actor, some degree of minilateralism would be predictable. Minilateralism can be defined as the 'creation of core groups and the multilateralisation of their agreements' (Kratochwil 1993: 468). A distinction should be made between minilateral procedures and the legitimacy of the procedures and their outcome. In this area there are no mechanics at play. Sometimes the procedure is accepted and thus legitimate, perhaps because of urgency or failed multilateralism. Within the EU, the creation of the Contact Group was accepted, although reluctantly and with caveats. At other times, even efficient minilateralism is not accepted because excluded states dislike the *fait accompli* presented, they conclude that better outcomes can be reached in a second try (Cancún), or they prefer the *status quo* to change worked out by means of minilateralism. For minilateralism to work, it is necessary that 'the many' accept agreements reached among 'the few'. If such acceptance is not put forward, there will be no multilateral agreement. EU policy-making circles have mixed views on the merits of minilateralism. On the one hand, some do not like the idea, for instance the former Development Commissioner, Paul Nielsson. After the Cancún failure meeting, he argued that 'Multilateralism is not about gathering international backing for pre-set national interests. Nor can it be about a few powerful nations trying to work out the parameters of international negotiations between themselves' (2003). Other critics point to the image of rubber-stamping, arguing that the lack of direct involvement in negotiated agreements makes failure of compliance more likely among those not actively involved. Furthermore, public legitimacy might be reduced because 'they – "our representatives" – just accept anything decided among the powerful'. If key states are insensitive to the preferences of rubber-stampers, minilateralism is less likely to be successful. For that reason, the doctrine 'rules for the world, exceptionalism for the US' has a hard time getting accepted.

There are, however, also positive dimensions to minilateralism. Nielsson made his comments after Cancún, not after the more successful follow-on meeting in Geneva. Yet the minilateral dimension was equally pronounced. Potentially, minilateralism makes multilateralism more efficient, it makes it easier to reach agreements and also in a more time-efficient manner. Furthermore, the approach makes compliance more likely because agreements reflect the interest of states with the highest stakes in a given issue. However, the best argument in favour of minilateralism is that the alternatives are often worse. Alternatives include no agreement or agreements reached by means of bilateralism. Obviously, sometimes no agreement is better than a bad agreement. But were LDCs better off with no agreement in Cancún compared to accepting the agreement prepared by the US and the EU? Unsuccessful multilateral diplomacy breeds frustration, as shown by the EU Trade Commissioner, Pascal Lamy, after Cancún, 'We will have to have a good hard think amongst ourselves.' According to an observer, Lamy 'wants to hint at an option that the EU may focus on bilateral and plurilateral talks' (*EUobserver*, 16 September 2003).

A question of identity

The relationship between identity, role and policy invites further reflection. It seems to me, that at least part of the existing confusion is caused by the fact that 'multilateralism' can play a role in each of these features. It obviously takes more space than is available here to explicate these complex linkages, so a brief tentative outline will have to do. First, I believe it is significant that the EU not only *responds* to global or regional changes by means of adapting *domestic* policies and institutions. On the contrary, the EU aims at shaping its international environment, protecting its interests and contributing to global solutions, and these international roles contribute to making the EU an international actor. It is also significant that the EU has aspirations to play a role *in* international organizations, i.e. not just *being* an international organization. This demonstrates that the EU is somehow 'special', aiming at playing a role as an actor in world politics. This given, it is not surprising that the EU for years has invested economic, political and organizational resources and gradually gained influence in multilateral institutions such as the UN, OSCE, FAO, WTO and many other organizations.[2] This aspiration contributes significantly to the EU's international identity, confirming that 'identity', 'role' and 'policy' are closely linked.

Clearly, the support of effective multilateralism plays a role in ongoing processes of collective identity formation. When asked the existential question 'Who are we in this contemporary world?', one possible answer is, 'We are the people who believe in the value of global governance, and therefore we make support of multilateral institutions a strategic objective.' When presenting reasons for investment in multilateral institutions, policy-makers frequently point out that the EU is founded on a multilateral edifice. In this fashion, they highlight that the aim comes from within the Union, that the Union is bound to assume such a role. However, the Union's embrace of multilateral institutions can also be seen as an unintended consequence of the Bush administration's choice of à la carte multilateralism. This only confirms the insight of theories of identity, that is, that identity grows on the basis of two basic questions, 'Who am I?' and 'Who am I in relation to others?' This can be further specified in the sense that identity, role and policy can be bridged and fruitfully analysed by focusing on the function of foreign policy 'principles' and official references to European values. That is, when senior officials like former Commissioners Christopher Patten and Pascal Lamy, as well as the High Representative, Javier Solana, identify European values and principles as something 'we can stand up for', they aim at creating a European public philosophy within the field of foreign affairs. In other words, they attempt to create the kind of principles to which George Kennan (1995) has previously referred. If successful, they will have created a compulsory component for any process of identity-making; and, at the same time, a precondition for a sustainable new EU international role with clout.

Multilateralism also plays a role for policy-making, that is, political action intended to achieve certain goals by employment of specific means. The strategic objective of supporting effective multilateralism is part of the European security strategy. However, if A Secure Europe (2003) is going to provide what its title promises, then the objective has to be spelled out in numerous policy documents, all serving a function at lower but more concrete levels of policy-making. A range of such specific policy documents have been adopted, but given the grandiose nature of effective multilateralism most are yet to come. There is no reason, in the present context, to go into a detailed account for policy-making. In contrast, there is reason to reiterate that if we look for policy coherence in cases where multilateralism is playing a role in processes of collective identity formation, then we will most likely reach misleading conclusions.

Projecting multilateralism globally: a feasibility test

The issue of domestic–international linkages is probably as old as the idea of a distinct international system. The entire literature that has been subsumed under the label of second image focuses on how states try to shape their international environment. The question about linkages between domestic and multilateral institutions is just a sub-set of that literature. It is therefore hardly surprising that sooner or later the perspective would be applied to the EU. In the present context, there are no reasons to account for the long story of views on the EU and the world. Instead I will focus specifically on linkages between the EU and international institutions.

It is easy to document that the EU invests heavily in multilateral institutions and that the Union is strongly committed to achieve effective multilateralism. However, this may prove to be insufficient. Indeed, there seem to be serious problems to making effective multilateralism a success. For a start, it is helpful to reconsider the key rationale of multilateralism. According to Ikenberry (2002):

> The attraction of institutional agreements for a leading state is that they potentially lock other states into stable and predictable policy orientations, thereby reducing the need to use coercion to secure the dominant state's foreign policy aims. But the price that the leading state must pay for this institutionalised cooperation is a reduction in its own policy autonomy and unfettered ability to exercise power.

In the case of the EU, such a rationale implies at least three problems. The first problem concerns the need to use coercion to secure the EU's foreign-policy aims. Coercion is often understood to be employment of military means and, as is well known, the EU simply does not possess such means. Even if coercion is understood more broadly, coercion may still pose a problem. Some argue that coercion is not what the EU is good at nor a quality the EU should develop. However, the argument should not be overstated. Coercive means are not absent from the EU's foreign-policy toolbox. Economic sanctions, financial instruments, policies of conditionality all belong to the coercive kind of instruments. In transatlantic trade conflicts, the EU has proved willing and capable of playing the tit-for-tat sanctions game. Concerning EU enlargement, the strongest coercive instrument is the prospect of membership, i.e. an instrument that has been capable of fundamentally changing the European continent. Despite these coercive instruments, the question remains whether the EU employs coercion to such an extent that multilateral agreements and institutions look favourable as an alternative. What applies to coercion also applies to the second problematic issue, 'a reduction in its own policy autonomy and unfettered ability to exercise power'. As regards the EU, both features surely exist but they cannot be said to be among the EU's dominant qualities. From the perspective of other states, the obvious question is why they should enter multilateral arrangements, created under the auspices of the EU, if there is not much to gain in terms of restraining or constraining the EU. The third problem is a so-called blow-back problem. Could it be that Ikenberry's rationale of multilateralism does not work very well in the case of the EU because it has been modelled on the US? In other words, is the problem related to the explanans rather than to the explanandum? Similarly, some would regard it a problem that the EU is not a state. However, the EU has proved to be a capable international actor, and its non-state nature is apparently a bigger problem for certain theories than for the EU.

Peter F. Cowhey has explored linkages between domestic politics and multilateralism, particularly 'when the promises of dominant powers are credible in a multilateral order' (1993: 158). He examines the close relationship between domestic politics and credibility, pointing out why for instance Japanese domestic politics makes Japan a relatively unsuitable sponsor of multilateralism. Such reflections seem most relevant to apply to the case of the EU and in the following I will briefly look into these matters. Making a priority of 'effective multilateralism' may well have been triggered as a response to the unilaterally-minded foreign policy of the Bush administration. But do European governments 'EU–domestically' perform in a fashion that makes their multilateral strategy attractive or credible to others? There are reasons to doubt this. In the day-to-day working of the EU, some multilateral principles and norms seem to be in trouble. Euro-stability pact politics has not been characterized by overwhelming interest in strict and equal compliance. Rather, it has been rules for smaller EU member states and *exceptionalism* for France and Germany. Furthermore, France has several times demonstrated outspoken reluctance to comply with sanctions, e.g. sanctions imposed on Zimbabwe in 2003. During the political war over Iraq, Jacques Chirac engaged in lecturing Central Europeans in a style similar to the one favoured at the time by Secretary of Defense Donald Rumsfeld. In its international policies, the Union has demonstrated consistent constraint in complying with multilateral agreements. The banana case is one long story about the Union refusing to comply with WTO rulings, and the hormone beef case demonstrates a similar disrespect for global institutions and rules.[3] Within the field of security, NATO has been a story about European free-riding for years. When Tony Blair provides reasons for improving European defence capacity by claiming it is 'time to pay back', he implicitly acknowledges that Europe for decades has been unwilling to provide for its own security. Within the policy area of development aid, European governments have signed up to UN standards, yet at the same time they have managed to reduce spending on aid throughout the 1990s. Furthermore, the CAP costs/EU aid ratio has always been highly asymmetrical, implying that for LDCs the benefits of aid lag far behind the devastating international effects of the CAP. By demonstrating the *Primat der Innenpolitik,* the EU's international credibility has been markedly constrained. All these examples suggest that if angels always comply with international multilateral agreements, the EU is no angel. Furthermore, if the Union sometimes is incapable of making multilateralism work 'at home', how can the Union possibly expect to be recognized as a credible sponsor of multilateralism internationally?

The EU and unilateral, bilateral and multilateral strategies

When revisiting the 'inherently multilateral' school of thought, we are reminded that domestically the EU is 'good' or 'weak' or genetically coded in a multilateral fashion. Therefore, so the argument goes, it is logical for the EU to opt for a strong commitment to the multilateral system. It is relatively easy to find evidence in support of the claim in its different versions. However, it is even easier to find evidence in support of the counter-claim, i.e. that there are no strong, determining linkages between the EU's domestic institutions and the engagement in multilateralism. In the following, I will go further into detail concerning three issues. What do European unilateralists look like? How can the prudent balance between multilateral and unilateral action be described? How can a differentiated approach be recognized?

Is EU unilateral strategy a contradiction in terms?

Does the EU's new role in international politics include a role as a unilateral actor? When addressing this issue, it is useful to compare contemporary American political currents. Joseph Nye points out that in the US there are few pure unilateralists or multilateralists. He goes on to present two kinds of American unilateralists:

> Some unilateralists advocate an assertive damn-the-torpedoes approach to promoting American values . . . Other unilateralists (sometimes called sovereigntists) focus less on the promotion of American values than on their protection, and they sometimes gain support from the significant minority of isolationist opinion that still exists in this country.
>
> (2002: 154–5)

Whereas the first grouping consists of people like Robert Kagan, William Kristol and Charles Krauthammer, the second group consists of people like Jesse Helms and John Bolton. Nye summarizes his analysis by pointing out that 'This battle between multilateralists and unilateralists, often played out in a struggle between the President and Congress, has led to a somewhat schizophrenic American foreign policy' (2002: 156). Nye's categories and distinctions seem helpful concerning the pattern of orientations within American foreign policy, but do they also apply to Europe? In my view, they may indeed be helpful in identifying foreign-policy orientations in Europe. But we do not know the degree to which they are helpful, because there has been no comprehensive research programme aiming at analysing dynamics in European foreign policy along these dimensions. While the part of a schizophrenic foreign policy sounds familiar, who would be Europe's isolationists or Europe's 'damn-the-torpedoes' unilateralists? Do we have unilateral sovereigntists in Europe? How do the major currents appear from a European perspective? How differently would these orientations be represented in various EU member states? Would there be any connection with European colonial and imperial legacies or, for that matter, with the tradition of providing development aid to the Third World? The point is that we do not have solid knowledge on these aspects. Because we do not have a clear picture of the balance between European multilateralists and their critics, we cannot know precisely neither how severe the crisis of multilateralism is or what the prospects are of making effective multilateralism a success.

If we assume there is no pure multilateral and unilateral approach, how can the EU navigate between the Scylla of multilateralism and the Charybdis of unilateralism? Again, Joseph Nye's (2002: 163) reflections are helpful, and he definitely explores the proper balance between multilateral and unilateral action concerning the US. In the present context, the issue is not whether he strikes the 'right' balance but to determine the degree to which such a balance is applicable to the EU. Due to lack of space, I cannot go into a detailed analysis. However, it seems to me that all Nye's dimensions do indeed make sense also in the context of EU strategies. For instance, concerning 'intrinsically co-operative issues', Nye's conclusion is as relevant to the EU as it is to the US. Europeans seem more prepared to accept the view that common problems need common solutions. If this applies, then Nye is making a point which is self-evident to the European ear.

Would a differentiated approach be suitable?

The EU need perhaps not be an either/or heroic multilateralist. It is worth while remembering that the US has been a 'good multilateralist' in its relations with Europe, but a bilateralist when cultivating relations with Asia. In a similar fashion, the EU could conclude that a differentiated approach would be appropriate. After all, the EU's global environment is highly differentiated, and power relationships are equally differentiated. Let us for illustrative purposes look at some of the world regions and highlight preferred strategies. The EU's 'near abroad' comes in two colours: one colour for potential members and another colour for non-potential members. Concerning the first colour, enlargement negotiations have always been strictly bilateral, and it is highly unlikely that the strategy will turn multilateral in the future. No multilateral conference will be called in order to determine whether Turkey or Ukraine should become members of the EU. The second colour is reserved for states and regions at close range but, none the less, unlikely ever to become members of the EU: Russia, North Africa, the Middle East, Iran and the Caucasus region. Clearly, the EU has interests in the development of this second tier and prefers states with stable and predictable policy orientations. For decades it has been futile to contemplate too specific objectives vis-à-vis the future arc of non-members, and policy-makers have in any case been preoccupied with redefining Europe 'domestically'. Yet the enlargement process will eventually come to an end. The carrot of accession, the EU's most powerful foreign-policy instrument for achieving milieu goals, will soon 'run out of targets'. Hence, the gradual but increasingly steady development of the EU's so-called neighbourhood policy (Wallace 2003). The approach chosen seems to be a mixture of multilateralism and bilateralism. Thus, the multilateral Barcelona process covers part of the area, the Mediterranean, whereas relations with Iran and Russia for example are cultivated in a bilateral fashion. The third kind of relationships includes so-called inter-regional relations, cultivated foremost in multilateral settings (ASEM, Mercosur, ASEAN, the Gulf Co-operation Council, etc.) but also by means of bilateral relations. Finally, EU relations with the US are foremost bilateral, whereas the US for its part can choose between bilateral relations with the EU (recognizing the EU as a collective actor) and with individual EU member states. No matter how specific relations can be characterized, there are eminently good reasons to conclude that the EU is far from being the 'religious' multilateralist the Union has been claimed to be, whether for purposes of praise or scorn. It follows that the relevant issue is not whether or not the Union should adopt a differentiated approach but rather to recognize the fact that such an approach has characterized the Union's foreign-policy practice for years.

As I have demonstrated above, EU practice is far from the multilateral caricature outlined by Robert Kagan and others. But EU practice is also far from the self-proclaimed role of true believer in multilateralism. In this context, Nye's general conclusion is worthy of a longer quotation. Writing about American foreign policy, he believes his country 'should have a general preference for multilateralism, but not all multilateralism. At times we will have to go it alone. When we do so in pursuit of public goods, the nature of our ends may substitute for the means in legitimising our power in the eyes of others' (2002). Based upon the above brief analysis of the Union's balance between multilateralism and unilateralism, it is difficult to avoid the impression that Nye inadvertently has characterized current EU foreign-policy practice. His warning that unilateralism elevated as a full-fledged strategy is likely to fail has less relevance for the EU and is, in any case, aimed at the unilateralists within the Bush administration.

Conclusion

Research on the EU's changing international role has accompanied the process of European integration ever since the very beginning of the process. The aim of the present chapter has been to examine the foreign-policy objective of 'effective multilateralism', to question general images of the EU and to avoid simplistic either/or dichotomies. The chapter demonstrates that the EU's increasing engagement in international affairs, including more and more global responsibilities and duties, makes it compulsory to reconsider old roles and to define new international roles. The current crisis of multilateralism makes it a formidable political challenge to get the multilateral system back on track. At the same time, it is a considerable analytical challenge to thoroughly understand the EU's strategic objective of supporting 'effective multilateralism', a label indicating how the EU wants to find solutions to global problems. The objective is therefore also an important aspect of the EU's vision of world order. An end to multilateralism would be an end to an institutional form that somehow mirrors EU domestic institutions, and it would also short-circuit the flow of influence running from EU institutions to global institutions, a kind of power well suited to the EU.

The chapter confirms, on the one hand, that the multilateral form is very familiar to the EU, indeed the edifice of the EU can be viewed as a specific kind of multilateralism. No wonder, therefore, that the EU prefers compatible if not similar institutional forms at the global level. It has frequently been claimed that the EU could function as a model for global governance. On the other hand, the chapter also shows that considerable variation in terms of time, policies and strategy points to no direct causation in terms of domestic–international linkages. The chapter proceeds by discussing the degree to which the strategic objective is feasible, and whether the EU is a credible sponsor of multilateralism. Moreover, the chapter demonstrates that the EU makes use of a plethora of foreign-policy strategies and that a differentiated approach – a mixture of multilateral, bilateral and unilateral strategies – better characterizes EU foreign-policy practice than is widely assumed. The adoption of this differentiated approach also suggests that the EU is far from being a uniformly weak power. On the contrary, it seems.

Finally, the chapter suggests that if the US no longer recognized the EU as an international actor, it would be a lethal blow to long-held EU aspirations. But it takes more than one American administration to dismantle an international institution like multilateralism. A successful dismantling would require other key states to consistently and systematically 'milk' multilateral institutions of more than the same states are willing to invest. Taking multilateral institutions for granted and expecting the impossible proved to be the end of the Concert of Europe. Perhaps we are witnessing the beginning of such institutional decay. If we are witnessing an end to multilateralism, all the EU's investments will have been wasted. The EU stake in multilateralism is therefore very high. To a considerable degree, it is a question of survival and, hence, a threat to one of the EU's new roles.

Notes

1 Concerning the 'existence denied' doctrine and two other contemporary foreign-policy doctrines, see Jørgensen (2004). For a comprehensive study of EU influence on international actors, events and developments, see Ginsberg (2001).
2 For EU–UN relations, see Jørgensen and Laatikainen (2004); Laatikainen and Smith (forthcoming).
3 Though often misunderstanding the essence of multilateralism, John Oudenaren (2003) provides several examples of EU unilateral action.

References

Aggestam, L. (2004) 'A European Foreign Policy? Role Conceptions and the Politics of Identity in Britain, France and Germany', PhD thesis, Stockholm, Department of Political Science, University of Stockholm.

A Secure Europe (2003) *A Secure Europe in a Better World*, Brussels: Council Secretariat.

Berger, R. (1971) 'Vor der Wiedergeburt Europas à la Wiener Congress? Die Europa-Vorschläge Staatspräsident Pompidous', *Europa-Archiv*, 19: 665–72.

Bull, H. (1982) 'Civilian Power Europe: A Contradiction in Terms', *Journal of Common Market Studies*, 21: 149–64.

Clark, W. K. (2002) *Waging Modern War: Bosnia, Kosovo, and the Future of Combat*, New York: Public Affairs.

Cooper, R. (2003) *The Breaking of Nations: Order and Chaos in the Twentieth Century*, London: Atlantic Books.

Cowhey, P. F. (1993) 'Elect Locally – Order Globally: Domestic Politics and Multilateral Cooperation', in J. G. Ruggie (ed.) *Multilateralism Matters*, New York: Columbia University Press.

Duchêne, F. (1972) 'Europe's Role in World Peace', in R. Mayne (ed.) *Europe Tomorrow*, London: Fontana/Collins.

Frattini, F. (2003) '"More democracy and more efficiency in the new UN", Italian Ministry of Foreign Affairs', http://www.esteri.it/eng, accessed 01–03–2005.

Galtung, J. (1973) *The European Community: A Superpower in the Making*, London: Allen and Unwin.

Ginsberg, R. H. (2001) *The European Union in International Politics: Baptism by Fire*, Lanham, MD: Rowman and Littlefield.

Grilli, E. (1993) *The European Community and the Developing Countries*, Cambridge: Cambridge University Press.

Hassner, P. (2003) *The United States: The Empire of Force and the Force of Empire,* Chaillot Papers 54, Paris: Institute of Security Studies, Western European Union.
Holbrooke, R. (1999) *To End a War,* New York: Random House.
Ikenberry, G. J. (2002) 'America's Imperial Ambition', *Foreign Affairs,* 81 (5): 44–60.
Ikenberry, G. J. (2003) 'Multilateralism and U.S. Grand Strategy', in S. Patrick and S. Forman (eds) *Multilateralism and U.S. Foreign Policy: Ambivalent Engagement,* Boulder, CO: Lynne Rienner.
Jørgensen, K. E. (2004) 'Three Doctrines on EU Foreign Policy', *Welt Trends,* 42: 27–36.
Jørgensen, K. E. and Laatikainen, K. V. (2004) 'The EU at the UN', paper presented to the second Pan-European Conference on EU Politics, Bologna.
Kagan, R. (2002) 'Power and Weakness', *Policy Review,* No. 113.
Kagan, R. (2003). *Paradise and Power: America and Europe in the New World Order,* London: Atlantic Books.
Kennan, G. F. (1995) 'On American Principles', *Foreign Affairs,* 74: 116–23.
Kratochwil, F. (1993) 'Norms versus Numbers', in J. G. Ruggie (ed.) *Multilateralism Matters: The Theory and Praxis of an Institutional Form,* New York: Columbia University Press.
Krause, J. (2004) 'Multilateralism: Behind European Views', *Washington Quarterly,* 27 (2): 43–59.
Krauthammer, C. (2004) *Democratic Realism: An American Foreign Policy for a Unipolar World,* Washington, DC: AEI Press.
Laatikainen K. V. and Smith, K. (eds) (forthcoming) *Intersecting Multilateralisms: The European Union at the United Nations,* Basingstoke: Palgrave.
Lake, D. A. (2003) 'The New Sovereignty in International Relations', *International Studies Review,* 5: 303–24.
Manners, I. (2002) 'Normative Power Europe: A Contradiction in Terms?', *Journal of Common Market Studies,* 40: 253–74.
Nielsson, P. (2000) Speech at UNCTAD X, Bangkok, 18 February.
Nye, J. S. Jr (2002) *The Paradox of American Power: Why the World's only Superpower Can't Go It Alone,* New York: Oxford University Press.
Oudenaren, J. van (2003) 'What is Multilateral?', *Policy Review,* No. 117.
Owen, D. (1995) *Balkan Odyssey,* London: Gollancz.
Ravenhill, J. (1985) *Collective Clientelism: The Lomé Conventions and North–South Relations,* New York: Columbia University Press.
Richardson, J. (2002) 'The European Union in the World: A Community of Values', *Fordham International Law Journal,* 26 (1): 12–35.
Ruggie, J. G. (1993) *Multilateralism Matter: The Theory and Praxis of an Institutional Form,* New York: Columbia University Press.
Ruggie, J. G. (2003) 'This Crisis of Multilateralism is Different', speech delivered at the UNA–USA National Forum on the United Nations, June.
Sjöstedt, G. (1977) *The External Role of the European Community,* Farnborough: Saxon House.
Wallace, W. (2003) *Looking after the Neighbourhood: Responsibilities for the EU-25,* London: LSE.

3 Interpreted values

A normative reading of EU role conceptions and performance

Sonia Lucarelli

Whilst any international actor faces problems in maintaining a certain coherence between its behaviour and its self-image (Holsti 1970; Aggestam 1999), in the case of the European Union (EU) these problems are amplified by its peculiar nature. First, if identity and self-image are never given once and for all, in the case of the EU they are highly in-the-making: role conceptions, therefore, are not simply the result of a self-image but also an instrument in the process of constructing a political identity. Second, for the same reason, role performance and impact feed back into the process of identity-building more than in the case of political systems in which political identity is more consolidated. Third, the institutional architecture of the EU makes it a peculiar actor whose ability to maintain coherence in role performance seems to depend on the degree of integration reached in each specific area of policy, something which clearly does not happen in traditional political systems (i.e. states). Fourth, coherence in self-image, role conception and performance is further challenged by the unsettled question of the geographic borders of the EU. Given all these difficulties, can we talk of a specific EU identity and self-image? Does this shape a distinctive international role for the EU? Where does distinctiveness rest and with which limits and implication for the overall process of integration? This chapter tackles these questions by taking the unconventional perspective of looking at the specific values and principles that emerge out of the analysis of the EU foreign policy. The analysis shows that what is distinctive of the EU is a *peculiar interpretation* of a set of values and principles that are shared by a large part of the international community.

The first part of the chapter deals with some theoretical problems related to the terms here employed, i.e. political identity, role and foreign policy. It then goes on to expose the self-representation of EU values and role as it emerges in some recent documents, with the aim of showing that what is the most peculiar feature of the EU is not its values and principles in absolute terms, but their specific interpretation. Then the chapter shows how the peculiar EU interpretation of values and role has a multiplicity of origins. Finally, in the concluding section, the chapter deals with some of the perils of role performance and their possible feed-back into the integration process.

Theory: role, identity, foreign policy and the EU

In recent years international relations (IR) theory has started to devote unprecedented attention to the role of norms, values and identity in foreign policy. This has been the result of a welcome rediscovery of both a theoretical dimension of Foreign Policy Analysis (FPA) (Hill 2003; Carlsnaes 2001; on EU foreign policy, Carlsnaes *et al.* 2004; M. E. Smith 2004) and links to theoretical debates in IR, particularly of constructivist inspiration. However, despite much attention to ideas, norms and identity, the analysis of the relationship between these concepts and foreign policy still deserves investigation. In the first place, what is the relationship between values and identity? *Which* identity are we talking about? *Whose* identity are we talking about? What is the function of various types of identity (political, cultural, religious) in the articulation and performance of a role?

In the first place, I focus attention on *political* identity rather than cultural or religious identity (Huntington 1996, 2004; A. Smith 1992). Political identity is a construct that is not, and should not, be derived directly from a common culture. This is particularly true in the case of the EU, an eminently political project whose *telos* was to construct peace though co-operation among former enemies, despite their cultural differences. Recent calls for the introduction of references to Europe's Christian roots in the preamble of the EU Constitutional Treaty respond to a misunderstanding of European identity, which is not and cannot be based on a common culture, but on shared political values.

Second, I deal with political identity as a sub-species of group identity, not a 'collective identity' as if there were a superior entity – the community – above individuals: it is not the EU as a community which possesses 'identity', rather each individual citizen has a European political identity as soon as he/she recognizes him/herself around a set of social and political values and principles, in the sharing of which he/she feels a sense of belonging to the EU political group (Cerutti 2001, 2003, 2005; Habermas 2001). The consequent feeling of 'us' as the members of a group is therefore shaped around core values and principles. However, in order for those values and principles to shape the identity of the citizens they need to be *interpreted* (Cerutti 2003: 28). I claim here that culture, history, legal practices, institutions and policies are the frameworks in which specific interpretations of political values take place. Put in this way, identity is in fact a *process* more than a given, a *process of self-identification* of the individuals in a group (Bloom 1990). In this process culture, history, legal practices, institutions and policy, including foreign policy, are important.

We can consider role conception and role performance (see the Introduction to this volume) as intrinsic elements of the self-identification process. The way one conceives one's international role is functional to the way in which one conceives oneself; at the same time, the way one 'performs' one's role feeds back into one's political identity. A credibility crisis can take place when the political entity of reference (a state; the EU) does not perform the foreign policy its citizens expect it to perform. However, the degree of impact of foreign policy (a form of role performance) on political identity – and the group's concern for such an impact – differs depending on the degree of maturity of the group's political identity. In the case of a political identity in the making like the EU, the process of construction of self-identification is particularly sensitive to the image that the political group gives of itself through its politics and policy, even including foreign policy.

Which values are we talking about? What are the values held by the Europeans? The World Values Survey (WVS) shows that West Europeans (the EU/Europe until 2004) score highly on both secular values and on self-expression values, that is, tend to be societies in which traditional religious and family values have ceased to be fundamental (i.e. secular values prevail over traditional values), and an increasing share of the population has started to shift its priorities from an overwhelming emphasis on economic and physical security towards an increasing emphasis on subjective well-being, self-expression and quality of life (i.e. self-expression values prevail over attention to economic and physical security) (Inglehart *et al.* 2004; see also http://www.worldvaluessurvey.org/library/). Although there is a relevant distance among European countries on both axes of values (traditional/secular and security/self-expression), with northern countries scoring highest on both dimensions and southern Catholic countries scoring less, on average all Western European countries but Ireland appear dominated by secular/self-expression values. A representation that coincides nicely with the EU's self-representation as a political group, as we shall see below.

Values in the EU's role conceptions and performance

The EU's values (here a shortened formula to refer to the values of the EU as a political group) as summarized in Article I-2 of the proposed Constitution, include human dignity, liberty, democracy, equality, the rule of law and respect for human rights. Clearly, such values are not very different from those considered fundamental components of the 'American creed' (freedom, democracy and human rights). What is interesting in the EU context is the extent to which the EU's self-representation around such values has shaped the EU as a qualitatively different actor in world politics. In other words, I argue that the identification of EU/European core values and the definition of an international role for the EU/Europe are part of the same identity-building process.

What is this self-representation made of? The EU/Europe tends to represent itself in a way which in scholarly terms has been defined, in turn, as a 'civilian power' (Duchêne 1972; Telò 2004; Whitman 1998), a 'structural power' (Keukeleire 2003); a 'normative power' (Manners 2002); a 'normative area' (Therborn 2001), that is, a polity which relates to the world in a qualitatively different way. This qualitative difference is recalled in many EU documents. In the Laeken Declaration one reads:

> Europe needs to shoulder its *responsibilities* in the governance of globalisation. The role it has to play is that of a power resolutely doing *battle against all violence*, all terror and all fanaticism, but which also does not turn a blind eye to the world's heartrending injustices.
>
> (European Council 2001, emphasis added)

The text of the proposed Constitution proclaims:

> 1 The Union's action on the international scene shall be guided by the *principles which have inspired its own creation*, development and enlargement, and which it seeks to advance in the wider world: *democracy, the rule of law, the universality and indivisibility of human rights and fundamental freedoms, respect for human dignity, the principles of equality and solidarity, and respect for the principles of the United Nations Charter and international law.*
>
> (Article III-292, Title V, emphasis added)

When it comes to the Union's aims, the Constitution affirms:

> The Union [. . .] shall work for a high degree of cooperation in all fields of international relations, in order to:
>
> a safeguard its *values, fundamental interests, security, independence and integrity*;
> b consolidate and support *democracy, the rule of law, human rights* and the principles of *international law*;
> c preserve *peace, prevent conflicts* and strengthen international security, in accordance with the purposes and principles of the United Nations Charter. . .;
> d foster the *sustainable economic, social and environmental development* of developing countries, with the primary aim of *eradicating poverty*;
> e encourage the integration of all countries into the world economy, including through the *progressive abolition of restrictions on international trade*;
> f help develop international measures to preserve and improve the quality of the *environment* and the sustainable management of global natural resources, in order to ensure *sustainable development*;
> g assist populations, countries and regions confronting natural or man-made disasters;

h promote an international system based on stronger *multilateral cooperation* and *good global governance.*

(Article III-292, Title V, emphasis added)

Although the Constitution has not entered into force, what is there stated is relevant as it is a sort of summing-up of the self-representation of the Union throughout the years. Since the Union is a process, an actor in the making, its self-representation and role articulation have progressively been reshaped. The self-representation proposed in the Constitution represents a negotiated synthesis of what other documents had already stated before. For instance, EU values and objectives have been stated before in specific sectors of EU's international conduct. In the 1980s, the European Community (EC) produced declarations regarding the importance of human rights and democracy in its relations with third countries, but it was only with the Maastricht Treaty (TEU) that the EC undertook treaty-based commitments to foster the developing countries' sustainable development; gradual integration into the world economy; the fight against poverty; observance of human rights and fundamental freedoms; and the development and consolidation of democracy and the rule of law (Article 130u). The fight against poverty was then made an overarching aim of the EU's development co-operation policy (DCP) in the Treaty of Amsterdam (TA, Article 177). A particular aspect of human protection, i.e. gender protection, has become mainstreamed in all EU policies since the TA, but it had been adopted in the form of equal pay for different sexes since the Treaty of Rome (Pollack and Hafner-Burton 2000). As far as 'prevention' is concerned, the preventative principle has been initially used in the field of environmental policy already in 1973 (COM 1973). More recently, an explicit reference to preventative action has been used in the security field (European Council 2003).

The self-representation of the EU present in the Constitution as well as other relevant documents such as the Laeken Declaration or the European Security Strategy, or ESS (European Council 2001, 2003) is the externalization of a preceding internal agreement on the EC/U values and aims, and a performative act which eventually contributes to shaping the collective understandings of the EU's identity and role, both processes in the making. The self-image which emerges from these documents has the following main characteristics:

- The EU is a political actor aiming at behaving on the basis of its interest, but also of the political values inscribed in its initial *telos,* also with a view to expanding such values worldwide.
- The expansion of such values, however, never assumes the tone of a crusade. The difference between the ESS (European Council 2003) and the US 2002 National Security Strategy (NSS; US Presidency 2002) in this respect is clear. As an illustration, take the different

treatment in the two documents of the terrorist threat: in the ESS terrorism is treated as a 'strategic threat' and not, as in the NSS, as a new global 'enem[y] of civilization' (US Presidency 2002, p. 11). It follows that the division of the world into liberty-loving countries and rogue states supporting terrorism finds no equivalent in the ESS.

- The EU recognizes that it has global responsibilities, but accepts a greater burden only in its neighbourhood (European Council 2003). For instance, in the ESS, the EU defines a precise responsibility only as far as Europe (and the Middle East) is concerned: here Europe has a duty to promote liberal values and well-governed societies. Beyond it there is a generic call for global responsibilities.
- The EU's global responsibilities are not framed by a religious discourse, rather they are presented as the response to the new duties created by the processes of globalization, which demand governance, with a view to inscribing these processes in a more just and solidarist order (see European Council 2001).

Documents, however, do more than this, in that they better specify those values around which European identity is shaped (or, better, is in the process of being shaped). As a matter of fact, documents, as well as political practice (role performance) implicitly and explicitly provide interpretations of such values – which, as we have seen, is a fundamental step in the self-identification process.

The analysis of EU *foreign policy* broadly defined (all those policies towards the external environment that are regarded by external actors as 'the EU's'), confirms the presence in EU foreign policy of a number of fundamental values that have been stated in the EU documents since early in the integration process (peace) or which have *de facto* represented founding values since the beginning although not being spelled out as values in the early days of integration (democracy, human dignity, justice, solidarity, liberty, equality, liberalism). More recently, the EU has added 'harmony with nature', as a value in itself. The principles that emerge from an analysis of EU foreign-affairs documents and policies include: conflict prevention, the rule of law, good governance, subsidiarity, sustainable development, the precautionary principle, the preventative principle, responsibility.

Most of these values and principles are by no means peculiar to the EU and are shared by many other international actors. However, frequently the EU interpretation of such values and principles diverges from that provided in other political contexts. What might diverge is (1) the translation of a value into different guiding principles, or (2) the peculiar interpretation of a value in the light of another (here, clearly, what counts is the hierarchical order among values in different political communities). Finally, (3) interpretations might diverge also as far as the translation of values and principles into political practices is concerned. Below are some examples of the specific EU interpretations of its values and principles.

1. An example of the first process is provided by the value of liberty in the context of freedom of speech: blasphemy and racist speech are regarded as belonging to the same category of 'hate speech' in the US, while in Europe they are distinguished as, respectively, attacks on ideas (legal) and attacks on a person (illegal). According to Guy Haarscher, two different interpretations of 'liberty' based on two different historical experiences are at stake (Haarscher 2001: 98–101), but clearly part of the explanation of this treatment of blasphemy in the US rests also on the place of religious values in the socio-political context: according to the WVS, Americans turn out to be far more traditional (i.e. religious, patriotic; against abortion, euthanasia, divorce and suicide) than any European country except Ireland (Inglehart *et al.* 2004).

A further example has to do with the rejection in the EU of the death penalty, which in the Charter of Fundamental Rights derives directly from the value of dignity (Chapter 1, Article 2.1). Here the 'right to life' (expression of the value of dignity) is read together with an interpretation of the value of justice, where justice does not translate into directly proportional punishment for the offence. The different stance of the EU and the US on this aspect is well known, and has created problems relating to release of prisoners from Europe to the US as a form of co-operation in the fight against terrorism.

2. As for the second process (specific interpretations of a certain value in the light of other values or principles), embedded liberalism – an economic liberalism that should support domestic economic stability and social security – is a telling case. Although some authors regard it as a shared pillar of the (Western) order since World War II (Ikenberry 1996), this is undeniably a European value more than anyone else's. The peculiar interpretation given in Europe to liberalism as a value and a pillar of order has made it possible for the European societies to develop the strongest Welfare State systems in the world, despite the liberalization of markets. This was made possible by two other values and a principle of the European tradition: solidarity, justice and the principle of the rule of law. The result has been a peculiar understanding of liberalism, which sees the logic of free trade embedded by the need to safeguard also the other two values. If this has been applied since the beginning within the EC/U and its member states, it has also begun to influence also the EU's foreign policy. The TEU affirmed that international co-operation, as an aim of the Common Foreign Policy and Security Policy (CFSP), should help developing countries in a smooth and gradual integration into the world economy, at the same time calling for their sustainable social and political development (Article 130u). Furthermore, some positions taken by the EU at the WTO negotiations can hardly be explained by looking at the material benefits, only as ways to support underdeveloped countries. Some observers point to the Commission's position on the TRIPs agreement (intellectual property rights) as a case in point (Van den Hoven

2006). Clearly, this does not tell the full story of the EU's positions at the WTO negotiations, where interests matter as much as values (if we admit that for analytical reasons they can be kept separate).

The principle of sustainable development, widely used in the EU framework, emerges out of a combination of three core values: justice, solidarity and what I labelled 'harmony with nature'. The label 'harmony with nature' has been chosen to convey the idea that human progress cannot be disconnected from its effects on a natural world of which humankind is part. From here originates the idea of the centrality of the implementation of the principle of sustainable development, both within the Union and as part of its environmental policy and development co-operation policy (COM 1992, 2001a). As a matter of fact the Treaty of Amsterdam made sustainable development an objective of EU policies (Baker 2000). Both this principle and the precautionary principle are core ideas in EU environmental policy, while they find little space in US policy in this field (Baker and McCormick 2004). The principle of prevention was stated as early as the Treaty of Rome (Article 174). Though the precautionary principle was mentioned in the Rome Treaty with reference to the environment, later the Commission underlined that it is an EU general principle applicable particularly to 'environmental protection, human, animal and plant health' (COM 2000: 9; cf. Baker 2006).

Within the context of EU environmental policy, particularly as far as global warming is concerned, there is a further specification of this principle and the principle of responsibility: 'responsibility towards the future generations' (see COM 2000: 7; Baker 2006). Reference to responsibilities towards future generations, on the contrary, remains vague both in the Charter of Fundamental Rights (limited to a sentence in the Preamble, with no specification of the rights of the future generations) and in the Constitution, whose Preamble recalls the individual's 'responsibilities towards future generations and the Earth'.

3. The third form of peculiar interpretation by the EU of largely shared values and principles has to do with the peculiarities of transposition of such values and principles into external political conduct. There are a number of peculiarities in EU practices, some of which are referred to in the literature:

- *Structural prevention.* The attempt to adopt a preventative approach to the emergence of economic and security problems. Such an approach is widely recognized as a typical one and a specific term has been coined for it – structural foreign policy (Keukeleire 2003) – in fact it also links to the idea of the EU as a civilian power (Telò 2004).
- *Holism.* This is the attitude that considers structural links among various causes of a problem as well as among various instruments to prevent or solve it. The way in which terrorism is treated in recent documents on this issue illustrates this inclination (cf. European Council 2003).

- *Mainstreaming.* The concept is closely connected to the previous two practices and refers to the decision to evaluate each policy on the basis of its ability to safeguard a certain value or principle, e.g. gender protection (gender mainstreaming); conflict prevention; environmental protection.
- *Institutionalization* and *regulation.* The EU shows a strong preference for what John Ikenberry calls 'constitutionalism', i.e. joint principles and commitment anchored in binding institutional mechanisms (Ikenberry 1996). This faith in institutional settings is coupled with a distinct attitude towards regulation. The EU tends to (over)regulate domestically and also to develop and support institutional regulatory frameworks internationally (if not globally). This leads the EU to support and develop treaties, conventions (those concerning human rights are now part of the EU Charter of Fundamental Rights and the EU Constitution) and international regimes (the international regime on climate change is particularly telling of this attitude). Similarly, this faith explains the EU's support for the creation of supranational institutions such as the International Criminal Court (ICC). Support for the ICC, although a bit controversial initially, has since been demonstrated in a number of ways, not least the attempt by the EU to gain the Asian, Caribbean and Pacific (ACP) countries' support for the ICC as part of the first review of the Cotonou Agreement (February 2005). In the case of the ICC, clearly not only the value of justice was at stake, but also the acceptance of supranationality.
- *Multilateralism.* To the EU, this has become something more than 'an institutional form that coordinates relations among three or more states on the basis of generalized principles of conduct' (Ruggie 1993: 11): it has become a value to safeguard. As with any value, it is at times infringed (cf. Jørgensen in this volume), but the overall attitude in EU foreign policy shows how multilateralism has become a core principle of political interaction both within the Union (among the member states) and in EU external relations. The relevance of multilateralism for the EU has been recently recalled by the Council (European Council 2003) and the Commission (COM 2003b). Multilateralism has eventually become part of the European political identity – as was the case for post-World War II Germany (Maull 1995–96, 2000; Narnisch and Maull 2001) – while it seemed to be more a *tool* in the case of US foreign policy.
- *Constructive engagement.* This refers to the preference on the EU side for exercising pressure on another side more though partnership and dialogue than through sanctions. This is what the EU and other observers claim is taking place in EU relations with Iran and China.
- *Legalism.* This is the tendency to evaluate legitimacy on the basis of the legality conferred by adherence to an institutional framework (UN) and international law (UN authorization).

The origins: where do the interpretations of values come from?

It would be impossible to trace here the origin of each value which is constitutive of the EU's self-image and, ultimately, role articulation: values and their interpretation have not one single origin but are the result of complex interactive dynamics which cannot be analysed in detail in this context. What I can do here is to point to five major dynamics in the process of interpretation (i.e. self-identification) and provide some examples.

The initial telos

Although various origins of the interpretations of EU values can be identified, one cannot avoid mentioning the most fundamental one: the initial *raison d'être* of integration, what has been called its *telos* (Habermas 2001). The integration process started as a nearly utopian project of peace through co-operation among former enemies, economic development and democratic consolidation (if not transition) of the member states. The dramatic experiences of the 'brief century', particularly as far as dictatorship and the Holocaust are concerned, had reinforced Europeans' faith in the value of democratic systems, human dignity and solidarity, and had equally created shared memories of suffering – although experienced on opposing fronts. Although the Union's *telos* is not as strong and visible as it was at the outset (as Joseph Weiler has argued, 2001; see also Habermas 2001), the founding values of the Union were never abandoned in the political system and continue to be visible in its foreign policy performance. To those founding values of democracy, liberty, solidarity and human dignity others have been added over time ('harmony with nature' and multilateralism are cases in point). One can see differing interpretations or contending priorities concerning values and/or principles among the various actors involved in the EU foreign policy-making. One can also see inconsistency both over time and across cases, but one is always left with the impression that there are constitutive elements of the EU political identity at work.

Culture and history

As we have already seen, it is by no means uncommon to find authors who consider political values (and political identity) as a direct emanation of religious beliefs (Huntington 1996). Although I do not share the view of complete dependence of political values on cultural (religious) values, it is undeniable that culture provides one of the most important frameworks in which values are interpreted. (Others include the institutional and legal context, domestic and international pressures and forms of 'contagion'.) The example of the different interpretation of the value of freedom of speech in the case of blasphemy and in the case of racist speech should be illustrative of the role of culture. Secularism is a deeply held value among Europeans, even those from Catholic countries (Inglehart *et al.* 2004), a value which defines the boundaries of appropriateness in EU institutions, as shown by the case of the rejection by the European Parliament of Rocco Buttiglione as EU Commissioner for having shaped his political language on the basis of religious beliefs (which had led him to consider gays as 'sinners'). Such deeply held secularism undoubtedly also has its origin in the peculiar European experience of the relationship between the political and the religious spheres to which corresponded two secular powers (the State and the Church). Secularism became a value only with the French Revolution, after decades of continuing conflicts between these two powers.

The years that followed, then, were consolidating years for the founding principle of a separation between State and Church, and between religious and political beliefs, but the road was long and hard (suffice to recall the vicissitudes of the relationship between the Italian state and the Vatican) and political institutions felt the need to institutionalize such a value and instil it in the consciences of its citizens. This process did not need to take place in the US, where, as Huntington recalls, the Pilgrim Fathers had no Church and no State to face (Huntington 2004). This different historical evolution of the same Christian religion had implications also as far as other values are concerned, such as 'embedded liberalism' and 'harmony with nature': Hutton (2002, reported in Welsh 2006) reads the EU's and US's different attitude to nature, property and eventually science as a consequence of the universal availability of landed property enjoyed by the Protestant settlers. The state-institutionalized defence of property rights has thus constrained the state in pursuit of a common good or interest. On the other side, the European feudal experience (feudal rights) coupled with the influence of Catholicism (solidarity) has created a different duty for European states to intervene for the pursuit of the public good and to guarantee elements of redistributive justice. This is how liberalism became 'embedded'. As for the relationship with nature, the wide availability of land in the US did not force the people and the states to consider it a fundamental element of survival and an element which imposed reciprocal relations with those exploiting the same territory or the neighbours, as was the case in Europe.

Contagion and learning

Contagion is the application of the same values/principles/styles to political areas other than those in which they were first applied, as a result of spill-over effects or processes of imitation. In contrast, learning refers to the actual cognitive development which derives from experience. Examples of contagion and learning are of multiple types. They can be:

- *Cross-issue*, that is, from one issue area to another. As we have seen, for example, the preventative and precautionary principles, first used in the field of environmental policy, have subsequently been considered core principles in other areas, even including security. A good example of cross-issue contagion is provided by the practice of mainstreaming. For instance, the TEU made respect for democracy and human rights general principles of EU law, and this then implied that all other activities, including development co-operation policy, should be subject to it. This is the context in which democratic conditionality becomes a practice of EU foreign policy. Analogously, equality, first applied to the area of equal payment (TEU) was later applied to many more areas, leading eventually to its mainstreaming with the Treaty of Amsterdam and, thereby, its application also in other areas, such as in development co-operation policy.
- *Diachronic*, that is, in the same area, over time. A learning process has occurred throughout the integration process, whereby the specific interpretation of EU values and principles has evolved. For instance, in the field of gender equality, not only the areas in which the value has been applied have grown over time, but the specific understanding of the terms 'gender' and 'equality' have undergone a process of learning influenced by the intellectual debate on these issues over the years. From an understanding of women in biological, individual terms, the EC started in the 1980s to recognize women as a group. Furthermore, from an initial use of positive discrimination, the EC moved on also to request positive action. Finally, since the 1990s, the EU has considered gender as a socially constructed biological difference, and has mainstreamed gender policies (Pollack and Hafner-Burton 2000). Changes occurred in the EU development co-operation policy from the initial association system established with the Treaty of Rome (an involuntary and unilaterally granted association system), to first the Yaoundé Agreement (voluntary and negotiated), eventually to arrive, through the various Lomé Conventions, at the 2000 Cotonou Agreement, which introduced criteria of allocation according to performance, conditionality and constructive dialogue. All such changes are presented by the EU as the result of a learning process (http://europa.eu.int/comm/development/body/cotonou/overview_en. htm).
- *Externalization of domestic values* occurs when principles and values developed in the domestic EU context are transposed into EU foreign policy. Examples have been already provided as far as the precautionary principle in environmental politics is concerned (now a core principle also of the EU's global environmental policy), equality,

responsibility, democracy and human rights, and so on. Possibly the most striking feature is represented by the practice of multilateralism, which in the EU case has become a value in itself (cf. Jørgensen in Chapter 2 of this volume). Through the integration process, the member states and European institutions have learned to behave in a multilateral way among themselves. Even in the most demanding areas, such as member states' foreign policy, 'states have increasingly learned to define many ... of their foreign policy positions in terms of collectively defined values and goals' (M. E. Smith 2004: 99). In other words, multilateralism has become a praxis of behaviour which represents 'normality'; defections from normality occur, but are denounced as infringements of acceptable behaviour. This faith in multilateralism has then important repercussions in the EU's foreign policy, as we have seen above.

Direct contribution of the member states

Member states have been the core actors behind the EU integration process, so all the values and principles which are now called 'EU's' derive from the member states' political systems and culture. However, there are differences whose explanation will be provided below. The greater emphasis of the EU's development and co-operation policy on people-oriented development, poverty reduction, gender equality and sustainable development derives also from the development tradition of some EU member states (Nöel and Thérein 1995). At the same time the allocation of resources, particularly in the initial years, reflected very much the member states' specific interests (former colonies in the past; countries strategic for security reasons since 2001), as the OECD figures on funds allocation testify (http://www.oecd.org/dac). Another good example of the influence of member states in the interpretation of EU values (particularly in terms of the transposition of a value into a specific role duty) is provided by the influence exercised by the then recently entered Nordic countries on the mainstreaming of conflict prevention in Göteborg in 2001.

The EU's unique institutional structure

The most common response to the argument that the EU tends to adopt a structural foreign policy is that there is nothing else it can do. To put it simply, this would be 'making a virtue of necessity', given the fact that the EU lacks a traditional foreign-policy capacity (the CFSP introduced by TEU did not create an EU capacity beyond the member states' will, nor has it given the EU independent military instruments), while it has developed instruments and decisional capacity of a non-military, non-diplomatic nature (namely, the external relations branch of EU foreign policy). Put in these terms, this institutional explanation of the peculiarities of the EU's international role is limited to its deficiencies: should it develop a full-fledged foreign and security policy it would behave in a traditional way. This reading is definitely reductionist, but one cannot deny the influence of the EU's institutional structure on the specific definition of values and role that has been undertaken by the EU. The idea that the EU behaves differently because it is differently constituted has now been rethought, underlining more its peculiar institutional structure than its incomplete character (cf. Manners and Whitman 2003).

In the first place it is the peculiar structure of the EC/U that has forced the member states to develop a multilateral form of interaction as the 'appropriate' one. As Michael E. Smith observes, 'institutional mechanisms have both *pre-empted* the formation of fixed national foreign policy preferences and ... *socialized* its elite participants into articulating a common European policy [on an expanding number of issues]'. Furthermore, the densely institutionalized social setting in which EU member states interact conditions them 'to rely on shared values, ideas or knowledge in making their decisions' (M. E. Smith 2004: 99–100). This implies that the institutional structure of the EU has shaped a political system in which multilateralism has become at the same time a diplomatic necessity and a value in itself; a system which constitutes the social and political tissue in which socialization around shared value interpretations could more easily take place (cf. Aggestam in Chapter 1 of this volume). Finally, this internal definition of multilateralism as a 'normal' condition of interaction is clearly an important fact in the EU's preference for what I have labelled institutionalization and regulation. Due to the EU's institutional structure, sovereignty in Europe is no longer a monolithic concept: pulling and sharing of sovereignty is a daily reality, a reality which can be more easily accepted in the creation of international institutionalized structures of global governance.

In the second place, the peculiar structure of the EU (supranational, intergovernmental, characterized by a multi-level system of governance) significantly influences the way in which it performs its international role in specific fields more influenced by the hybridity of its structure. For instance, in the field of development co-operation policy the EU is both a bilateral donor and a multilateral: in this it is unique among development co-operation institutions (Bonaglia *et al.* 2006). This implies that, although some features of EU development co-operation appear clearly, as we have seen, there is no fully homogeneous EU model of development co-operation. Furthermore, legal provisions are ambiguous enough to allow for different interpretations by the member states. This may account for some of the inconsistencies but probably also for some specific interpretations which result from the necessary compromised position between the different actors involved.

A European dream fulfilled? In place of a conclusion

It has been argued here that the EU is a peculiar actor in world politics. Its peculiarity derives from (1) a European interpretation of some widely shared values and principles (e.g. embedded liberalism, harmony with nature; the pervasiveness of the preventative and precautionary principles, etc.); (2) the peculiar role conceptions shaped around these values and principles (somehow missionary without being crusading; secular; responsible); (3) the specific mode of transformation of roles into role performance (structural prevention, holism, mainstreaming, institutionalism and regulation, multilateralism, constructive engagement, legalism). The origin of such a peculiarity is claimed to be multiple (initial *telos*, culture and history, contagion and learning, institutional structure).

However, is this 'difference' relevant? In other words, does it lead to a perceptible difference in impact? Only partly. This is the reason why the idea of the EU as a qualitatively different international actor has attracted criticism, particularly but not only outside Europe (Kagan 2003), but it is also one of the reasons to affirm that the EU is still largely an actor whose self-identification arises largely from its external performance.

The first difficulty in showing that 'difference matters' has to do with clear incoherencies between role conception and role performance. Not only does the EU frequently not implement the sanctions that conditionality would imply (see K. Smith in Chapter 9 of this volume), but sometimes it fails to match deeds with fact. For instance, figures on the allocation of funds in development co-operation policy show that money does not get to the worst-off states, partly because the introduction of the democratic conditionality clause puts those countries in a difficult position. This raises a second problem, which is definitely not exclusively the EU's, which is the existence of values which do not conflict among themselves but whose implementation leads to conflicting policies: should the EU privilege partnership and constructive engagement or conditionality? Should it aim more at fighting poverty or tyranny? This is one cause for lack of coherence, to which are clearly to be added the different interests of the member states, the peculiar institutional structure of the EU which disperses foreign-policy responsibilities, and others.

There is then the difficulty faced by the EU in showing effectiveness. It is not by chance that Solana introduced in the ESS a reference to *effective* multilateralism, to show that impact counts. The EU difficulty is a double one: the actual limits to the EU's impact, but also the EU's difficulties in *communicating* difference. Ineffectiveness is by far the most criticized aspect of EU distinctiveness. The origins of this are largely claimed to be the inefficient decision-making machinery, the lack of a sanctioning system (or unwillingness to use it when available), a political culture and historical experience which have led the EU to imagine the world in its own image, thereby losing the capacity to see it for what it is and choose the tools accordingly (Kagan 2003). As most of the traditional institutional criticisms are well known, I prefer to spend a few words on the latter. I believe that it would be a great mistake not to take advantage of Kagan's simplistic though provocative analysis of the EU as a Venusian polity to reflect on his message. More than anything else, I believe that there are serious signs that the EU (and the member states therein) has lost the capacity to cope with conflict. It is not simply a question of having or not having military forces, but a question of contemplating politics in all its variety; a question of seriously recognizing that the Kantian world we would like to construct is not a reality in the largest part of Earth; it is a question of asking ourselves how to cope with this world when all other instruments fail to match the objective. Relying on the UN Charter is simply no response, as the Charter does not provide a political response to the problem, nor does the rest of international law. *Legalism* is a severe limit to the EU's ability to formulate new positions on the use of force in the changed international scenario. Nor is an answer provided by following the US, as some EU member states have done in the case of the Iraq war of 2003, dismissing – if temporarily – other European shared values.

The second difficulty in showing that 'difference matters' has to do with the repercussions of the self-identification process. As we saw at the beginning, political identity and self-image influence role conception and performance, but at the same time role performance feeds back into the process of self-identification, particularly in the case of imperfectly consolidated polities. The EU's failure to show effectiveness (which, in any case, is difficult to show in the case of long-term measures) and the availability of examples of incoherence (which are immediately denounced through the media far more than success stories) diminish the EU's credibility and legitimacy before its citizens. Faith in the interpretation of values that are presented as constitutive of the EU as a political group is at risk. If we couple this with the new, epochal enlargement of 2004, and the impossibility of predicting now the ability of EU institutions to both constrain and socialize the new member states, the 'European dream' (Rifkin 2004) will continue to be a dream, a process-in-the-making for a long time to come. The basis is there, the outcome of the process not fully so.

References

Aggestam, L. (1999) 'Role Conceptions and the Politics of Identity in Foreign Policy', Arena Working Paper 99/8, Oslo: Centre of European Studies, University of Oslo.

Baker, S. (2000) 'The European Union: Integration, Competition, Growth – and Sustainability', in W. M. Lafferty and J. Meadowcroft (eds) *Implementing Sustainable Development: Strategies and Initiatives in High Consumption Societies*, Oxford: Oxford University Press.

Baker, S. (2006) 'Environmental Values and Climate Change Policy: Contrasting the European Union and the United States', in S. Lucarelli and I. Manners (eds) *Values and Principles in European Union Foreign Policy*, London: Routledge.

Baker, S. and McCormick, J. (2004) 'Sustainable Development: Comparative Understandings and Responses', in N. J. Vig and M. C. Faure (eds) *Green Giants? Environmental Policy of the United States and the European Union*, Cambridge, MA: MIT Press.

Bloom, W. (1990) *Personal Identity, National Identity and International Relations*, Cambridge: Cambridge University Press.

Bonaglia, F., Goldstein, A. and Petito, F. (2006) 'Values in European Union Development Cooperation Policy', in S. Lucarelli and I. Manners (eds) *Values and Principles in European Union Foreign Policy*, London: Routledge.

Carlsnaes, W. (2002) 'Foreign Policy', in W. Carlsnaes, T. Risse and B. Simmons (eds) *Handbook of International Relations*, London: Sage Publications.

Carlsnaes, W., Sjursen, H. and White, B. (eds) (2004) *European Foreign Policy Today*, London: Sage Publications.

Cerutti, F. (2001) 'Towards the Political Identity of the Europeans: An Introduction', in F. Cerutti and E. Rudolph, *A Soul for Europe*, I: *On the Political and Cultural Identity of the Europeans: A Reader*, Leuven: Peeters.

Cerutti, F. (2003) 'A Political Identity of the Europeans?' *Thesis Eleven*, 72: 26–45.

Cerutti, F. (2005) 'Constitution and Political Identity in Europe', in U. Liebert (ed.) *Postnational Constitutionalisation in the Enlarged Europe: Foundations, Procedures, Prospects*, Baden-Baden: Nomos.

Duchêne, F. (1972) 'Europe's Role in World Peace', in R. Mayne (ed.) *Europe Tomorrow: Sixteen Europeans Look Ahead*, London: Fontana.

European Commission (1973) 'First Programme of Action on the Environment', *Official Journal*, Vol. 16. No. C112, 20 December.

European Commission (2000) *Communication on the Precautionary Principle*, COM (2000), 1, final.

European Commission (2001) *Environment 2010: Our Future, Our Choice*, COM (2001), 31, final.

European Commission (2003) *The European Union and the United Nations: The Choice of Multilateralism*, Communication from the Commission to the Council and the European Parliament, Brussels, COM (2003), 526 final.

European Council (2001) *Laeken Declaration on the Future of Europe*, attachment to the Presidency Conclusions, European Council Meeting in Laeken, 14–15 December 2001 (SN300/01 ADD1).

European Council (2003) *A Secure Europe in a Better World: European Security Strategy*, European Council Meeting in Brussels, 12 December 2003.

Haarscher, G. (2001) 'Europe's Soul: Freedom and Rights', in F. Cerutti and E. Rudolph (eds) *Soul for Europe*, I: *On the Political and Cultural Identity of the Europeans: A Reader*, Leuven: Peeters.

Habermas, J. (2001) *So, Why Does Europe Need a Constitution?* Policy Papers Series on Constitutional Reform of the European Union 2/2001, Florence: European University Institute.

Hill, C. (2003) *The Changing Politics of Foreign Policy*, Basingstoke: Macmillan.

Holsti, K. (1970) 'National Role Conceptions in the Study of Foreign Policy', *International Studies Quarterly*, 14: 233–309.

Huntington, S. (1996) *The Clash of Civilizations and the Remaking of World Order*, New York: Simon and Schuster.

Huntington, S. (2004) *Who are We? The Challenges to America's National Identity*, New York: Simon & Schuster.

Hutton, W. (2002) *The World We Are In*, London: Little Brown.

Ikenberry, G. J. (1996) 'The Myth of Post-Cold War Chaos', *Foreign Affairs*, 75: 79–91.

Inglehart, R., Basanez, M., Diez-Medrano, J., Halman, L. and Luijkx, R. (2004) *Human Beliefs and Values: A Cross-cultural Sourcebook based on the 1999–2002 Values Surveys*, Mexico City: Siglo XXI.

Kagan, R. (2003) *Paradise & Power: America and Europe in the New World Order*, London: Atlantic Books.

Keukeleire, S. (2003) 'The European Union as a Diplomatic Actor: Internal, Traditional and Structural Diplomacy', *Diplomacy and Statecraft*, 14: 31–56.

Manners, I. (2002) 'Normative Power Europe: A Contradiction in Terms?', *Journal of Common Market Studies*, 40: 235–58.

Manners, I. and Whitman, R. (2003) 'The "Difference Engine": Constructing and Representing the International Identity of the European Union', *Journal of European Public Policy*, 10: 380–404.

Maull, H. (1995–96) 'Germany in the Yugoslav Crisis', *Survival*, 37: 99–130.

Maull, H. (2000) 'Germany and the Use of Force: Still a "Civilian Power"?', *Survival*, 42: 56–80.

Narnisch, S. and Maull, H. W. (eds) (2001) *Germany as a Civilian Power? The Foreign Policy of the Berlin Republic*, Manchester and New York: Manchester University Press.

Nöel, A. and Thérein, J. Ph. (1995) 'From Domestic to International Justice: The Welfare State and Foreign Aid', *International Organization*, 49: 523–53.

Pollack, M. and Hafner-Burton, E. (2000) 'Mainstreaming Gender in the European Union', *Journal of European Public Policy*, 7: 432–56.

Rifkin, J. (2004) *The European Dream*, Oxford: Polity Press.

Ruggie, J. G. (1993) 'Multilateralism: The Anatomy of an Institution', in J. G. Ruggie (ed.) *Multilateralism Matters: The Theory and Praxis of an Institutional Form*, New York: Columbia University Press.

Smith, A. (1992) 'National Identity and the Idea of European Unity', *International Affairs*, 68: 55–76.

Smith, M. E. (2004) 'Institutionalization, Policy Adaptation and European Foreign Policy Coordination', *European Journal of International Relations*, 10: 95–136.

Telò, M. (2004) *L'Europa potenza civile*, Rome and Bari: Laterza.

Therborn, G. (2001) 'Europe's Breaks with Itself: The European Economy and the History, Modernity and World Future of Europe', in F. Cerutti and E. Rudolph (eds) *A Soul for Europe*, II: *On the Cultural and Political Identity of the Europeans: An Essay Collection*, Leuven: Peeters.

US Presidency (2002) *The National Security Strategy of the United States of America*, Washington, DC: Office of the President.

Van Den Hoven, A. (2006) 'European Union Regulatory Capitalism and Multilateral Trade Negotiations', in Sonia Lucarelli and Ian Manners (eds) *Values and Principles in European Union Foreign Policy*, London: Routledge.

Walzer, M. (1992) *What it Means to Be an American*, New York: Marsilio.

Weiler, J. (2001) 'I rischi dell'integrazione: *deficit* politico e fine delle diversità', in A. Loretoni (ed.) *Interviste sull'Europa: integrazione e identità nella globalizzazione*, Roma: Carocci.

Welsh, Ian (2006) 'Values, Science and the European Union: Bio-technology and Transatlantic Relations', in Sonia Lucarelli and Ian Manners (eds) *Values and Principles in European Union Foreign Policy*, London: Routledge.

Whitman, R. (1998) *From Civilian Power to Superpower? The International Identity of the European Union*, Basingstoke: Macmillan.

4 The symbolic manifestation of the EU's normative role in world politics

Ian Manners

The unfreezing of both the international order and the intellectual order in the post-Cold War era has encouraged fundamentally different ways of conceiving and understanding the roles of the European Union (EU) in world politics. In particular, the influences of social theory developed during the 1960s and 1970s were turned to by scholars eager to overcome the 'failure of international relations as an intellectual project' (Buzan and Little 2001). In this chapter, in line with the analytical framework developed in the book's introductory chapter, I will engage in a five-part consideration of the symbolic manifestation of the EU's normative role in world politics. By drawing on social theory I first suggest how understanding symbolism can help us to explain the EU's normative role through the use of role theory, negotiated order and symbolic manifestation. I then proceed to use this understanding in a discussion of common EU role conceptions, including a normative role. Third, I look at the origins of the EU's normative role by discussing its constitutive norms, together with some examples of their symbolic manifestation. Next, I examine how the EU's normative role is institutionalized through a consideration of the EU's symbolic manifestation in three distinct forms – totems, rituals and taboos. Finally, I conclude by discussing six examples of the EU's normative role performance and role impact. In this chapter I argue that a fuller understanding of the EU's roles in world politics, and in particular its normative role, requires us to engage in the study of the symbolic manifestation of these roles. In this respect the chapter will both develop a theoretical aspect of EU roles considered in the earlier part of the book and complement the more empirical contributions of the chapters in the later part of the book.

Role theory, negotiated order and symbolic manifestation

As Kal Holsti recognized in 1970, 'the notion that individual behaviour may be patterned to fit the expectations of others goes back to the beginning of this century' and he identified the work of John Dewey and George Herbert Mead as laying the foundations of understanding the social psychology of role theory (Holsti 1970: 236–7). Mead's development of symbolic interaction theory to help explain the importance of significant symbols and role-playing in the emergence of self and other is central to understanding the interaction between role theory, negotiated order and symbolic transactions (see Mead 1934). Drawing on the work of the pragmatists and symbolic interactionists of the 1930s, scholars in the 1950s and 1960s began to develop the co-constitutive relationship between role theory (with its emphasis on ontological independence) and negotiated order (with its emphasis on structural conditions). In particular Erving Goffman (1959), together with Peter Berger and Thomas Luckmann's (1966) work on role theory, raised questions about the relationship between self and institutional order in social life (see Berger and Luckmann 1967: 89–96, and Calhoun 1995: 197–8). The symbolic interactionist work of Anselm Strauss marked the next stage in these developments by introducing the notion of 'negotiated order':

> The negotiated order on any given day could be conceived as the sum total of the organisation's rules and policies, along with whatever agreements, understandings, pacts, contracts, and other working arrangements currently obtained.
>
> (Strauss 1978: 5–6, in Thomas 1984: 214)

Strauss's argument that 'all social order has a negotiated element', and that negotiations always occur 'under specific structural conditions', has proved to be influential in anthropology, sociology and organizational management (see Strauss *et al.* 1963, Munch 1986 and Benjamin 2003). Of particular interest here is the argument that the interactions between actors and negotiated order are heavily influenced by symbolic power – 'the power to determine the situation in which interactions take place' (Hallett 2003: 130).

The study of the EU's role in world politics has been influenced in important ways by this work on role theory and negotiated order. In particular, the application of role theory to the foreign policies of EU member states (see Aggestam 1999, 2004) and the EU itself (see Lerch 2001, 2003a, b) has proved of value. In parallel the application of negotiated order to the EU (see M. Smith 1996, 2000) has also made a valuable contribution. In line with the aim of this volume, my focus in the rest of the chapter will be on understanding how the symbolic manifestation of the EU influences its role in shaping the negotiated order of world politics. Before doing so, I shall briefly return to the discussion of international role conceptions of the EU as developed by Richard Whitman and myself in order to clarify the normative role of the EU in world politics.

Role conceptions: the EU's normative role

In recent years I have argued that the debate over the international role of the EU has been dominated by a dichotomy between the ideal types of 'civilian power Europe' and 'military power Europe' (see Manners 2000a, 2002). As Richard Whitman and myself have discussed elsewhere, whereas discussions regarding the civilian and military roles of the EU tend to focus on the question of *capabilities*, my argument in favour of the EU's normative role requires a discussion of *culturation* and *conciliation* (Manners and Whitman 2003: 390–1).

Understanding *culturation* demands that we consider the extent to which the EU's civilian role provides continuity (albeit on a larger scale) of many, if not all, the norms of Westphalian international relations – in particular the inside/outside distinction between those within and without Europe (Manners 2002: 238; Manners and Whitman 2003: 390). Similarly, although discussions of the EU's civilian role clearly emphasize the strengthening of international society and international law, they rarely go as far as arguing for the transformation of the international system into one normatively cultured by, for example, Kantian cosmopolitian ethics and Habermasian discourse ethics. Finally, proponents of a greater civilian role for the EU are generally in favour of economies of scale when enlarging and deepening the EU – that somehow a federal union of 25 and more member states would be able to resist the seduction of looking and behaving like a great power. My argument behind the EU's normative role is that only constant reflexive monitoring by us all of the EU's particular historical evolution, hybrid polity and constitutional configuration will ensure that the processes of European integration result in a more normative Union for the good of all, rather than simply a bigger EU state for the good of some.

Understanding *conciliation* demands that we consider the extent to which the EU's military role ensures the continuity (albeit in a different form) of many, if not all, the norms of Westphalian international relations that favour intervention in the symptoms of conflict over conciliation in the causes of conflict (Manners 2002: 238; Manners and Whitman 2003: 390). Empirically, these two approaches can be differentiated in terms of whether conflict is resolved through shorter-term intervention in the conflict (i.e. changing the conflict itself) or through longer-term conciliation of the parties (i.e. changing the norm of conflict). My argument behind the EU's normative role is that understanding and resolving conflict involves addressing the structural causes of conflict and the associated extreme constructions of difference. Richard Whitman and I have illustrated these three relationships between the EU's primary roles in world politics as shown in Figure 4.1.

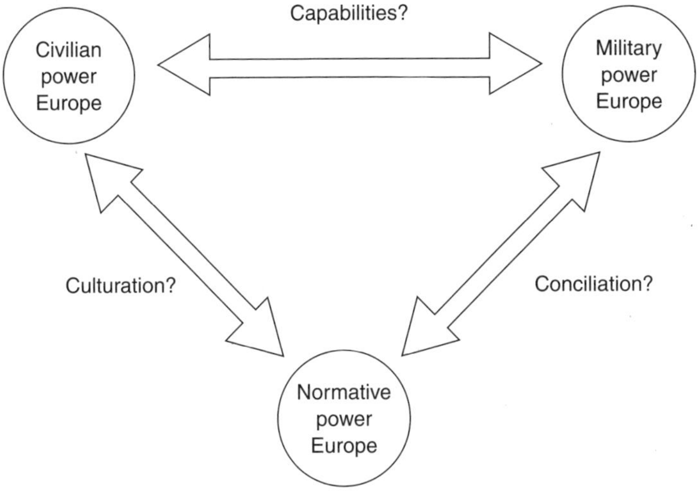

Figure 4.1 Role conceptions of the EU (source: Manners (2000a: 30); Manners and Whitman (2003: 391)).

Role origins – the EU's normative constitution

> Article I-2. The Union's values
> The Union is founded on the values of respect for human dignity, liberty, democracy, equality, the rule of law and respect for human rights, including the rights of persons belonging to minority groups. These values are common to the Member States in a society in which pluralism, non-discrimination, tolerance, justice, solidarity, and the principle of equality between women and men prevail.
>
> Article I-3. The Union's objectives
> 4 In its relations with the wider world, the Union shall uphold and promote its values and interests. It shall contribute to peace, security, the sustainable development of the earth, solidarity and mutual respect among peoples, free and fair trade, eradication of poverty and protection of human rights and in particular children's rights, as well as to strict observance and development of international law, including respect for the principles of the United Nations Charter.

As articles I-2 and I-3 of the Constitution for Europe illustrate, over the past 50 years the EU has developed a series of founding values and wider objectives that contribute to its constituting the normative elements of its international identity (Manners and Whitman 1998, 2003). These values and objectives (Figure 4.2) are reflected in nine norms that I have

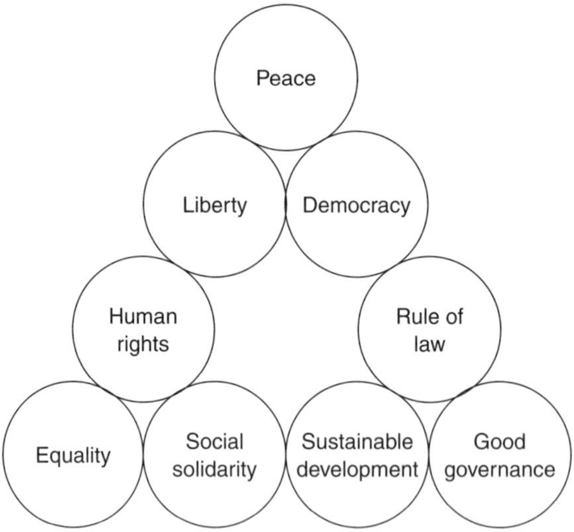

Figure 4.2 The EU's normative constitution (source: Manners (2005b)).

previously argued are constitutive of the EU's normative role in world politics (Manners 2000a: 32–4; 2002: 242–3). In the context of my discussion of the EU's normative role in world politics, I shall briefly revisit these norms and reflect on how they are symbolically manifested.

The first EU norm is *peace* – Robert Schuman's opening words on 9 May 1950 provided the historical *raison d'être* for European integration; 'world peace cannot be safeguarded without the making of creative efforts proportionate to the dangers which threaten it'. Reiterated again in the preambles of the European Coal and Steel Community (ECSC), the Treaty establishing the European Community (TEC), and the Treaty on European Union, Article I-3 of the Constitution for Europe establishes peace as the EU's primary objective: '1. The Union's aim is to promote peace, its values and the well-being of its peoples.' As the Nobel Peace Prize laureate John Hume has observed, the EU norm of peace is crucially symbolized in world politics by the existence of the EU itself:

> it is now clear that European Union is the best example in the history of the world of conflict resolution and it is the duty of everyone, particularly those who live in areas of conflict, to study how it was done and to apply its principles to their own conflict resolution.
>
> (John Hume 1998)

The second EU norm is *liberty* – freedom within a social context. Liberty, similar to the norms of democracy, rule of law and human rights, was codified as founding norms by the revised Article 6 of the consolidated Treaty on European Union after the Amsterdam summit in 1997. The Charter of Fundamental Rights of the European Union adopted at the Nice European Council in December 2000, and incorporated into the Constitution for Europe, develops the EU understanding of liberty. Title II of the Charter sets out 14 rights and freedoms, starting with Article II-66: 'Everyone has the right to liberty and security of the person.' The EU norm of liberty is symbolized in world politics by the rights, freedoms and responsibilities held and exercised by EU citizens and institutions, for example the rights of EU citizenship and the four freedoms of the single market.

The third EU norm is *democracy* – the promotion of a particular form, organization and philosophy of political life. The participation and requirements of democracy have been a constitutive norm of the EU since its birth, with Schuman arguing in the French National Assembly in 1948 that 'we intend to prepare for its [Germany's] admission to a peaceful, democratic organisation of European nations'. Thus, from the inception of the ECSC and ECs until 1970, democracy was the membership norm of the EC. This norm was first codified in the 1970 Luxembourg Report which stated that membership of the EC was open only to democratic states with freely elected parliaments. During the 1990s, the EU was far more explicit in the promotion and requirements of democracy for membership (Copenhagen Criteria, 1993), for development aid (conditionality clauses, 1995), and in its foreign-policy provisions. The EU norm of democracy is symbolized in world politics by its promotion and conditionality in relations with its closest partners, for example as part of the transition and accession processes with Central and Eastern Europe.

The fourth EU norm is *human rights* – one of the most visible and promoted norms of the post-Cold War era. Alongside democracy and the rule of law, respect for human rights was made explicit in the December 1973 Copenhagen document on 'European identity' (Manners and Whitman 1998: 236). Within Europe, human rights law had been progressively developed through the ECHR, and the interpretations of the European Court of Justice. By the 1990s, similar to democracy, human rights were given prominence in the Treaty on European Union and are now promoted through a variety of means, including conditionality clauses in enlargement and development aid. The EU norm of human rights is symbolized in world politics by the high-profile positions taken by the EU at, among others, the UN Commission on Human Rights and visible presence of the EC's observer status to the Commission.

The fifth EU norm is the *rule of law* – the political foundations provided by just legal systems and equal protection for all. The rule of law is seen as essential for ensuring the stability and success of the other norms of liberty, democracy and human rights. Hence, these four norms are to be found promoted together through development aid, CFSP and the

Copenhagen membership criteria. The Constitution for Europe ensures that the rule of law continues to be promoted in external action and international relations, but with additional references to 'respect for the principles of the United Nations Charter and international law' (Article III-292). The EU norm of the rule of law is symbolized in world politics by the EU's threefold commitment to the communitarian law of the *acquis communautaire*, international law developed through the principles of the UN charter, and cosmopolitan law involving a 'commitment to individual rights and principles in accordance with the ECHR [European Convention on Human Rights] and the UN' (Manners 2002: 241).

The sixth EU norm is *equality* – the legal prohibition of discrimination together with proactive policies to promote equality. The norm of equality has become one of the most promoted norms discussed here, moving from a relatively narrow focus on preventing discrimination based on nationality to the far broader and prominent principles of equality in Article I-2 of the Constitution for Europe. In the 1990s, equality norms expanded beyond nationality to include equality between men and women (TEC, Article 2), the protection of minorities (Copenhagen Criteria), and 'action to combat discrimination based on sex, racial or ethnic origin, religion or belief, disability, age or sexual orientation' (TEC, Article 13). The EU norm of equality is symbolized in world politics by the mainstreaming of Article 13 actions through the creation of institutions such as the European Monitoring Centre on Racism and Xenophobia and the Gender Equality Institute, as well as the promotion of equality at conferences such as the 1995 Fourth World Conference on Women in Beijing and the 2001 World Conference against Racism, Racial Discrimination, Xenophobia and Related Intolerance in Durban.

The seventh EU norm is *social solidarity* – the promotion of the social economy, the social partnership and social justice within the EU, and in relations with the developing world. Alongside the norms of democracy, the rule of law and respect for human rights, social solidarity has been emphasized as a norm in the 1973 Copenhagen Declaration, the 1986 Foreign Ministers' Declaration, the 1991 Council Resolution, the 2000 Charter of Fundamental Rights of the Union, and the Constitution for Europe. The Charter of Fundamental Rights makes these norms explicit with its Title IV on solidarity, including workers, the family, health and social security rights. The EU norm of social solidarity is symbolized in world politics by the fairly recent and relatively unique EU commitment to 'free and fair trade' as found in policy developments and the Constitution for Europe since it was placed on the agenda of the Doha Development Agenda of the WTO by a combination of anti-globalization activists and developing countries.

The eighth EU norm is *sustainable development* – a commitment to 'development which meets the needs of the present without compromising the ability of future generations to meet their own needs' (Brundtland

1987: 5). This commitment, and the difficulties of reconciling economic and environmental interests, have evolved slowly since the initial 1972 declaration by heads of member states on Europe's environment (Baker 1997: 92). The December 1988 Declaration on the Environment, the June 1990 Declaration on the Environmental Imperative and the Treaty on European Union all contributed to the codification of the principle of sustainable development in the Fifth Action Programme on the Environment and Sustainable Development (Manners 2000b: 77; Lightfoot and Burchell 2005: 76). The EU norm of sustainable development is symbolized in world politics by its clear and unambiguous commitment to the 1997 Kyoto Protocol to the 1992 United Nations Framework Convention on Climate Change.

The ninth EU norm is *good governance* – the provision of open, participatory and democratic governance without creating hierarchical, exclusionary and centralized government. The norm of good governance is the most recent norm to develop within the EU, reflecting its external promotion through enlargement and development policies, and the concerns of internal accountability and democracy within the EU. The norm has its origins in the dual concerns to encourage stable institutions through the accession process (Copenhagen Criteria, June 1993) and the international spread of human rights, democracy and development through good governance (Council Resolution, November 1991). The EU norm of good governance is symbolized in world politics by the post-Iraq commitment to 'a rule-based international order' involving 'spreading good governance, supporting social and political reform, dealing with corruption and abuse of power, establishing the rule of law and human rights are the best means of strengthening the international order' (Council of the European Union 2003: 10).

The EU's normative role in world politics is symbolically constituted by the complex interaction of these nine norms. This pyramid of the EU norms motivating and mediating the Union's normative role in external action can be illustrated as in Figure 4.2.

Role institutionalization: the EU's symbolic manifestation

Having briefly revisited the nine norms that I argue constitute the EU's normative role, I will now turn to how this role is institutionalized through its symbolic manifestations in world politics. Most of the work analysing the EU's roles in world politics has tended to focus on policies rather than its symbolic manifestation. I am not suggesting that an emphasis on EU policies towards the rest of the world is misplaced, simply that the symbolic manifestation of the EU's normative role reveals much more about the political reality and social institutionalization of the EU's international identity – 'symbols do not simply *reflect* our political reality: they actively *constitute* it' (Shore 2000: 89). It is possible to identify three differing manifestations of this symbolic constitution of reality through icons ('totems'), actions ('rituals') and beliefs ('taboos'). The choice of sacred discourse to describe this trichotomy of manifestations is a reflection of the symbolic power I am trying to explain, rather than a commitment to anything other than humanity as an organizing belief.

Symbolic totems

> Article I-8. The symbols of the Union
> The flag of the Union shall be a circle of twelve golden stars on a blue background.
> The anthem of the Union shall be based on the 'Ode to Joy' from the Ninth Symphony by Ludwig van Beethoven.
> The motto of the Union shall be: 'United in diversity.'
> The currency of the Union shall be the euro.
> 9 May shall be celebrated throughout the Union as Europe Day.

Symbolic totems are the tangible iconic manifestations of EU symbols in the world. They are the most obvious, and most discussed, manifestation of the EU's physical presence in world politics. As Article I-8 from the Constitution for Europe illustrates, the most apparent 'symbols of the Union' are to be found as a result of the Adonnino committee's work in 1984 – a flag, anthem and day of celebration (the motto and currency are more recent developments). Although the anthem, motto and day are very much unrecognizable totems for most EU citizens and non-citizens, the flag and the currency have now achieved a much wider resonance. Although not venerated in quite the same way, the EU border sign, passport and driving licence/identity card all perform similar roles in making tangible the EU as a physical presence with psychological consequences. Of particular importance to the discussion of the EU in world politics are the totems of the standard EU map and the Commission Representations. The standard EU map serves as a multi-linguistic totem of who is in and who is out, together with comparisons between the EU, the US and Japan of area, population and gross domestic product. The Commission Representations serve as the second most important totem (behind the flag) of the EU's physical presence in approximately 130 cities around the world.

Symbolic rituals

Symbolic rituals are observable, although often intangible, symbolic manifestations of the EU in the world. They are also potentially equally obvious, although in reality less discussed, manifestations of the EU's practices in world politics. EU symbolic rituals are more deeply embedded than the symbolic totems of the 1980s and 1990s discussed above. In particular, the ritualistic practices surrounding the 'birth' of the Community located in Franco-German 'rapprochement' and involving the 'founding fathers'. Thus the rituals of France and Germany since the Elysée Treaty (1963) include the explicitly visual practices of joint acts of remembrance and hand-holding at war memorials, the joint positions/declarations generally agreed prior to IGCs (Nice excepted) and the ultimate act of solidarity – President Chirac of France representing Germany at an EU summit in October 2003. In more explicitly EU rituals, the observation and veneration of the 'founding fathers' serve as a symbolic manifestation of the 'birth' of the Community in *Messianiac* acts. The clear identification of Jean Monnet, Robert Schuman, Konrad Adenauer, Alcide De Gasperi and Paul-Henri Spaak, together with the possible inclusion of Altiero Spinelli and Walter Hallstein, as the 'founding fathers' renders more solid the symbolic rituals of post-war reconciliation. In addition to the ritualistic veneration of these 'fathers' (through institutions, societies and literature), the homes of Monnet and Schuman have become museums and places of worship to European integration. Other European rituals place emphasis on European years and cities through the joint programmes with the Council of Europe which celebrate the annual 'European Year of…', including languages, people with disabilities, education or citizenship (in the 2000s), and the 'European City of Culture'. Undoubtedly the most important ritual for understanding the EU in world politics is the physical performances by the variety of 'representatives' of the Union, ranging from the Presidents of the Commission, Council and Parliament, to the High and Special Representatives. These performances may merely be verbal, as in declarations in front of the press in Brussels, or they may be more physical, as in the High Representatives' 'missions' on foreign-policy tasks around the world.

Symbolic taboos

Symbolic taboos are found in usually unobservable and intangible discourses, which reflect the manifestations of meanings and beliefs about the EU. These are the least well studied and understood manifestations of the EU's meanings in world politics. Important as totems and rituals are, it is EU symbolic taboos that shape and explain much of the EU's social institutions, and more importantly the way in which these manifest in world politics. Symbolic taboos are very different from simple discourses within and without the EU – they undoubtedly reinforce 'the importance of symbols as repositories of meaning and agents of consciousness' (Shore 2000: 77). However, symbolic taboos go further in providing a series of inviolable and sacrosanct understandings about what the EU is and what the EU does. In this respect symbolic taboos are constitutive of what the EU is and what it is not, and thus what the EU could and could not do. In this respect symbolic taboos predetermine what might eventually turn into policy possibilities.

Symbolic taboos include those phrases and sayings that are instantly recognizable as the central discourse around which EU politics and policies revolve – from the treaties and declarations to the practical realities of the policies. Examples of these taboos include the discourses of the integration process itself and those of the EU in the world. Within the former, the mere utterance of phrases such as 'Europe will not be made all at once, or according to a single plan', 'not merely unthinkable, but materially impossible', 'common high authority', 'pooling of sovereignty', and '*acquis communautaire*' provide both the rationale and the means through which integration is to be achieved. In each case, it is very difficult to imagine the breaking of the spirit, if not the letter, of these taboos in the integration process. More recent taboos are not as firmly sanctified but still provide the means through which the EU now exists. These include the 'four freedoms', 'single currency', 'ending of the division of the European continent', 'Copenhagen criteria', 'environmental imperative', 'unity through diversity' and 'progressive framing of a common defence policy'. In its relations with the rest of the world, taboo discourse includes phrases such as 'partnership and co-operation', 'near neighbourhood', 'network of agreements', 'rules-based system', 'Petersburg tasks' and even 'battlegroups'.

Role performance and impact: signs of the EU's normative role

To conclude, I will try to provide just a few examples of what I consider to be signs, both indicative and symbolic, of the EU's normative role in world politics. To do this I will revisit the factors that shape EU norm diffusion in world politics, using some of the symbolic manifestations to illustrate. As I have suggested previously, the six factors shaping norm diffusion are contagion, information, procedure, transference, overt presence and cultural filter (Manners 2000a: 35–6; 2002: 244–5).

The *contagion* diffusion of norms takes place almost entirely through the role of symbolic manifestations in diffusing ideas from the EU to other political actors. An example of the contagion of symbolic manifestations of the EU's normative role can be found in the ways in which symbolic taboos within the EU regarding the idea and means of regional integration have diffused to other continents. Hence symbolic discourses such as the creation of a 'common high authority', 'four freedoms' and even a 'single currency' are seen in other regions of the world as being so strong that they are worthy of imitation. Thus in both South America (Mercosur, created in 1991) and Africa (the move from the Organization of African Unity to the African Union in 2002) we see regional organizations being created in order to imitate the perceived worth of the EU's symbolic taboos. The African Union (AU) is particularly interesting in the way it sought to imitate the EU model –

'during the Lusaka Summit several references were made to the African Union being loosely based on the European Union model, in which respect it was said that Africa "should not re-invent the wheel" (South African DFA 2002). Institutionally the AU mimics the EU, with its administrative Commission, Executive Council of member states' foreign ministers, Permanent Representatives Committee, Pan-African Parliament and Court of Justice.

The *informational* diffusion of norms occurs through references to totems, rituals and taboos in the messages and readings regarding the EU's normative role. The role of the EU in the immediate aftermath of European or global tragedies serves as a good example of such informational diffusion. For example, take these four public statements as symbolic manifestations of the EU's normative role:

> President Romano Prodi is visiting Enschede today to express European solidarity with the families stricken by the terrible accident that occurred on Saturday 13 May.... The Commission has therefore studied the possibility of providing financial support for the devastated areas from the Structural Funds to assist the Dutch authorities with the reconstruction and restoration.
>
> (Commission 2000)

> Dr Javier Solana, EU High Representative for the CFSP, expresses his sadness at the death of EUMM monitors.... Dr Solana said 'I deeply regret the death yesterday of the two ELTNM monitors and their interpreter. The men and women of the EUMM are carrying out a difficult but essential task with exemplary courage and dedication in the interest of peace and stability in the whole region. The men that died yesterday have paid the highest price for this ideal.'
>
> (Council 2001a)

> This barbaric attack was directed against the free world and our common values. It is a watershed event and life will never be quite the same again. European institutions and Governments will work closely together with our American friends and partners in the defence of freedom.
>
> (Prodi 2001)

> The General Affairs Council decided yesterday that Friday 14th September 2001 would be a European day of mourning for the victims of the terrorist attacks in the USA.... Staff of the EU Institutions as well as citizens of Brussels are invited to make the silence a collective act ... on Rond Point Schuman shortly before 12:00 noon tomorrow so that the silence can be observed.
>
> (Council 2001b)

These statements illustrate a number of extremely important symbolic manifestations at work. In particular, they suggest that EU leaders are able to demonstrate many of the symbolic rituals closely associated with the exercise of domestic and foreign policy. Equally interesting is the way in which the rituals communicate solidarity, collectivity and distinctive norms, such as social solidarity and sustainable peace in the 'free world' (see Manners 2005a on 'sustainable peace').

The *procedural* diffusion of norms takes place through the institutionalization of relationships between the EU and third parties, also involving the range of symbolic manifestations. The relationship between the EU and the ACP countries, as renewed and reinterpreted at Cotonou, Benin, in 2000 serves as an interesting example of the symbolic manifestation of the EU's normative role. The Cotonou Agreement was accompanied by an image of many hands holding a 'solidarity jar' (a large jar with many holes) aloft. Sat on the lip of the solidarity jar is a globe with Europe and Africa to the fore, and the inscription 'ACP–UE, XXV years' across the Mediterranean Sea on the globe. The accompanying declaration read thus:

> *The symbolism of the solidarity jar*
> The symbol chosen by the host country to illustrate the Cotonou Agreement simultaneously embodies the power of union and the importance of solidarity – the pierced jar will hold water only if the people come together to plug its holes with their fingers. This symbolic image, borrowed from Ghezo, former king of Dahomey (as Benin used to be known), fits perfectly with the values which have always underpinned relations between the European Union and the ACP countries – values which are now more than ever crucial to the successes of the future partnership.
>
> (*The ACP–EU Courier* 2000).

The symbolic manifestation of the EU's normative role in this image and declaration should be apparent, but what is more interesting is that the symbol was chosen by Benin using indigenous art. Thus, the procedural diffusion between the EU and the ACP is institutionalized, for good or ill, by the idea and image of the 'power of union', the 'importance of solidarity' and the need for 'partnership'.

Transference diffusion concerns the transmission of norms when the EU is involved in the transfer of material and immaterial assets such as humanitarian aid and technical assistance. An interesting example of the symbolic manifestation of the EU's normative role was to be seen in Ramalla, Palestine, in 2002. During most of 2002 Yasser Arafat, the former premier of the Palestine Authority (PA), had been holed up in his Authority headquarters in Ramalla. During that time, the Israeli government systematically demolished all of the buildings in the Ramalla compound, except Arafat's, in an attempt to force Arafat to bring a halt to the second *intifada*. In parallel the US and EU negotiators worked hard to resolve the conflict and ensure that both Arafat and the PA were not destroyed. At the end of the siege, in late 2002, as Arafat finally walked away from the compound, the images were transmitted live to the rest of the world. In the background of these scenes, the last image of Ramalla was two flags flying over the demolished compound and peace process – the Palestinian Authority and the European Union. Like the role of all of these symbolic manifestations of the EU's normative role, the important thing to note is not the success of the EU but the extent to which it is psycho-sociologically associated with the process. (See Deutch and Kinnvall 2001; and Hansson and Kinnvall 2004 for considerations of the social psychology of political symbolism.)

The *overt* diffusion involving EU norms occurs as a result of the physical presence of the EU in third states and international organizations. An example of interest here is the symbolic manifestations of the EU in the United Nations. Since the end of the Cold War the members of the EU have become increasingly cohesive in their support of common EU positions both within the General Assembly and in the other UN organs. Of particular interest symbolically is not the extent to which EU member states' representatives hold regular meetings to co-ordinate their positions, or the role of the EU Council presidency in speaking *for* the EU, but the few symbolic examples of when EC representatives have the opportunity to act as physical manifestations *of* the EC when they are given the opportunity to speak in special sessions and specialist organs such as the Food and Agriculture Organization (FAO). Although relatively rare, this symbolic ritual also performs the act of diffusing other symbolic taboos, in particular 'speaking with one voice'.

The *cultural filter* does not facilitate so much as shape and transform the diffusion of EU norms. Kinnvall argues that the cultural filter is based on the interplay between the construction of knowledge and the creation of social and political identity by the subjects of norm diffusion (Kinnvall 1995: 61–71). The cultural filter becomes crucial in understanding how and by what means EU symbolic manifestations are interpreted during representation and reception. Equally important, as illustrated below, the cultural filter is reflexive in that the EU itself adapts both its symbols and its methods to its normative self-understanding. As I have discussed elsewhere (Manners 2000a, 2002), since 1998 the EU has played an important, if not leading, role in pursuit of the international abolition of the death penalty. It is important also to note the way in which the cultural filter in the third countries, such as the US, has remained robust against EU norm diffusion in this case. Because of the litigious–individualistic nature of US society, the EU has focused its norms at the legal and individual level, as the brief of *amicus curiae* ('friend of the court') helps illustrate. *Amicus curiae* briefs are submitted by *amici* ('friends' who are not party to the case), and with the consent of both parties, with the intention of informing the court of information not available from the parties or other *amici* (see Wilson 2004: 1–2, esp. n. 1). To give just one example of the EU use of an *amicus curiae* in the case of Donald Roper v. Christopher Simmons:

> The European Union considers the principles of liberty, democracy, respect for human rights and fundamental freedoms, and the rule of law, to be of vital importance both nationally and in the international community. . . . The EU and its Member States share the widespread opinion of the international community of states that the execution of persons below 18 years of age at the time of their offences violates widely accepted human rights norms and the minimum standards of human rights set forth by the United Nations. Furthermore, the EU and its Member States are opposed to the death penalty in all cases and accordingly aim at its universal abolition.
>
> (Wilson 2004: 1–2)

> *Justice Kennedy*. Let – let's focus on the word 'unusual'. Forget 'cruel' for the moment, although they're both obviously involved. We've seen very substantial demonstration that world opinion is – is against this, at least as interpreted by the leaders of the European Union. Does that have a bearing on what's unusual? Suppose it were shown that the United States were one of the very, very few countries that executed juveniles, and that's true. Does that have a bearing on whether or not it's unusual?
>
> (Supreme Court 2004: 14)

> Our determination that the death penalty is disproportionate punishment for offenders under 18 finds confirmation in the stark reality that the United States is the only country in the world that continues to give official sanction to the juvenile death penalty. As respondent and a number of *amici* emphasize, Article 37 of the United Nations Convention on the Rights of the Child, which every country in the world has ratified save for the United States and Somalia, contains an express prohibition on capital punishment for crimes committed by juveniles under 18. . . . Brief for European Union *et al.* as *Amici Curiae* 12–13. . . . It is proper that we acknowledge the overwhelming weight of international opinion against the juvenile death penalty. . . . The opinion of the world community, while not controlling our outcome, does provide respected and significant confirmation for our own conclusions.
>
> (Kennedy 2005: 21–4)

As these three extracts illustrate, the *amicus curiae* submitted by Richard Wilson on behalf of the EU was used as a demonstration of 'world opinion' during the US Supreme Court's oral arguments in order to determine whether the US was being 'cruel and unusual' in executing juveniles. As Supreme Court Justice Kennedy acknowledged in writing the majority opinion in favour of abolishing the execution of juveniles under 18 at the time of the crime, world opinion provides a 'respected and significant confirmation for our own conclusions'. This final example helps illustrate the way in which the symbolical manifestation of the EU's normative role is mediated in the context of the cultural filter. More specifically, it demonstrates an interesting case of the EU disregarding 'national sovereignty' and acting directly in a domestic legal setting. Thus while the norm is human rights, the symbol is the transgression of state sovereignty.

Conclusion

Although these six brief examples of the symbolic manifestation of the EU's normative role in world politics are only fleeting, I hope I have been able to illustrate this chapter's central argument. My argument has been that a fuller understanding and analysis of the EU's roles in international politics, in particular its normative role, requires us to engage in the study of the symbolic manifestation of the EU's international identity. The search for, and interpretation of, symbolic manifestations such as informational public statements, overt physical presence at the UN, and the cultural filter of the US legal system, are important in allowing us to understand the processes through which the EU's normative role is symbolically manifested. In contrast, the extent to which symbolic manifestations of the contagion of the EU regional integration model, procedural institutionalization of the Cotonou Agreement, and transference to the PA, are more important in helping us to analyse and judge the impact of the EU's normative role.

Returning to the interplay between role theory, negotiated order and symbolic manifestations, it appears that a fuller awareness of the EU's normative role has to account for the co-constitutive relationship between self-understanding and structural conditions. First, EU self-understanding involves the way in which the symbolic manifestations discussed in this chapter contribute to the social and psychological construction of self-identity, and thus role. However, as Richard Whitman and I have discussed elsewhere, the EU must be understood as in terms of its 'complex and multifaceted international identity' involving 'a complex and fluid negotiation of multiple relational identities' (Manners and Whitman 1998: 238; 2003: 400). This complexity and multiplicity of identities is clearly reflected in the plurality of roles which the EU plays at any one time, in any one place. In this respect bounded distinctions of self–other, and by implication role, must be problematized by the realities of the late/postmodern era and the hybrid polity perspectives which the EU represents almost a century after the pragmatists and interactionists first began to develop role theory. Second, the structural conditions in which the EU sits and shapes are also constituted and understood through the symbolic manifestations of the negotiated order of social life. In order to understand the normative role of the EU, an appreciation of both the less tangible social institutionalization of power relations *and* the more tangible network of global relations is desirable. Finally, it is the interplay between the symbolic power to determine role-playing situations and the structural conditions shaping the negotiation of order that ultimately leads us to the greatest symbolic manifestation of the EU's normative role in world politics – 'the power of constituting the given' (Bourdieu 1991: 170).

Note

I am very grateful to Annika Björkdahl, Dirk De Bièvre, Ole Elgström, Stefano Guzzini, Ulla Holm, Pertti Joenniemi, Knud Erik Jørgensen, Catarina Kinnvall, Sonia Lucarelli, José Magone, Stefania Panebianco, Jess Pilegaard, Ulrich Sedelmeier, Helene Sjursen, Karen Smith, Michael Smith, Emma Stewart and Angela Wigger for their helpful comments.

References

Aggestam, L. (1999) 'Role Conceptions and the Politics of Identity in Foreign Policy', ARENA Working Papers 99/8, Oslo: Centre of European Studies, University of Oslo.

Aggestam, L. (2004) *A European Foreign Policy? Role Conceptions and the Politics of Identity in Britain, France and Germany*, Stockholm: Department of Political Science, Stockholm University.

Baker, Susan (1997) 'The Evolution of European Union Environmental Policy: From Growth to Sustainable Development?', in Susan Baker, Maria Kousis, Dick Richardson and Stephen Young (eds) *The Politics of Sustainable Development: Theory, Policy and Practice within the European Union*, London: Routledge.

Benjamin, O. (2003) 'The Power of Unsilencing: Between Silence and Negotiation in Heterosexual Relationships', *Journal for the Theory of Social Behaviour*, 33 (1): 1–19.

Berger, P. and Luckmann, T. (1967) *The Social Construction of Reality: A Treatise in the Sociology of Knowledge*, London: Penguin.

Bourdieu, P. (1991) *Language and Symbolic Power*, Boston, MA: Harvard University Press.

Brundtland, G. H. (1987) *Our Common Future/World Commission on Environment and Development*, Oxford: Oxford University Press.

Buzan, B. and Little, R. (2001)'Why International Relations has Failed as an Intellectual Project and What to do About it', *Millennium*, 30 (1): 19–39.

Calhoun, C. (1995) *Critical Social Theory: Culture, History and the Challenge of Difference*, Oxford: Blackwell.

Commission of the European Union (2000) 'Explosion in Enschede (Netherlands): President Romano Prodi visits the scene of the disaster', Press Statement IP/00/489, Brussels, 17 May.

Council of the European Union (1991) Resolution of the Council on Human Rights, Democracy and Development, 28 November.

Council of the European Union (2001a) 'Dr Javier Solana, EU High Representative for the CFSP, expresses his sadness at the death of EUMM monitors', Press Statement 01333/00, Brussels, 20 July.

Council of the European Union (2001b) Joint Information to the Press by the European Union Institutions, Press Statement S0148/01, Brussels, 13 September.

Council of the European Union (2003) *A Secure Europe in a Better World: European Security Strategy*, Brussels, 12 December.

Courier (2000) 'Special Issue on the Cotonou Agreement', *ACP–EU Courier*, September.

Deutch, M. and Kinnvall, K. (2001) 'What is Political Psychology?', in K. R. Monroe (ed.) *Political Psychology*, Mahwah, NJ: Lawrence Erlbaum.

Goffman, E. (1959) *The Presentation of Self in Everyday Life*, New York: Doubleday.

Hallet, T. (2003) 'Symbolic Power and Organizational Culture', *Sociological Theory*, 21 (2): 128–49.

Hansson, S. and Kinnvall, C. (2004) 'Women as Symbols in Religious Discourses: Feminist Perspectives on Gender and Indian Religions', *Chakra: Tidskrift för Indiska Religioner*, 1: 7–20.

Holsti, K. (1970) 'National Role Conceptions in the Study of Foreign Policy', *International Studies Quarterly*, 14 (3): 233–309.

Hume, J. (1998) The Nobel Lecture given by the Nobel Peace Prize Laureate 1998 – John Hume, Oslo, 10 December, http://www.nobel.no/eng_lect_98h.html.

Kennedy, A. (2005) Opinion of the Court, Roper v. Simmons, Supreme Court of the United States, No. 03-633, 1 March.

Kinnvall, C. (1995) *Cultural Diffusion and Political Learning: The Democratization of China*, Lund: Lund University Press.

Lerch, M. (2001) 'The Important Role of Roles: a Theoretical Framework for Understanding the External Identity of the European Union'. Paper presented to panel on 'Identity and Foreign Policy in Europe', ECPR fourth Pan-European International Relations Conference, Canterbury.

Lerch, M. (2003a) 'European Identity in International Society: A Constructivist Analysis of the EU Charter of Fundamental Rights', *Constitutionalism Web-Papers, ConWEB*, No. 2.

Lerch, M. (2003b) *Universelle Rechte – Europäische Pflichten? Eine konstruktivistische Analyse der Rolle der Europäischen Union in der internationalen Menschenrechtspolitik*, Marburg: University of Marburg.

Lightfoot, S. and Burchell, J. (2005) 'The European Union and the World Summit on Sustainable Development: Normative Power Europe in Action?', *Journal of Common Market Studies*, 43 (1): 75–95.

Manners, I. (2000a) *Normative Power Europe: A Contradiction in Terms?* Working Paper 38/2000, Copenhagen: Copenhagen Peace Research Institute, http://www.copri.dk/publications/WP/WP 2000/38-2000.doc.

Manners, I. (2000b) *Substance and Symbolism: An Anatomy of Cooperation in the New Europe*, Aldershot: Ashgate.

Manners, I. (2002) 'Normative Power Europe: A Contradiction in Terms?', *Journal of Common Market Studies*, 40 (2): 235–58.

Manners, I. (2005a) 'The Value of Peace', in M. Aziz and S. Millns (eds) *Values in the Constitution of Europe*, Aldershot: Ashgate.

Manners, I. (2005b) 'The Constitutive Nature of Values, Images and Principles in the European Union', in S. Lucarelli and I. Manners (eds) *Values and Principles in European Union Foreign Policy*, London: Routledge.

Manners, I. and Whitman, R. (1998) 'Towards Identifying the International Identity of the European Union: A Framework for Analysis of the EU's Network of Relationships', *Journal of European Integration*, 21: 231–49.

Manners, I. and Whitman, R. (2003) 'The "Difference Engine": Constructing and Representing the International Identity of the European Union', *Journal of European Public Policy*, 10 (3): 380–404.

Mead, G. H. (1934) *Mind, Self and Society*, Chicago: University of Chicago Press.

Münch, R. (1986) 'The American Creed in Sociological Theory: Exchange, Negotiated Order, Accommodated Individualism, and Contingency', *Sociological Theory*, 4: 41–60.

Office for Official Publications of the European Communities (2004) Treaty Establishing a Constitution for Europe, *Official Journal of the European Union* 2004/C 310/01.

Prodi, R. (2001) Statement by President Prodi on the attacks against the United States, Press Statement IP/01/1265, Brussels, 12 September.

Shore, C. (2000) *Building Europe: the Cultural Politics of European Integration*, London: Routledge.

Smith, M. (1996) 'The European Union and a Changing Europe: Establishing the Boundaries of Order', *Journal of Common Market Studies*, 34 (1): 5–28.

Smith, M. (2000) 'Negotiating New Europes: the Roles of the European Union', *Journal of European Public Policy*, 7 (5): 806–22.

South African DFA (2002) 'Transition from the OAU to the African Union', Department of Foreign Affairs, Republic of South Africa, http://www.au2002.gov.za/docs/background/oau_to_au.htm.

Strauss, A. (1978) *Negotiations: Varieties, Contexts, Processes, and Social Order*, San Francisco: Jossey-Bass.

Strauss, A., Schatzman, L., Ehrlich, D., Bucher, R. and Sabshin, M. (1963) 'The Hospital and its Negotiated Order', in E. Freidson (ed.) *The Hospital in Modern Society*, New York: Free Press.

Supreme Court of the United States (2004) Donald Roper v. Christopher Simmons, No. 03-633, Oral Arguments, 13 October.

Thomas, J. (1984) 'Some Aspects of Negotiated Order, Loose Coupling and Mesostructure in Maximum Security Prisons', *Symbolic Interaction*, 7: 213–31.

Wilson, R. (2004) *Brief of Amici Curiae of the European Union and Members of the International Community in Support of Respondent*, Donald Roper v. Christopher Simmons, No. 03-633 in the Supreme Court of the United States.

5 Values or rights?

Alternative conceptions of the EU's 'normative' role

Helene Sjursen

It is far from uncommon to encounter the concept of 'role' in the EU foreign-policy literature. However, it is most often used as a general way of describing the EU's international behaviour or assessing its influence, and is rarely connected to explicit theoretical assumptions. Hence it is often treated as interchangeable with references to the EU's international 'actorness', 'identity', 'nature', etc. The ambition of this volume is to bring role *theory* into the analysis of EU foreign policy. Roles are normatively regulated and refer to the expectations that are attached to a position or post. Consequently, using role analysis as a framework for studying the EU's foreign policy should direct researchers towards examining questions such as how the EU's foreign policy writes itself into an international society with a number of formal and informal norms and rules that create expectations with regard to its behaviour. This would certainly provide an alternative way of accounting for what the EU does in the international system to that of realist analyses, which tend to assume that actors are driven exclusively by utility considerations and to neglect that they might (also) be conditioned by normative expectations. However, one might question whether role theory is sufficient or satisfactory in terms of making sense of, and accounting for, many of the empirical claims made about the EU's foreign policy.

Role theory has often been criticized for being conventionalist. It draws a picture of actors as conformists: actors' behaviour is considered to be shaped by a set of norms that create expectations about what ought to be done. It has more difficulties in capturing the actors' potential autonomy and also change. How do actors overcome the situatedness of their role? The EU is often described as a 'different' or 'unique' actor in the international system. Another way of describing 'uniqueness' would be to say that the EU's foreign policy is '*un*conventional', and the question then becomes to what extent a concept that takes as its fundamental starting point that actors' behaviour is shaped by a given normative order can account for this. In so far as it might be correct that the EU breaks with the established normative order of international society, how would role theory account for this? It would seem, at best, that we need something in addition to role analysis to make sense of, and scrutinize, such claims about EU foreign policy.

In this chapter I suggest that discourse theory and the concept of communicative rationality may help to theoretically account for an actor's putative break with an established normative order. It suggests that actors are capable of 'criticising the norms that they are socialised under, and [of] choos[ing] different modes of action from what they are expected to and used to' (Eriksen 1999: 226). Such a description might capture something apparently relevant to the EU – and which role theory might have more difficulties in accounting for. Furthermore, discourse theory should be helpful in terms of disentangling some of the ambiguities and biases of the arguments about the 'normative' role of the EU. In fact, a large part of the literature that concerns itself with the particularity of the EU's foreign policy also makes claims about the EU being a 'normative power', an 'ethical power', a 'civil power', etc. However, these claims often seem insufficiently accounted for in theoretical terms and also appear to convey a rather indiscriminate view of norms (Sjursen 2006). There are numerous norms and they may point to very different types of foreign policies, hence conceptualizing the EU as 'normative'/'ethical', etc., can be only a first step towards saying something about EU foreign policy. What is more, all foreign policies may be said to have an 'ethical' or a 'normative' dimension. What (if anything) is then so special about the EU? Thus, while sceptical of the prospects of role theory as the solution that may allow us to capture all aspects of the 'unidentified international object' that is the EU, I adhere to the editors' claim that 'there is likely profit and analytical purchase in pursuing new ways of analysing EU foreign policy' (Introduction to this volume).

Taking the conception of actors as communicatively rational as a starting point, I suggest an analytical distinction between two conceptions of foreign policy. Both would be broadly consistent with the argument that the EU's international role can be described as 'normative', 'ethical' or 'civilizing', yet they would lead to different expectations with regard to what kind of foreign policy the EU might develop. Whereas the first conception – of a *value-based* foreign policy – entails a common foreign and security policy that is established mainly to ensure and protect the sustainability of a particular community with a particular (European) identity, the second conception – of a *rights-based* foreign policy – would suggest that the efforts to build a common foreign policy should be understood as the expression of a concern for promoting certain principles not only inside the EU but also at the international stage. Hence they give very different meanings to the idea of a 'normative' role for the EU.[1]

The main task of the chapter is to work out more concretely what might be the core characteristics of a European foreign policy that would fit with these two conceptions. The potential empirical relevance of the two conceptions will also be considered, although it is not the purpose of the chapter to systematically assess their empirical validity.

Communicative rationality

It has become quite common, rightly or wrongly, to stress the particularity, or difference, of EU foreign policy, although there is no complete consensus on what exactly this particularity consists in or how best to account for it. Authors emphasize different dimensions when they present this general argument. However, the idea that the EU is a 'normative', 'ethical' or 'civil' power has gained increasing ground, and the 'particularity' of the EU is often linked to an image of a putative 'normative' dimension (Manners 2002; Aggestam 2004; Smith 2000; Whitman 1998; Rosencrance 1998). Assuming that there is some validity to such conceptualizations of the EU, what kind of theoretical tools might be used to account for this? As sociological role theory concerns itself with conceptions of appropriate behaviour, it allows us to incorporate a concern for norms and for normative commitments in the analysis. Thus, at first sight, one might conclude that this is a useful avenue to take in order to account for a normative dimension in the EU's foreign policy. However, given that role theory tends to emphasize and focus on how actors 'insert' themselves into existing normative patterns, it may be more difficult for role theory alone to account for a 'normative/ethical/civil' power that is also considered different, behaving in ways that are distinct both from traditional Great Powers and from classic international organizations. For this purpose, a theory that *both* takes the putative normative dimension to political processes seriously *and* considers norms to have a rational basis is useful (Eriksen and Weigård 2003). This is so not least because at the core of the EU's 'normative' power is considered to be its 'ability to change conceptions of normal' (Manners 2002: 239). Consequently, among the many confusions and uncertainties that arise as a result of the 'normative/ethical/civilian' power argument is that of why the EU should respect certain norms, why certain norms are considered valid, as well as why others should be rejected.

From a discourse theoretical perspective norms are not only practical arrangements, held together through 'mutual agreement about their advantageousness or through the use of coercive power' (Eriksen and Weigård 1997: 224–5). In contrast to a realist or a functionalist perspective norms are held to be autonomous sources of motivation owing their validity to their impartial justification, i.e. that they can be defended in an open, free and rational debate (among all affected). It is through a communicative process in which norms are rationally assessed that their relevance and binding character are established. In this sense this perspective provides a useful theoretical underpinning of conceptions of the EU as a 'normative/ethical/civilian' power, as well as for claims about the EU as a different or unconventional actor, seeking to shape international rules and norms and not only to write itself into a given normative order.

In order to capture the possibility that actors are able to reflect on the validity of different norms, and why they should be complied with, actors are considered communicatively rational. This means that actors are considered rational when they are able to justify and explain their actions in relation to intersubjectively valid norms, that is, norms that cannot be reasonably rejected in a rational debate (Eriksen and Weigård 2003). This conception comes from Jürgen Habermas's theory of communicative action. Habermas considers that our communication through linguistic expressions – 'speech acts' – 'play a central role in regulating and reproducing forms of social life and the identities of actors' (Cronin and de Greiff 1998: x).[2]

Actors are conceived of as understanding-oriented and thus able to shift from a purely self-regarding to an other-regarding mode of interaction. This is not, however, the same thing as a conception of actors as altruistic. Rather the actor is conceived of as having

> the ability to critically reflect on her own understandings of reality, interests, preferences, and maxims of behaviour; to estimate the consequences for other actors should she decide to pursue her own interests; and to participate in a discourse with others regarding the interpretation of interest and norms for the coordination of behaviour and interaction.
>
> (Lose 2001: 185)

This opens not only the possibility of a change of viewpoints as a result of interaction and communication, and the possibility that actors agree to certain decisions even if they go against their own material interest. It also implies that following a norm – or not – may be the result of a conscious choice made in a process of argumentation with other actors, rather than simply being, for example, a habit. The validity of the norm would be tested, rejected or accepted through the discursive process.

Whereas an actor's concern for material gains could be accounted for through a rational-choice perspective, answers to questions regarding 'who we are' (identity questions) or what is the right conduct from a moral perspective are more difficult to reconstruct from such premises. Consequently, the conception of actors as communicatively rational is helpful in particular by bringing the potential communal and/or normative dimension in European foreign policy out more clearly. It provides analysts with a clear alternative starting point for hypothesizing about the EU's foreign policy to that of rational-choice-inspired approaches. Hence it is a valuable additional tool of analysis to those found in the realist or rational-choice literature, as well as those in the neo-liberal institutionalist literature in international relations, which share with its neo-realist counterparts the essential assumption of actors as rational utility maximizers (Risse-Kappen 1995).

Most important for the theme of this book, due to the emphasis on the actors' capability of reflecting on the validity of norms and coming to agreement through exchanges or arguments about what is the right thing to do, it provides us with a theoretical starting point for understanding how actors might overcome the situatedness of a given role, or break with established normative patterns. A further value-added of the communicative approach is that it specifies the micro-mechanism that often seems to be lacking in the literature on the putative normative dimension in EU foreign policy. Due to its emphasis on norms and ideas, this approach follows the principal arguments of the so-called 'constructivist' perspective on security, but strengthens it by providing a theory of the validity of norms.

To communitarians, communicative processes are context-bound; they are possible only in collectivities that have a 'thick' sense of identity. In such collectivities the relevant form of justification of a policy would be referring to what the appropriate conduct is given the particular identity of the particular community in question. Norms would express common understandings of the 'good life'. This would fit with a value-based foreign policy and probably also be much in line with the expectations of role theory. It would be the thickness of the social environment – a common cultural identity – that would explain the emergence of, and commitment to, common norms. However, whereas much of the EU foreign-policy literature, and role theory, highlight the potential role of identity in shaping norms, the conception of actors as communicatively rational can help us to capture also those processes in which actors rely on arguments that have a certain universal validity, as well as the possibility that arguments can function as a mobilizing force for change. From a communicative perspective it is possible to theoretically account for social norms and institutions *also* being upheld because actors consider them valid regardless of the culture from which they emerge. This would allow us to theoretically account for actors' efforts to 'overcome' the situatedness of their role.

In line with this, an analytical distinction between different types of norms, between values and rights or higher order norms, may be highlighted. Values or conceptions of what is good may vary according to cultural or social contexts. They are particular to a specific community or a specific collective identity. To establish what is right, fair or just on the other hand can be kept separate from this:

> The question of fairness does not refer to an axiological value, but to a moral norm – a deontological principle. It is concerned with what we are obliged to do when our actions have consequences for others. Rights then refer to higher order principles and claim universal validity.
> (Eriksen and Weigård 2003: 134–5)

Whereas it would not be reasonable to expect transcultural agreement about values, the same is not necessarily the case with regard to higher-order norms such as 'equality, freedom, solidarity, self-realisation and human dignity' (Eriksen and Weigård 2003: 138).

Based on this distinction, I suggest two alternative conceptions of the EU's foreign policy: 'value-based' and 'rights-based'. The rest of this chapter is devoted to working out more concretely what the core characteristics of these two conceptions of the EU's foreign and security policy would be. What kind of foreign policy might one expect according to these two conceptions and to what extent do they fit with our empirical knowledge of European foreign policy?

Indicators of a value-based or a rights-based foreign policy[3]

Three core indicators will be discussed: (1) the institutional structure of the common foreign policy; (2) the legitimacy-basis of the common foreign policy; and (3) the conception of international relations on which collective foreign-policy initiatives (towards states outside the EU) might rely. The third indicator is considered particularly important in terms of suggesting to what extent we can argue that the EU is a distinct international actor. Assuming that the core organizing principle of international society is that of external sovereignty, one might define a 'different' actor as one that breaks with this principle not only – as the EU does – in its internal organization but also in its general international orientation. Concretely, this would mean that it would strive for the development of a higher-order law – above the states – thus breaking with the Westphalian logic of external sovereignty.[4]

First, however, what kind of institutional arrangements might one expect in a rights-based and in a value-based foreign policy?

Institutional arrangements

Starting with the *rights-based* foreign policy, it follows from the definition of actors as communicatively rational and understanding-oriented that they will be capable of agreeing to establish institutions and rules for interaction that are mutually binding and that may constrain their ability to promote particular interests. The mobilizing factor for the establishment of such institutions or rules would be the joint conviction of the actors involved that they would provide the best way, or the best procedures, for solving common problems. It is perhaps less obvious whether or not this perspective would lead to expectations of supranational or, rather, intergovernmental institutions and international governance (Bohman 1999). However, the most likely option would probably be *supranationalism*, defined as the establishment of a mutually binding legal arrangement – connected to sanctions – between the actors. Such mutually binding institutions would be necessary in order to ensure collective action, which is to take away the motives for actors not to comply with common rules. They sanction non-compliance; hence make it less costly to act in a morally adequate way. Without mutually binding legal norms, there is always a risk of defection and a concern that some actors contribute more than they receive (whereas others are free-riders). In order to avoid such risks common rules are necessary.

Here, the rational-choice perspective might agree with the communicative perspective. However, it diverges on the potential for actors to actually come to agreement on common rules. Furthermore, the two perspectives differ on the reasons why actors might agree in the first place, as well as comply once they have come to an agreement. Whereas the rational-choice perspective would expect agreement only if the rational utility calculations of each individual actor suggest that agreement is beneficial, the communicative perspective assumes that agreement is possible on the basis of the better argument. In the aftermath, then, the legal agreement is maintained not only because of its ultimate ability to force actors to comply but because it is considered legitimate – it is considered to provide fair terms of co-operation for all the actors involved. Regardless of their material resources they are subjected to the same duties and have the same rights. The law is considered to have a moral element that makes it possible to obey it based on a moral assessment about what is fair, or what is in the interest of the common good (Eriksen and Weigård 2003). It ensures a fair process of decision-making.

With regard to a *value-based* foreign policy the consensus that would provide the basis for compliance is limited, as it is based upon a we-feeling, a sense of common identity and the idea of special obligations to fellow members within the community. Allegiance to a common foreign and security policy would be the result of a sense of common destiny and a clear distinction between what is European as opposed to other human collectives. In such a unit, supranational institutions would be unproblematic; however, given that the glue that is considered to hold the states together is that of a common identity, such institutions might not be a necessary requirement. *Transnational arrangements* would most likely suffice.

Legitimacy basis

With regard to the legitimacy basis for a value-based and a rights-based foreign policy, there would also be differences. In both cases, however, the democratic checks and balances of the member states would not be a sufficient source of legitimacy, as a degree of supranationality is considered. In the case of a *value-based* conception, one would rely on a sense of solidarity as the principal source of legitimacy for the foreign and security policy. The requirements for democratic checks and balances would perhaps be considered less strong, as the need for a common foreign and security policy would be legitimized with reference to the need to defend and protect a particular life-form from potential threats and intrusions. In fact, the value- or identity-based conception does not as such presuppose democracy. It is only if the community in question endorses democratic principles as a constitutive part of its common identity that democratic legitimacy would be expected. What one would expect first of all is a certain requirement of consistency between the particular understanding of the characteristics of a particular entity and the policy choices made. To many, this might be particularly relevant with regard to foreign and security policy. Indeed, it is sometimes even argued that with regard to issues that pertain to national security, openness and democratic accountability can be problematic, and efficiency requirements are more important. Physical survival – national sovereignty – is what is ultimately considered to be at stake, and is thus considered to take primacy over requirements for democratic checks and balances.[5] This is reflected also in the national constitutions of several EU member states in the sense that foreign and security policy is often considered to be the prerogative of the executive and the decision to go to war is sometimes even almost exclusively in the hands of the executive branch (Wagner 2005). National parliaments on the whole spend less time scrutinizing foreign-policy issues than traditional domestic political matters. The point here, however, is less that the advocates of the limited need for democratic controls and procedures in foreign and security policy seem to lean on the need for efficiency in order to justify limited democratic control, but that they tend to do so, and succeed in doing so, due to assumptions of cultural and ethnic cohesion within a nation-state. Questions of foreign policy are often framed in terms of 'us' and 'them', and are expected to provoke a reflex of solidarity and unity of purpose that does not require the same kind of democratic checks and balances as those issues that pertain only to relations within the collective 'us'. A similar reflex would then be what one would expect as a legitimacy basis for a *value-based* European foreign policy.

With regard to the legitimacy basis for a *rights-based* conception of foreign and security policy it would, as noted, also need to draw on something else than the domestic political processes in the member states, due to its supranational elements. However, it would not in the same way as in a value-based conception be possible to expect an automatic sense of solidarity and support for a common foreign and security policy due to a common identity. A rights-based common foreign and security policy would need to be accountable to a wide variety of interests and perspectives. In order to ensure such accountability, a broad public debate, where all those affected could in principle be heard, would be required. This presupposes a European public sphere as well as legally entrenched rights of citizenship at the supranational and not only at the national level.

Finally, what kind of perspective on international relations might be expected in a rights-based and a value-based foreign policy?

Perspective on international relations

With regard to the *value-based* foreign policy, it might actually be closer to what we traditionally consider foreign policy to be about – even though the emphasis would be on norms. This is so in the sense that the potential for conflict with other actors would be a consideration; however, whereas this is traditionally conceptualized in terms of actors in pursuit of (self-) interests in an anarchical international system, here it would be a matter of actors protecting specific values and a particular way of life in a world of culturally differentiated spheres. As already noted, with regard to the foreign policies of states, it is often the case that the idea of protecting particular interests and a particular identity are rolled into one. This is illustrated with the concept of 'national interest', which is constantly used by national foreign policy-makers to justify what they do. Although the existence of a clearly identifiable national interest is in many cases an illusion,[6] the implicit assumption of the existence of such a national interest lurks behind many analyses and discussions of foreign policy. However, an analytical distinction may be made between interest and values and this provides a more nuanced set of analytical tools.

Expectations of achieving agreement on common normative concerns across different cultural spheres would be limited in a value-based foreign policy. In accordance with the communitarian argument that communicative processes are context-bound, and only possible in collectivities that have a 'thick' sense of identity, the relevant form of justification of a policy would be referring to what the appropriate conduct is given the particular identity of the particular community in question. Claims to universality would, from such a perspective, appear simply as disguises for particular interests or cultural understandings. Hence, most likely, a value-based foreign policy would not aspire to more than minimal common legal norms at the international level. However, to the extent that a 'normative', 'ethical', 'civilian' power would actively promote norms in the international system, it might have a legitimacy problem and the risk of provoking controversy might be high.

In a *rights-based* foreign policy it would be reasonable to expect that the emphasis would be on the cosmopolitan elements in the international system and on the need to further strengthen them. This perspective rests on the assumption that it is possible to come to transcultural agreement on certain higher-order norms.[7] The emphasis would be on 'overcoming power politics' through the establishment of higher-order norms above the nation-states, rather than on contributing to the power political 'game' through the strengthening of existing (perceived) balances of power or establishing a new balance of power. More concretely, this would mean not only a focus on multilateral institutions and the need for a strengthening of international law. The onus would be on arrangements that would bind actors also at the international level and put (legal) constraints on the ability of actors to pursue self-interested behaviour and exercise power for their own material or political gain. Hence, a rights-based foreign policy would emphasize not only the value of international law but also the importance of a reorientation of international law towards a strengthening of the status of human rights. It is on the basis of human rights as universal principles that a supranational legal structure can be established, and one might expect a search for a redefinition of state sovereignty that would allow a certain reconciliation between the principles of external sovereignty, which in practice can lead to the acceptance of tyranny, and the principles of human rights (Eriksen and Weigård 2003). New developments such as the establishment of the International Criminal Court would be an example of the kinds of initiative that a rights-based foreign policy would emphasize.

Empirical relevance

To what extent, if at all, do the things we know about the EU's foreign and security policy fit with the conception of a value-based and/or a rights-based foreign policy as outlined above? Intuitively, the answer would be that such conceptions of foreign policy have little empirical relevance. We are not used to think or talk about foreign policies in terms that explicitly highlight their normative dimension. Practitioners who do so are considered at best naïve and lacking in knowledge about the 'realities' of international politics, at worst dangerous idealists, promoting moral principles without regard for political and cultural particularities. With regard to political scientists who emphasize such dimensions, they are suspected of uncritically accepting the arguments of cynical policy-makers who hide their real agendas behind rhetorical statements about the importance of rights and values. The arguments in favour of rejecting the empirical relevance of a value-based or rights-based conception of European foreign policy are further strengthened by the fact that the institutional structure of the EFP remains intergovernmental and that in both a value-based and a rights-based foreign policy we would expect intergovernmentalism to be overcome, or at least supplemented, by other institutional arrangements. Also the Constitutional Treaty seems to confirm that intergovernmentalism is firmly entrenched in European foreign, security and defence policy, even though the pillar system is formally abolished. Nevertheless, other empirical findings seem to suggest something else. Hence the need for further scrutiny.

Institutional arrangements

Although this is not translated into formal institutional structures, increasingly findings suggest that the institutional nexus of policy-making and the many actors involved in the field of foreign and security policy depart from a simple intergovernmental organizing model. The Commission's activities affect traditional foreign-policy issues and it is often difficult to distinguish between its domain and that of the member states. Further, the frequency of meetings amongst national representatives in the various institutional settings organized under the Council and located in Brussels may have contributed to what observers refer to as processes of Brusselsization, which suggest a *de facto* move in the direction of supranationalism (Allen 1998; Howorth 2000). The time spent on the preparation of these meetings as well as their duration may imply a deliberative mode of interaction. Committee studies of other EU areas, as well as IR studies, have documented changes in role perception, learning and alteration of preferences in such sites (Joerges and Vos 1999; Egeberg *et al.* 2003; Risse 2000). Also, the transformatory capacity of the CFSP vis-à-vis national foreign policies is highlighted by several authors (Tonra 2001; Pijpers 1996). The existence of clearly distinguishable national preferences has become less obvious. Conceiving of a process in which preferences are defined through interaction with representatives of other states comes closer to the concept of communicative rationality and of actors 'who co-ordinate their plans through argumentation, aimed at reaching mutual agreement' (Eriksen and Weigård 2003). Together with the accumulation of previous stances on foreign policy issues providing a common framework for action and decision, the fact that the obligation to consult all other parties has (according to observers such as Nuttall 2000) become the standard in the CFSP – even though it is obviously not always respected – is another observation that can perhaps be better accounted for by the concept of communicative rationality. Finally, the planned abolition of the pillar system, the new post of Foreign Minister and the plans to develop an EU external action service all seem to take EU foreign policy beyond intergovernmentalism. The new Foreign Minister, for example, will have a mandate from the Council but will spend most of his/her time in the Commission and only intermittently meet the national Foreign Ministers. From an organizational perspective this would imply that his/her prime reference and identity will be linked to the Commission rather than the member states. In turn such phenomena point to developments in EFP that may be in line with the expectation of a value-based or rights-based foreign policy.

Legitimacy basis

With regard to the legitimacy basis of EU foreign policy, there seems to be substantial evidence to support the mainstream intergovernmental perspective and little to support the *rights-based* conception. This is so in particular if we define 'all interested parties' as we have done here as the European citizens rather than the member states. There is little evidence, so far, of a European public sphere in foreign policy. One exception would be the public response in Europe to the US war in Iraq. However, this was not translated into a common policy at the European level.

Does the conception of the EU's foreign and security policy as *value-based* fare any better in regard to the issue of legitimacy basis? Interestingly, here, when the then US Secretary of State Henry Kissinger, fearful of European discussions of establishing closer co-operation on foreign policy within the EC, launched what he called the Year of Europe, in an attempt to strengthen transatlantic relations, the response of the European Community was to issue, in July 1973, the Copenhagen declaration on European identity. Whilst stressing the importance of the US's nuclear umbrella for Europe, the declaration states not only the importance of equality between the US and Europe but also that the transatlantic dimension should not affect the then Nine (EC member states') determination to establish themselves as a distinct and original entity.[8] However, the declaration stressed the diversity of cultures within the framework of a common European civilization.[9] Hence, although this says something about the desire for an autonomous EU foreign policy being present very early on in the history of European Political Co-operation (EPC), which later became the CFSP, it cannot be seen as an indicator of a common identity. A more recent case that might indicate a certain sense of Europeanness is that of enlargement to Central and Eastern Europe. Here, a particular sense of duty to solidarity with the other part of Europe contributes to explain what drove the EU to commit itself to enlarge in spite of the costs it was expected to entail. This sense of duty to solidarity with the 'other half of Europe' does point to a certain sense of identity – however thin (Sjursen 2002). Nevertheless, again this is hardly sufficient to assume or expect the existence of a reflex of solidarity or loyalty that could on its own constitute the legitimacy basis for a value-based European foreign and security policy.

Perspective on international relations

Finally, with regard to the perspective on international relations, are the value-based or rights-based conceptions of a European foreign and security policy matched by empirical observations? This is what the literature on the EU as a 'normative', 'civilian', 'civilizing' or 'ethical' power seems to suggest. However, this literature seems based on a rather indiscriminate view of norms. The argument is that the EU promotes norms, values and ideas in general in the international system. They could be norms that are particular to the EU (and thus consistent with a value-based conception of foreign policy), or they could be norms that are universally acceptable (in consistence with the rights-based conception). This means that if the EU defines itself, and is defined by others, as a 'force for the good' (European Security Strategy 2003) then this could (in accordance with a value-based foreign policy) be a subjective definition linked to a particular European understanding and defined in a particular European cultural context. It might not match what is defined as 'good' or 'valuable' in other parts of the world, which would be conditioned by other cultural or social norms. So 'normative power' Europe could act in accordance with normative concerns yet be perceived as acting in the same way as 'historical empires'. This is rarely problematized in this literature. On the other hand, the EU's emphasis could also be on universal principles such as human rights, thus suggesting that the EU is moving in the direction of a 'rights-based' foreign policy.

The empirical evidence is not clear. On the one hand, protection of human rights has indeed been included as an important goal in the EU's external policy.[10] This has, among other things, led to a human rights clause becoming standard content of all trade agreements established with other countries since 1992 (Menéndez 2004). And as Ian Manners shows in his study of the EU's campaign for the abolition of the death penalty, the EU 'has played an important, if not crucial, role in bringing about abolition' (Manners 2002: 248). Manners here points to the EU's activities not only towards countries that have been or seek to become members of the EU, but also to states who would not have that ambition. However, Börzel and Risse's survey of the EU's policy on democracy promotion seems to suggest a certain value-bias in the sense that the EU has developed a specific model of democracy promotion that it seeks to export without much consideration for the target state. Hence they argue that 'In fact, the EU follows quite clearly a specific cultural script' (Börzel and Risse 2004: 2). This would suggest that the EU has more of a value-based approach. The strong emphasis on diplomatic instruments and economic aid is more difficult to place. As Smith argues: 'the EU still clearly prefers positive civilian to coercive military measures' (Smith 2003: 111). This is also visible in the EU's security strategy, where the emphasis is on 'preventative engagement', diplomatic action and multilateralism as cornerstones of the EU's approach to international security. In sum, the literature on the EU's 'normative' role seems to rely on an indiscriminate view of 'norms', 'ethics' or 'values', thus lacking the necessary criteria to distinguish between different kinds of norms and their validity and legitimacy. Hence, it cannot really sustain the argument that the EU is not a 'normative power similar to traditional colonial powers seeking to impose a particular world view' (Manners 2002), neither is there sufficient evidence to assess whether the EU is going either in a value-based or in a rights-based direction.

Conclusion

In this chapter I have suggested that turning to role theory may not be enough if we are to theoretically account for the claims about the EU being a 'normative/ethical/civilian' power in the international system. To the extent that such claims imply that the EU is a different kind of actor, and even more so an actor that is considered to contribute to shape conceptions of what is 'normal', we need a theory that can account for actors' ability to escape the situatedness of their role, and for their (putative) break with established normative patterns. Against this backdrop I have pointed to the potential contribution of discourse theory and the concept of communicative rationality. The concept of communicative rationality may contribute by providing the micro-foundations necessary for us to theoretically account for the importance of norms, as well as for actors' ability to rationally assess their validity.

In line with the distinction between norms as embedded in a particular cultural context and higher-order principles that may claim universal validity, I have developed two alternative conceptions of the EU's foreign policy – both of which might fit with the idea of European foreign policy as 'normative', 'ethical' or 'civilizing'. This above distinction is important not least because it demonstrates a core problem with the 'normative', 'ethical', 'civilian' power argument, which is that it does not have any criteria for assessing the legitimacy of such power. This is particularly problematic because of the implicit assumption conveyed in this literature that 'normative' power is a 'good thing'.

It has not been the aim of the chapter to make any hard empirical claims about the EU's foreign policy, although the potential empirical relevance of the two conceptions of foreign policy has been briefly considered. Rather, the chapter has been inspired by the concern that in order for us to move forward with regard to the 'normative', 'ethical', 'civilizing' power argument, a firmer theoretical basis, a clarification of analytical concepts and clear critical standards is necessary. The aim has been to contribute to this endeavour.

Notes

1 Both these conceptions break with the mainstream view of the EU's foreign policy as intergovernmental and established only to serve the national interests of member states. This chapter does not deny the empirical relevance of this mainstream conception, it simply chooses to focus on developing alternative conceptions. Unless such alternative conceptions are developed, it is difficult to properly assess also the relevance of the mainstream argument. Furthermore, increasingly the literature suggests that such a conception of EFP is insufficient. For a discussion that includes the intergovernmental model see Sjursen (2005).

2 See also Habermas's discourse principle, discussed in Eriksen and Weigård (2003: 147) and based on Habermas (1996: 107).

3 This section builds on Sjursen (2005).
4 Role theory could explain such a break with established norms by arguing that the international norms have changed. However, although developments in the direction of cosmopolitanism might be visible in today's international system, we are far from facing a cosmopolitan world. Hence it would still be a matter of actors selecting or choosing between different norm sets and thus the challenge remains to theoretically account for the choice that has been made.
5 This is of course problematic from a normative perspective, but that is not the issue here.
6 Or, to quote a former state secretary in the Norwegian Ministry of Foreign Affairs, 'the national interest is something you invent on your way to the airport'.
7 This is not an uncontested claim. See for example Brown (1999).
8 Declaration on European Identity by the Nine Foreign Ministers, Copenhagen, 14 December 1973. Printed in Hill and Smith (2000: 92–7).
9 Ibid., para. 2.
10 See in particular *Human rights in third countries. Summaries of legislation.* http://europa.eu.int/scadplus/leg/en/lvb/r10100.htm, but also *European Security Strategy* (2003).

References

Aggestam, L. (2004) 'A European Foreign Policy? Role Conceptions and the Politics of Identity in Britain, France and Germany', doctoral dissertation, Stockholm: Department of Political Science, Stockholm University.

Allen, D. (1998) '"Who speaks for Europe?" The Search for an Effective and Coherent External Policy', in J. Peterson and H. Sjursen (eds) *A Common Foreign Policy for Europe?* London: Routledge.

Bohman, J. (1999) 'International Regimes and Democratic Governance: Political Equality and Influence in Global Institutions', *International Affairs,* 75 (3): 499–513.

Börzel, T. A. and Risse, T. (2004) 'One Size Fits All! EU Policies for the Promotion of Human Rights, Democracy and the Rule of Law', paper prepared for the Workshop on Democracy Promotion, 4–5 October, Center for Development, Democracy, and the Rule of Law, Stanford University.

Brown, C. (1999) 'Universal Human Rights: A Critique', in T. Dunne and N. J. Wheeler (eds) *Human Rights in Global Politics,* Cambridge: Cambridge University Press.

Cronin, C. and De Greff, P. (eds) (1998) *The Inclusion of the Other: Studies in Political Theory: Jürgen Habermas,* Cambridge, MA: MIT Press.

Egeberg, M., Schaeffer, G. and Trondal, J. (2003) 'The Many Faces of EU Committee Governance', *West European Politics,* 26 (3): 19–40.

Eriksen, E. O. (1999) 'Towards a Logic of Justification: On the Possibility of Post-national Solidarity', in M. Egeberg and P. Lægreid (eds) *Organizing Political Institutions,* Oslo: Scandinavian University Press.

Eriksen, E. O. and Weigård, J. (1997) 'Conceptualising Politics: Strategic or Communicative Action?', *Scandinavian Political Studies,* 20 (3): 219–41.

Eriksen, E. O. and Weigård, J. (2003) *Understanding Habermas: Communicative Action and Deliberative Democracy,* London and New York: Continuum.

European Security Strategy (2003) *A Secure Europe in a Better World.* Brussels, 12 December.

Habermas, J. (1996) *Between Facts and Norms. Contributions to a Discourse Theory of Law and Democracy*, Cambridge, MA: MIT Press.

Hill, C. and Smith, K. (eds) (2000) *European Foreign Policy: Key Documents*, London: Routledge.

Howorth, J. (2000) 'European Defence and the Changing Politics of the European Union: Hanging Together or Hanging Separately', *Journal of Common Market Studies*, 39 (4): 765–89.

Joerges, C. and Vos, E. (eds) (1999) *EU Committees: Social Regulation, Law and Politics*, Oxford: Hart Publishing.

Lose, L. (2001) 'Communicative Action and the World of Diplomacy', in K. Fierke and K. E. Jørgensen (eds) *Constructing International Relations*, New York: Sharpe.

Manners, I. (2002) 'Normative Power Europe: A Contradiction in Terms?', *Journal of Common Market Studies*, 40 (2): 235–58.

Maull, H. W. (2000) 'Germany and the Use of Force: Still a Civilian Power?', *Survival*, 42 (2): 56–80.

Menéndez, A. (2004) 'Human Rights: European Charter of Fundamental Rights', in W. Carlsnaes, H. Sjursen and B. White (eds) *Contemporary European Foreign Policy*, London: Sage Publications.

Nuttall, S. (2000) *European Foreign Policy*, Oxford: Oxford University Press.

Pijpers, A. (1996) 'The Netherlands: The Weakening Pull of Atlanticism', in C. Hill (ed.) *The Actors in Europe's Foreign Policy*, London: Routledge.

Risse, T. (2000) '"Let's Argue!" Communicative Action in World Politics', *International Organization*, 54 (1): 1–39.

Risse-Kappen, T. (1995) *Co-operation among Democracies*, Princeton, NJ: Princeton University Press.

Rosencrance, R. (1998) 'The European Union: A New Type of International Actor', in J. Zielonka (ed.) *Paradoxes of European Foreign Policy*, The Hague: Kluwer Law International.

Sjursen, H. (2002) 'Why Expand? The Question of Legitimacy and Justification in the EU's Enlargement Policy', *Journal of Common Market Studies*, 40 (3): 491–513.

Sjursen, H. (2005) 'Towards a Post-national Foreign and Security Policy?', in E. O. Eriksen (ed.) *Making the European Polity: Reflexive Integration in the EU*, London and New York: Routledge.

Sjursen, H. (2006) 'The EU as a "Normative Power": How Can This Be?', *Journal of European Public Policy*, special issue, 13 (2): 235–51.

Smith, K. E. (2000) 'The End of Civilian Power EU: A Welcome Demise or a Cause for concern?', *International Spectator*, 23 (2): 11–28.

Smith, K. E. (2003) *European Union Foreign Policy in a Changing World*, Cambridge: Polity Press.

Tonra, B. (2001) *The Europeanisation of National Foreign Policy: Dutch, Danish and Irish Foreign Policy in the European Union*, Aldershot: Ashgate.

Wagner, W. (2005) *The Democratic Legitimacy of European Security and Defence Policy*, Occasional Paper 57, Paris: Institute for Security Studies.

Whitman, R. (1998) *From Civilian Power to Superpower? The International Identity of the European Union*, Basingstoke: Macmillan.

6 Muscles from Brussels

The demise of civilian power Europe?

Richard Whitman

The central focus of this chapter is an assessment of the concept of 'civilian power Europe', which has been associated with the characterization and examination of the international role of the European Union (EU) for almost 30 years. The chapter commences by outlining the notion of civilian power Europe as originally formulated, and then proceeds to examine how the idea has been used, adapted and refuted across time. The purpose of this examination is to facilitate an exploration of whether the idea has continuing utility in the early twenty-first century. The chapter examines the notion of civilian power both as a concept for the analysis of the international role of the EU and also as a role that the EU has sought to cultivate. In line with the understanding of roles in the Introduction to this volume, civilian power Europe (CPE) can also be explored as a pattern of behaviour which is expected of the EU by its member states and third parties and has become considered as the appropriate form of behaviour through which the EU should conduct its international relations.

Central to the analysis of civilian power Europe is a consideration of whether the conception has been undermined or transformed by processes of change in post-Cold War Europe, by the creation of the Common Foreign and Security Policy (CFSP) and by the subsequent development of the European Security and Defence Policy (ESDP). In order to probe these issues, the chapter focuses on three central analytical elements: the environment within which the EU has had to operate, the processes through which its policies are formed, and the instruments with which it pursues these policies. On the basis of this analysis, the chapter concludes that the notion of CPE still has considerable empirical and theoretical purchase when the EU is considered in the context of the post-enlargement contemporary international relations of Europe. Furthermore, a consideration of the idea demonstrates the need to develop a clear conception of the international capabilities of the EU if appropriate forms of understanding of the international role of the EU are to be developed.

The rise (and fall?) of civilian power Europe

The debate on how to categorize the international significance of the EU has its origins over 30 years ago. It was first conducted in the early 1970s by attempting to construct a new conceptual category to fit the, then, EC. The debate focused around the issue of whether the then EC was a 'civilian power' (Duchêne 1972, 1973) or a putative 'superpower' (Galtung 1973) The significance of these approaches is that they focused upon a distinctive (or potentially distinctive) international role for the EC.

François Duchêne's notion of a 'civilian power Europe' has subsequently resonated through the debate on the international role of the EC/EU (Laursen 1991; Lodge 1993; Tsakaloyannis 1989; Smith 2002; Treacher 2004). The notion of civilian power Europe as first advanced by Duchêne was an exercise in futurology: his central contention was that maintaining a nuclear and superpower stalemate in Europe ought to, and would, devalue military power and give scope to 'civilian forms of influence and action'. In his words:

> Europe would be the first major area of the Old World where the age-old processes of war and indirect violence could be translated into something more in tune with the twentieth-century citizen's notion of civilised politics.
>
> (Duchêne 1972)

Duchêne's conception of a European civilian power rested upon the inconceivability of a nuclear-armed European federation and the banishing of war from Western Europe:

> The European Community's interest as a civilian group of countries long on economic power and relatively short on armed force is as far as possible to *domesticate* relations between states, including those of its own members and those with states outside its frontiers. This means trying to bring to international problems the sense of common responsibility and structures of contractual politics which have been in the past associated exclusively with 'home' and not foreign, that is *alien*, affairs.
>
> (Duchêne 1973: 19–20)

Duchêne's standpoint was both an empirical observation (on the forms of power exercised by the EC member states collectively) and a normative assertion about the then EC (the 'domestication' or 'civility' role) (Stavridis 2001: 44). The intermingling of these two elements has been the hallmark of discussions about the notion of civilian power Europe, and they will be taken forward throughout this chapter.

The most trenchant, and articulate, criticisms of the notion of civilian power Europe were provided by Hedley Bull at the height of the Second Cold War. The central component of Bull's criticism was that clear-cut: 'the power or influence exerted by the European Community and other such civilian actors was conditional upon a strategic environment provided by the military power of states, which they did not control' (Bull 1982: 151). Furthermore, there was not one 'Europe' but only a Europe of state governments – a concert of states. The inference to be drawn from Bull's argument was that only with a European military capability would there be European actorness. However, for Bull supranational authority in the area of defence policy would be a source of weakness, rather than strength, because only nation-states could inspire the loyalty to make war (Bull 1982: 163).

Despite changes since the end of the Cold War, and the development of both the CFSP and the ESDP, the notion of civilian power still represents a touchstone for debates on the international role of the EU because of the premise that it is conducting a distinctive form of diplomacy, in both form and substance. For some commentators the debate around civilian power Europe was the dominant discourse *constructing* the EU in the 1990s (Larsen 1991). This can be read as practitioners' articulation of a distinct role for the EU in international relations. Describing, or making the case for, a CPE has been a hallmark of pronouncements of members of the European Commission and the member states in recent years, illustrated for example in Romano Prodi's call for the EU to become a 'global civil power' (Prodi 2000). In short, there has been an act of *role-taking* sustained by a strong self-image of what role the EU should occupy in international politics.

Analytically, this chapter argues that civilian power Europe still offers contemporary insights, on three grounds. First, the wider European environment in terms of international society within which the Union operates is crucial for understanding its own significance. Second, the Union's pursuit of a distinctive diplomacy would appear to reflect concern with process: the notion of 'civilianizing' relations by creating forms of institutionalized association, partnership and co-operation which has been a conscious undertaking by the EU. Third, assessing CPE requires a consideration of the form of power exercised and instruments used by the EU, implying that a focus on role performance is vital to understanding the currency of the concept.

Environment: the EU and a changing international society

In the 'new dawn' at the end of the Cold War and before the conflicts of former Yugoslavia were in their ascendancy, there was something of a renaissance of the concept of civilian power. More generally arguments were made that the exercise of power within international relations was much less dependent upon military force and that forms of 'soft power' were to the fore (Nye 1990). Arguments were rehearsed about a change in the structure and substance of international relations that suggested a changing landscape, in which civilian forms of power were more appropriate. Hanns Maull took Richard Rosecrance's notion of 'trading states' and developed this as a systematic re-statement of civilian power. For Maull the implications for civilian power (as applied to Germany and Japan) were:

> a the acceptance of the necessity of cooperation with others in the pursuit of international objectives;
> b the concentration on non-military, primarily economic, means to secure national goals with military power left as a residual instrument serving essentially to safeguard other means of international interaction; and
> c a willingness to develop supranational structures to address critical issues of international management.
>
> (Maull 1990: 92–3)

Interestingly, a decade after these ideas were articulated to examine Germany and Japan, they provide an accurate characterization of the contemporary EU's international role and identity. However, this characterization tells us little about how this 'power' in civilian power is generated and exercised and, therefore, does not assist us in an understanding of the EU's power within the international arena. There is also something of a paradox in that the notion of CPE underwent a *renaissance* due to a changed environment of international relations within Europe that the EU did not play an immediate role in reshaping. Subsequent to the end of the Cold War the EU has, however, played a role in reshaping the structure of the international politics of Europe. This situation requires further consideration of the power exercised by the EU.

To assist in understanding how power is exercised in this particular international environment, the concept of 'international society' (developed by the English school) offers insight (Diez and Whitman 2002).[1] Whereas an international system operates more or less mechanically and of necessity, international society represents a conscious effort to transform and regulate relations among its constitutive units, alerting us to the norms and institutions in the international realm that, while being set up by its members for a specific purpose, also shape their identity. This is a useful characterization of the process at work in the relationship that the EU has developed with Central and Eastern Europe, and more recently with South Eastern Europe.

It is also important for our purposes that within the EU such a society is particularly well developed, in that the set of common rules is particularly dense. This suggests that the EU forms a specific sub-system of the current international system, in which the societal element is stronger than elsewhere. During the Cold War the 'rules' of the superpower conflict severely constrained the extent to which EC/EU norms and values could be conveyed, and were received, beyond Western Europe. The conception and image that the regimes in Eastern Europe held of the EC/EU acted as a constraint on the latter's role performance, and only underwent a shift following the first formal agreements with the EC/EU in the very late 1980s. These agreements represented a perceptual shift by granting recognition of the EC/EU as an actor of significance; they also illustrate how the membership of *EU international society* should be distinguished from formal membership of the EU. All international societies are delineated through the *self-identification* of their members with common interests and values, and furthermore the acceptance of being *bound by rules and institutions*. As a consequence, although EU membership formalizes being part of EU international society, in principle EU and European international society cannot be distinguished solely on the basis of formal membership. The decisive criterion for distinction rather is the degree of identification and of the acceptance of being bound by the rules and norms of the respective international society.

EU international society discourse embraces all states that self-identify with the common interests and common values of the EU and accept common sets of rules in the relations with other members of the society. States that define themselves as candidates for entry, or re-entry, into 'Europe' do not all fall within the category of candidate member states for the EU (for example, Ukraine). Therefore the EU international society discourse embraces more states than those that are formally applicant states to the EU. The degrees of self-identification can also be differential. This is true not only beyond the borders of the EU, but also for EU members. More important for our purpose here, however, considering EU international society in this manner places both EU member states and prospective member states of the EU within the same international society. This illustrates well the power effect that the EU can exercise over a group of non-member states.

However, the exercise of the power by civilian power Europe does not begin and end in Europe. This interrelationship can be illustrated, for example, through the EU's CFSP, which has to conform with the values of both European and global international society and to be implemented through their respective institutions (Whitman 1998a). As discussed above, EU member states form the core of EU international society. The gradated relationship of other states to the core is dependent upon both the self-identification with the common interests and values of the core and the degree to which they accept the EU rules and institutions. This places EU applicant states in a dominion or suzerain relationship within EU international society, where the EU can extend its governance regime beyond its formal borders (Friis and Murphy 1999; M. Smith 1996a). The fuzziness of the borders of the EU's system of governance is therefore a result of a two-way relationship (Christiansen *et al.* 2000).

On the one hand, the choice by the EU to use particular kinds of trade and aid instruments to deepen the relationship with a third-party state, such as a membership applicant, can be understood as being reflective of the position that the EU allocates to that third party within its 'gradated empire' (Manners and Whitman 1998). Considered in these terms, the act of the EU promulgating views about the structure of the relationship that it wishes to develop with third parties (for example, the issuing of common strategies under the CFSP or Commission Communication setting out new strategies towards countries or regions) takes on a different significance.

On the other hand, the effectiveness of such policies and the nature of the power relations within the EU international society are not dependent on the EU and its member states alone. Rather, the self-identification of those states to which the policies are directed, and its overlap with the values and interests of the EU core, are equally important to determine these states' position in the EU's 'empire', and the EU's possibilities to impose its system of governance on them (Diez 2000).

Analysed in these terms, considerations of whether the EU possesses a foreign policy in state-like terms (or not) become second-order to considerations of the form of the relationship that the EU and the states surrounding it have created for themselves. The key observation here is that the relationship is one that is created in classic Duchênean terms as 'domesticating relations'. Expressed in terms of the ideas outlined in the Introduction to this volume it is both an enhancement of the role performance potential of the EU and an increase in the impact of that role.

Process and civilian power

Another factor that is crucial for assessing the development of the Union's roles is process. There is a substantive body of literature on the international roles of the EU that focuses upon an exposition of the content of specific policies conducted by the EU for projection externally from the Union and theoretical explanations or assumptions as to the manner in which that policy was formulated. This body of literature consists primarily of individual case studies, although these are supported by a limited amount of comparative case study work. The focus upon the process of decision-making that is central to this approach also represents an enduring division in accounts of the international roles of the EU.

In attempting to map the external relations of the EC/EU, accounts invariably focus upon the legal foundations for a particular agreement or set of agreements (Macleod *et al.* 1996). Although commentators disagree as to whether the CFSP represents a meaningful 'foreign policy', its joint actions and common positions have been subject to case study scrutiny (Holland 1995, 1997; Denza 2002). Accounting for the role of the decision-making process has been central to analysis of EPC/CFSP (Hill 1996). Other case studies seeking to account for a foreign-policy 'event' and EC/EU action, or inaction, have delved in the domestic sources of member states' foreign-policy stances (Stavridis and Hill 1996).

A number of other case studies have also argued for a theoretical uniting of both EPC/CFSP and external relations into a single framework. This argument proceeds from the premise that the nature of foreign policy itself has undergone transformation as a consequence of changes in the nature and structure of the international system that have rendered distinctions between 'high' and 'low' politics less pertinent and in the Introduction to this volume is characterized as a pluralist turn in IR thinking (H. Smith 1995; M. Smith 1998). The contention of such a standpoint as applied to the EU is that separate consideration of processes (pillars one, two and three), both empirically and conceptually, is at the cost of neglecting study of the factors that are common to both sets of policies and has led to neglect of frameworks that may accommodate both sets of processes with a few exceptions (Ginsberg 1989; Whitman 1998b).

The situation is further complicated by the fact that certain internal EC/EU policies (that are neither external relations or CFSP) have external implications. This is best illustrated by the analysis of the impact of the Single Market programme (Redmond 1992). The concept of *externalization* conceived by Schmitter conveys a mutually supporting direct link between internal integration and external responses (Schmitter 1969). Such an analysis has been extended to illustrate processes beyond states to encompass non-state and sub-national actors (Hocking and Smith 1997). This has given rise to the notion that alongside the policy-making processes of external relations and CFSP the EC/EU's international activities represent an on-going *negotiated order* involving actors within and without the EU engaged in an institutionalized negotiation process which is itself embedded in the international arena (M. Smith 1996b). This notion of process captures the means through which the EU's power is exercised.

The consideration of process introduces the member states as a key factor of influence in the exploration of civilian power Europe. Since the notion of civilian power Europe was first articulated the six-state EC has expanded to a 25-member state EU. The consideration of the process through which EC/EU policy is formulated represents a crucial insight into the rationale for the Union both developing and utilizing different instruments of implementation in the international system. This is a dimension of the development of a European foreign policy that the author has explored at length elsewhere (Manners and Whitman 2000). However, it should be noted that with respect to the ESDP this is an area which has been chronically under-explored. The extent to which the individual states are advocates of a civilian power Europe is a research project in search of researchers.

Hill characterized *cohesiveness* in decision-making (taking decisions and holding to them) as one strand of capabilities available to the Union (Peterson and Sjursen 1998: 28). Other work on decision-making suggests that decision-making processes demonstrate contradictory characteristics – greater 'Brusselization' (Allen 1998), but also a widening of the actors and influences (M. Smith 1998). Cohesiveness may therefore be better measured through agreement measured by greater recourse to instruments than cohesion in decision-making processes.

The development of a 'reflex of consultation' has been the hallmark of the CFSP across time and has not been generated solely by the creation of institutional arrangements through treaty revisions (Manners and Whitman 2000). It is too early to assess whether the new political and military bodies created post-Helsinki and codified in the Treaty of Nice such as the *COPS*, the Military Committee (populated by representatives of the member states' commanders-in-chief) and its chair, and the Military Staff (the precursor of a European staff headquarters); and their relationship to the Secretary General/High Representative will generate the same reflex as the decision-making structure.

Identifying instruments of implementation

A greater understanding of the capabilities of the Union is necessary if the international role of the EU is to be accurately comprehended and the 'health' of CPE to be accurately assessed. This is primarily because the notion of CPE has rested upon the form that the EU's diplomacy has taken. An assessment of the EU's capabilities is thus a core component of the conceptions and images that the EU has of itself and those held by other parties. The 'system of implementation' identified by Hill as necessary for actor capability can be characterized as a set of instruments that are available to the EU (Hill 1993, 1998).

These instruments are not formally identified by the Union as its 'system of implementation', but provide a typology by which we might establish a framework to consider the extent to which the EU is fulfilling its aspiration to assert its international identity. The *ability to agree* and *resources* identified by Hill as the other two elements of his capabilities have been explored by the author at length elsewhere (Whitman 1998b). Therefore this section of the chapter tackles only one side of the capability–expectations gap and largely ignores the question of the expectations of third parties. It concerns itself with questions of supply rather than demand. The argument thus seeks to identify a typology of instruments available at the disposal of the Union and through an exposition of one of these it seeks briefly to further explore civilian power Europe.

It is, of course, possible to tell the story of the development of the CFSP in terms of Treaty amendments and/or to detail the development of Common Strategies, Joint Actions and Common Positions across time.

The author has attempted this analysis elsewhere (Whitman 1998c). However, this renders little assistance in exploring whether the EU has developed instruments for the conduct of its foreign policy compatible with the notion that the EU acts as a civilian power.

Space precludes an examination of the full set of instruments which can be classified as: *informational, procedural, transference* and *overt*. Each of these elements has been described elsewhere and illustrated by reference to examples drawn from the CFSP (and external relations as the hallmark of the last decade has been the drawing together of CFSP and external relations instruments of implementation) since the foundation of the EU in November 1993 (Manners and Whitman 1998). The focus here is on overt instruments, since these can be taken as a litmus test of whether the EU has moved 'civilian' instruments to give effect to the EU foreign policy.

Such overt instruments refer to the physical presence of the EU and its representatives outside the Union. This can be either on a permanent basis, for example the establishment of the external delegations of the Commission, or more transitory, for instance visits of the troika or the dispatch of monitors, and special representatives, to the Middle East and the Great Lakes, for example. The Union also has its own network of external delegations, which would be transformed by the External Action Service envisioned in the Constitutional Treaty.

Empirical observation suggests that the EU has gone more 'overt' since the early 1990s. The 'new' troika established under the Treaty of Amsterdam (Presidency of the Union, the High Representative and the member of the Commission responsible for external relations) represented an attempt to create a more efficient mechanism than the 'old' CFSP troika and 'bi-cephalic troika' (the troika plus the Commission). The Treaty of Amsterdam, in creating the new High Representative for CFSP and reformulating the troika, has created a more robust set of representational arrangements, in the same vein. The appointment of the High Representative in October 1999 created a new overt instrument for the CFSP which is, arguably, the most significant development within the CFSP since 1993. The manner in which this position has been defined, by the first post-holder, Javier Solana, has shaped this instrument into a key dimension of the implementation of the CFSP. However, the small budget at Solana's disposal and his small staff means that he is a 'stand-alone' actor requiring the assistance of the European Commission to execute policy. The Commission, under the former Commissioner Chris Patten, performed a similar overt role with being the most public face of international activity by the Commission boosted by the reorganization of the European Commission's RELEX services. The proposal to combine the High Representative and Commission roles in the position of an EU Foreign Minister with an EU External Action Service proposed in the EU Constitutional Treaty would further unify the face of EU foreign policy.

In addition, since 1996 the role of the EU Special Representative, and since 2003 the Personal Representative, have become regular features in the CFSP toolkit.

The Joint Actions of the CFSP have also led to the creation of a number of new overt instruments used by the Union, including the convoying of aid in Bosnia-Herzegovina and the sending of observers to the Russian and South African elections, the EU administration of Mostar and the European Union Monitoring Mission (EUMM). The instruments were codified and developed with the Helsinki European Council Conclusions – and then taken further at the Feira and Göteborg European Councils – with the commitment to develop the civilian aspects of crisis management (Presidency Conclusions 2000). The headline goals set for a non-military Rapid Reaction Facility have focused upon re-establishing the civilian structures necessary to ensure political, social and economic stability and to give a civilian capacity to the rapid reaction military force (by mobilizing non-military personnel: police, customs officials, judges, etc.) and with its own Headline Goals (Presidency Conclusions 1999). Operationally, the EU's take-over of the International Police Task Force (IPTF) in Bosnia on 1 January 2003 was the first crisis management operation through this mechanism initiated under the ESDP. All of these developments have been read as being reconcilable with the idea of civilian power Europe (Youngs 2002).

Other developments in the military security field can be read as more problematic for the notion of the EU as a civilian power. For Hill, the key development of actor capability for the EU was the ability to have recourse to military force. The central significance of military power for challenging the civilian power thesis is now an active public policy debate. In the use of the CPE as an analytical concept this debate has proceeded for over a decade: the creation of the CFSP with a defence aspiration was originally read as signalling the intent of the member states of the Union to move beyond a civilian power Europe and to develop a defence dimension to the Union's international identity (Lodge 1993). The crucial change that has happened with respect to the EU's ESDP since the late 1990s is the move from aspirations to operational capacity. The European Council meeting in Helsinki in December 1999 set the 'headline goal' for a military force that could be deployed rapidly and that would be capable of carrying out the full range of Petersberg tasks which delineated the extent of the EU's military aspirations (Presidency Conclusions 1999). From December 1999 onwards considerable work was put into finding the mechanisms to realize the operational objectives set at Helsinki. In May 2003 the EU announced that it now possessed 'operational capability across the full range of Petersberg tasks, limited and constrained by recognized shortfalls'. In the view of Javier Solana these do fall short of the Helsinki Headline Goal. Subsequently, in June 2004 the European Council agreed a new plan, 'Headline Goal 2010', as a part of the Capability Development Mechanism that is scheduled to be achieved by 2010 (Council of the European Union 2004). Since then there has been the launch of the proposal for Battle Groups which are intended to be operational by 2007. All of this demonstrates a classic EU approach to developing a policy area, which is to generate institutions and then set them to realizing key deadlines which are reviewed at successive European Council meetings. Hence the Headline Goal was followed by a European Capabilities Action Plan and work to plug gaps identified by the capabilities improvement process.

Although the headline goal has been revised from the form that was originally articulated – to take account of the practicalities of realizing the objective – it is still a significant undertaking. For the purpose of the argument here, the forces committed under the headline goal represent the emergence of the first non-NATO military structure in post-Cold War Europe. Even though the operational capability has not yet achieved the headline goals, the EU has now engaged in a number of modest operations. The EU has undertaken five such operations to date, most recently embarking on an operation in Georgia and a significant operation in Bosnia. The undertaking of three small-scale operations – Concordia, Artemis, Proxima and the EU Police Mission in Bosnia (EUPM) – has given the EU a nascent operational presence, albeit confined largely to South Eastern Europe. The six-month Concordia operation in Macedonia, launched in March 2003, was the first 'Berlin-plus' operation having access to NATO planning facilities, structures and military assets. The Artemis operation consisted of the deployment of 1,800 French-led troops to Bunia in the Democratic Republic of Congo as a holding operation until UN forces could be deployed. The Proxima operation was the follow-on policing mission to Macedonia deployed in mid-December 2004 for 12 months. The EUPM in Bosnia was the first civilian Petersberg operation undertaken by the EU established at the beginning of January 2003 and due to expire at the end of December 2005. This 500+ strong police mission was complemented by the Althea (EUFOR) 'Berlin-plus' operation to replace SFOR at the end of 2004 consisting of 7,000 EU troops to replace the 12,000 strong SFOR force. The latter raises the question as to whether 'size matters' in determining whether there has been the transcendence of the civilian power idea. What would represent its death-knell?

Civilian power redux? Environment, process and instruments

The creation of the ESDP has, unsurprisingly, led to the conclusion that it spells the end of civilian power Europe (K. E. Smith 2002). A contrasting view is that militarization of the EU may facilitate the EU acting 'as a real civilian power in the world, that is to say as a force for the external promotion of democratic principles' (Stavridis 2001). It is, perhaps, too early to assess the success of the ESDP and, therefore, use this as grounds upon which to dispel the idea of civilian power Europe. However, Maull's re-analysis of civilian power Germany after participation in the war in Kosovo in 1999 is of some utility here in illustrating that recourse to military means does not invalidate the notion of civilian power Europe per se (Maull 2000). A less sanguine view on possible EU military power is that there is continuing relative military weakness of Europe vis-à-vis the US – but that should not be conflated with a lack of EU international power. As Andrew Moravcsik has argued:

> Europeans already wield effective power over peace and war as great as that of the United States, but they do so quietly, through 'civilian power'. That does not lie in the deployment of battalions or bombers, but rather in the quiet promotion of democracy and development through trade, foreign aid and peacekeeping.
>
> (Moravcsik 2002)

The argument that the EU enjoys a competitive advantage in international relations, as opposed to other actors, is more in conformity with Hill's position on a distinct international role(s) for the EU in his Capabilities–Expectations Gap thesis.[2] However, suggesting that the weakness of the EU's military capability validates the notion of civilian power Europe is an incomplete argument. As the argument above illustrates very clearly, there are a number of elements that are neglected by a focus solely on instruments. Therefore developing and strengthening the military instrument is not sufficient to validate or invalidate the notion of civilian power Europe. As noted above there has to be a focus upon the *environment* – the international structures, processes and actors within which the EC/EU is embedded and through which it operates – the *process* through which that policy is decided and the development of *instruments* for the implementation of the Union's foreign policy, both in formal treaty terms and in terms of their acceptance and use by member states.

If it is accepted that the EU has not yet strayed beyond the confines of what can be accommodated within the idea of CPE, what would call the utility of the concept into question? The first factor would be a shift in the environment in which CPE operates. One such change would be if the EU member states decided to develop the EU's international role in such terms that the ESDP was separate and separable from NATO. This would most likely be a cause of, or the reaction to, a divide between Europe and the US.

A second change would be a shift in the role that the member states wish to cultivate for the EU in international society. The notion advanced by President Chirac that Europe should act as pole of international relations in a multipolar world is not a view that has wide currency among the EU member states. The war in Iraq illustrated that there is not an immutable view on the role that the EU should play in relation to the US as a key actor in international relations. Differential attitudes to the war in Iraq cut across both the then 15 EU member states and those states that joined the coalition and fought under Operation Iraqi Freedom. Out of the 25 EU member states, 13 had troops deployed. The remaining 12 states were either 'oppositionists' or 'neutrals'.

What is remarkable, however, is that the status quo in the EU's foreign, security and defence policy remained largely unaffected by the war in Iraq. During the war there was 'business as usual'. The day-to-day process of EU foreign policy continued (especially if foreign policy is considered in the broadest sense, embracing foreign economic policy) – common positions, joint actions, political dialogue, systematic consultation all continued. The war also did not have an impact upon the development of the new EU Security Strategy. The strategy presented by Javier Solana at the Thessaloniki European Council in June 2003 underwent considerable debate before being formally agreed at the European Council in December 2003 (Council of the EU 2003). The security strategy had three strategic aims: to create an extended zone of security and stability around the EU; to build an international order via multilateralism; to tackle the 'not so new' security threats (especially WMD). Importantly, the security strategy also advanced the notion of a strategic culture that fosters early, rapid and where necessary robust intervention. This document is not the equivalent of a US National Security Strategy but has stimulated commentators to push for an EU strategic concept (Lindley-French and Agieri 2004). The contrast with the US National Security Strategy is, however, instructive in that it represents a clear codification of the member states' collective position on the forms of power that they wish to exercise in international relations. The role that they define for themselves is that they aspire for a civilian power Europe to go global.

The ESDP: the death of civilian power Europe?

This chapter has argued that civilian power Europe is still a 'live' concept with empirical and theoretical purchase when the EU is considered in the context of the contemporary international relations of Europe. The manner in which the ESDP has evolved to date does not make it possible definitively to conclude that the EU has departed from civilian power Europe. Indeed, for some member states the Petersberg orientation of the policy area is fully in conformity with civilian power norms. The focus of this chapter, though, has been to give analytical primacy to the EC/EU and not to it's member states, which has recently been the focus of other scholars (Howorth 2004).

A key strand of the varieties of civilian power that have been articulated is the environment of international relations constraining, or facilitating, this role. A key question to be posed is whether 9/11 and its aftermath will result in a transformation that will change the terrain upon which the EU operates. This is a question which is of both empirical and theoretical interest if the concept is to retain purchase.

The focus upon instruments used by the EU to assert its identity on the international scene outlined above is inevitably sketchy. However, it is intended to illustrate that focusing solely upon the instruments through which the EU conducts its international relations provides a limited insight into the full international significance of the EU. A full appreciation of the EU's capacity to operate as 'civilian power Europe' demands an appreciation of the environment within which these instruments are deployed, and of the EU's position in that environment. It also requires attention to the process of policy formulation and to the instruments that can be mobilized for the pursuit of policy.

The concern with the recourse to civilian forms of power by the EU has remained despite the changed environment of international relations in Europe with the demise of the Cold War overlay and the conflicts in the former Yugoslavia. The re-Europeanization of security in Europe has been accompanied by the EU advancing the project of a military security identity through the ESDP since the Treaty on European Union. Civilian forms of power have largely been retained, and arguably strengthened in Europe, and remain the hallmark of the European international identity beyond the continent. It can be argued that EU military power is developing, as suggested by Hanns Maull in defining the characteristics of a civilian power, as a 'residual instrument serving essentially to safeguard other means of international interaction' (Maull 1999). In short, CPE remains a role to which the EU continues to aspire.

Notes

1 The distinction between the concepts of international system and international society is central to the English School account of international relations. For Bull a 'A society of states (or international society) exists when a group of states, conscious of certain common interests and common values, form a society in the sense that they conceive themselves to be bound by a common set of rules in their relations with one another, and share in the working of common institutions' (Bull 1977: 13).

2 Hill's approach was to explore the international role of the EC/EU by delineating its functions in the international system before making a decision about the 'form' of the EC. Hill viewed the EC's functions as fourfold: the stabilizing of Western Europe; managing world trade; being the principal voice of the developed world in relations with the South; providing a second Western voice in international diplomacy.

References

Allen, D. (1998) '"Who Speaks for Europe?" The Search for an Effective and Coherent External Policy', in J. Peterson and H. Sjursen (eds) *A Common Foreign Policy for Europe? Competing Visions of the CFSP*, London: Routledge.

Allen, D. and Smith, M. (1990) 'Western Europe's Presence in the Contemporary International Arena', *Review of International Affairs*, 16: 19–37.

Bull, H. (1982) 'Civilian Power Europe: A Contradiction in Terms?', *Journal of Common Market Studies*, 21 (1): 149–70.

Bull, H. and Watson, A. (eds) (1984) *The Expansion of International Society*, Oxford: Clarendon Press.

Carlsnaes, W. and Smith, S. (eds) (1994) *European Foreign Policy: The EC and Changing Perspectives*, London: Sage Publications.

Christiansen, T., Petito, F. and Tonra, B. (2000) 'Fuzzy Politics around Fuzzy Borders: The European Union's "Near Abroad"', *Cooperation and Conflict*, 35 (4): 389–415.

Council of the European Union (2004) 'EU Headline Goal 2010 Approved by the General Affairs and External Relations Council on 17 May 2004'. Endorsed by the European Council of 17 and 18 June 2004, http://ue.eu.int/uedocs/cmsUpload/2010%20Headline%20Goal.pdf.

Council of the European Union (2003) 'A Secure Europe in a Better World', Brussels, 12 December.

Denza, E. (2002) *The Intergovernmental Pillars of the Union*, Oxford: Oxford University Press.

Diez, T. (2000) 'The Imposition of Governance, and the Transformation of Foreign Policy through EU Enlargement', paper presented at the workshop 'Governance by Enlargement', Darmstadt, Germany, 23–25 June.

Diez, T. and Whitman, R. (2002) 'Analysing European Integration: Reflecting on the English School – Scenarios for an Encounter', *Journal of Common Market Studies*, 40 (1): 43–67.

Duchêne, F. (1972) 'Europe's Role in World Peace', in R. Mayne (ed.) *Europe Tomorrow: Sixteen Europeans Look Ahead*, London: Fontana.

Duchêne, F. (1973) 'The European Community and the Uncertainties of Interdependence', in M. Kohnstamm and W. Hager (eds) *A Nation Writ Large? Foreign-Policy Problems before the European Community*, London: Macmillan.

Friis, L. and Murphy, A. (1999) 'The European Union and Central and Eastern Europe: Governance and Boundaries', *Journal of Common Market Studies*, 37 (3): 429–54.

Galtung, J. (1973) *The European Community: A Superpower in the Making*, London: Allen & Unwin.

Ginsberg, R. H. (1989) *Foreign Policy Actions of the European Community: The Politics of Scale*, Boulder, CO: Lynne Rienner.

Hill, C. (1993) 'The Capability–Expectations Gap, or Conceptualising Europe's International Role', *Journal of Common Market Studies*, 31 (3): 305–28.

Hill, C. (ed.) (1996) *The Actors in Europe's Foreign Policy*, London: Routledge.

Hill, C. (1998) 'Closing the Capabilities–Expectations Gap?', in J. Peterson and H. Sjursen (eds) *A Common Foreign Policy for Europe? Competing Visions of the CFSP*, London: Routledge.

Hill, C. (2003) *The Changing Politics of Foreign Policy*, London: Palgrave.

Hocking, B. and Smith, M. (1997) *Beyond Foreign Economic Policy: The United States, the Single European Market and the Changing World Economy*, London: Pinter.

Holland, M. (1995) *European Union Common Foreign and Security Policy: From EPC to CFSP Joint Action and South Africa*, London: Macmillan.

Holland, M. (ed.) (1997) *Common Foreign and Security Policy: The Record and Reforms*, London: Pinter.

Howorth, J. (2004) 'Discourse, Ideas, and Epistemic Communities in European Security and Defence Policy', *West European Politics*, 27 (2): 211–34.

Laffan, B. (1996) 'The Politics of Identity and Political Order in Europe', *Journal of Common Market Studies*, 34 (1): 81–102.

Larsen, H. (1991) 'The EU: A Global Military Actor', *Cooperation and Conflict*, 37 (3): 283–302.

Laursen, F. (1991) 'The EC in the World Context: Civilian Power or Superpower?', *Futures*, 747–59.

Lindley-French J. and Agieri, G. A. (2004) *European Defence Strategy*, Gutersloh: Bertelsmann Stiftung.

Lodge, J. (1993) 'From Civilian Power to Speaking with a Common Voice: The Transition to a CFSP', in J. Lodge (ed.) *The European Community and the Challenge of the Future*, 2nd edn, London: Pinter.

Macleod, I., Hendry, I. D. and Hyett, S. (1996) *The External Relations of the European Communities: A Manual of Law and Practice*, Oxford: Clarendon Press.

Manners, I. (2000) 'Normative Power Europe: A Contradiction in Terms?', *Journal of Common Market Studies*, 40 (2): 235–58.

Manners, I. and Whitman, R. G. (1998) 'Towards Identifying the International Identity of the European Union: A Framework of Analysis of the EU's Network of Relationships', *Journal of European Integration*, 21 (2): 231–49.

Manners, I. and Whitman, R. G. (eds) (2000) *The Foreign Policies of European Union Member States*, Manchester: Manchester University Press.

Maull, H. W. (1990) 'Germany and Japan: The New Civilian Powers', *Foreign Affairs*, 69 (5): 91–106.

Maull, H. W. (2000) 'Germany and the Use of Force: Still a "Civilian Power"?', *Survival*, 42 (2): 56–80.

Moravcsik, A. (2002) 'The Quiet Superpower', *Newsweek*, 17 June, p. 27.

Nye, J. S., Jr (1990) 'Soft Power', *Foreign Policy*, 80: 153–71.

Peterson, J. and Sjursen, H. (eds) (1998) *A Common Foreign Policy for Europe? Competing Visions of the CFSP*, London: Routledge.

Presidency Conclusions (1999) Helsinki European Council, 10 and 11 December, SN 0300/1/99. EN.

Presidency Conclusions (2000) Santa Maria da Feira European Council, 19 and 20 June, SN 200/1/00. EN.

Presidency Conclusions (2001) Göteborg European Council, 15 and 16 June, SN 200/1/01 REV 1. EN.

Prodi, R. (2000) '2000–2005: Shaping the New Europe', speech to the European Parliament, Strasbourg, 15 February, Speech/00/41.

Redmond, J. (ed.) (1992) *The External Relations of the European Community: The International Response to 1992*, London: Macmillan.

Schmitter, P. (1969) 'Three Neo-functional Hypotheses about International Integration', *International Organization*, 23 (1): 161–6.

Sjöstedt, G. (1977) 'The Exercise of International Civil Power: A Framework for Analysis', *Cooperation and Conflict*, 12: 21–39.

Smith, H. (1995) *European Union Foreign Policy and Central America*, London: Macmillan.

Smith, K. E. (2002) 'The End of Civilian Power EU: A Welcome Demise or Cause for Concern?', *International Spectator*, 35 (2): 11–28.

Smith, M. (1996a) 'The European Union and a Changing Europe: Establishing the Boundaries of Order', *Journal of Common Market Studies*, 43 (1): 5–28.

Smith, M. (1996b) 'The EU as an International Actor', in J. Richardson (ed.) *European Union: Power and Policy-making*, London: Routledge.

Smith, M. (1998) 'Does the Flag Follow Trade? "Politicisation" and the Emergence of a European Foreign Policy', in J. Peterson and H. Sjursen (eds) *A Common Foreign Policy for Europe? Competing Visions of the CFSP*, London: Routledge.

Soetendorp, B. (1994) 'The Evolution of the EC/EU as a Single Foreign Policy Actor', in W. Carlsnaes and S. Smith (eds) *European Foreign Policy: The EC and Changing Perspectives*, London: Sage.

Stavridis, S. (2001) '"Militarising" the EU: The Concept of Civilian Power Europe Revisited', *International Spectator*, 36 (4).

Stavridis, S. and Hill, C. (eds) (1996) *Domestic Sources of Foreign Policy: Western European Reactions to the Falklands Conflict*, Oxford: Berg.

Treacher, A. (2004) 'From Civilian Power to Military Actor: The EU's Resistible Transformation', *European Foreign Affairs Review*, 9 (1): 49–66.

Tsakaloyannis, P. (1989) 'The EC: From Civilian Power to Military Integration', in J. Lodge (ed.) *The European Community and the Challenge of the Future*, London: Pinter.

Whitman, R. G. (1998a) 'The Common Foreign and Security Policy: Past Practice and Future Prospects', *Current Economics and Politics of Europe*, 8 (1): 35–57.

Whitman, R. G. (1998b) *From Civilian Power to Superpower? The International Identity of the EU*, London: Macmillan.

Whitman, R. G. (1998c) 'Creating a Foreign Policy for Europe? Implementing the Common Foreign and Security Policy from Maastricht to Amsterdam', *Australian Journal of International Affairs*, 52 (2): 165–83.

Youngs, R. (2002) 'The European Security and Defence Policy: What Impact on the EU's Approach to Security Challenges?', *European Security*, 11 (2): 101–24.

7 The EU's role as a promoter of human rights and democracy

Enlargement policy practice and role formation

Ulrich Sedelmeier

This chapter addresses a specific role of the EU in international politics: its role as a promoter of human rights and democracy. It focuses on the origins of this role conception and identifies one particular pathway to create new roles for the EU in international politics, namely as a – partly unintended – consequence of collective policy practice in its external relations. I argue that one distinct source, or driving force, behind this role is the process of eastern enlargement. The EU's policy practice – its enlargement policy and the related discourse – contributed to the formation of this specific role of the EU.

EU policy-makers not only set compliance with the principles of human rights and democracy as membership conditions for candidate countries, but articulated and institutionalized them as characteristics of the EU's collective identity. Although unintended by some EU actors, this policy practice created internal and external expectations about behaviour that is appropriate for this role conception, namely adherence to these principles in European foreign policy.

The distinctive origin of this role has implications for role performance, which translates this role conception into policy outcomes. Key obstacles for an 'ethical' foreign policy that is consistent with this role conception are that it is a collective, rather than shared, property of EU actors, and that its standards of appropriate behaviour still remain rather diffuse. Norm entrepreneurs in the EU are therefore crucial for role performance and its impact on European foreign policy.[1] This role conception provides a normative environment that empowers the advocates of foreign-policy options that can be legitimized with references to this particular role and this specific identity. The motives of such policy advocates might be either principled or instrumental, and their strategies might rely either on persuasion or shaming. In turn, these differences in the characteristics of advocacy might determine their success and the sustainability of its policy impact.

The EU's role as a promoter of human rights and democracy

One of the most prominent new roles of the EU in international politics since the end of the Cold War is the promotion of human rights and democracy. Its origins date back a long way, such as the affirmation by the ECJ in the 1960s that respect for fundamental rights was part of the EC's legal heritage (Alston and Weiler 1999: 4). However, most developments in this area are more recent. They included the declaration of the Luxembourg European Council in December 1997 on the fiftieth anniversary of the Universal Declaration of Human Rights, the adoption of the European Initiative for Development and Human Rights in 1999, and the Charter of Fundamental Rights adopted at the Nice European Council in December 2002. The draft constitutional treaty includes both this charter and a commitment to the EU's accession to the European Convention on Human Rights.

The EU's commitment to promoting human rights and democracy internationally include the Luxembourg European Council declaration of June 1991 that stated that 'the Community and its Member States undertake to pursue the policy of promoting human rights and fundamental freedoms throughout the world'. The Maastricht Treaty on European Union articulates as one objective of the Common Foreign and Security Policy 'developing and consolidating democracy, the rule of law and respect for human rights and fundamental freedoms'. The most concrete expression was the Commission's communication on 'the European Union's role in promoting human rights and democratisation in third countries' (European Commission 2001), which the Council endorsed in June 2001.

The EU's policies for the promotion of rights and democracy could be separated into three strands. First, the EU-financed programmes designed to promote democracy and human rights directly, such as the PHARE democracy programme which is aimed at the countries of East Central Europe. Second, the EU uses asymmetrical interdependence to attach conditions to its offers of membership or trade agreements with third countries. Democracy and human rights are one central element of the EU's political conditionality (see e.g. Smith 1998). The third strand is least developed: it concerns an 'ethical dimension' of foreign policy (Light and Smith 2001; Smith 2001) that sanctions abuses of human rights and democracy in third countries. Its weakest form is to condemn violations of these principles in common declarations and démarches, which are more traditional tools of CFSP. Stronger forms range from diplomatic sanctions (e.g. suspending official contacts) and arms embargoes to approving military interventions to end human rights abuses.

The first two strands can be described respectively as 'reinforcement by support' and 'reinforcement by reward', while the latter includes 'reinforcement by punishment' (see e.g. Schimmelfennig *et al.* 2003 for this distinction). Needless to say, this third is most onerous and least developed in the EU (notwithstanding an assessment of whether the first two are effective, efficient, or coherently applied). It is not only the most costly in material terms, but EU actors might also differ in their views about the trade-offs involved with regard to countervailing norms.

In this chapter, I do not attempt to provide a comprehensive account of the origins and sources of this role conception or the EU's human rights policy (see e.g. Smith 2003: 98–144). General causes include structural changes in international normative context since the end of the Cold War, as well as the advocacy of by particular member states (especially the Nordic states) and EU institutions (especially the European Parliament). Rather, this chapter is primarily interested in one particular source: the impact of the EU's enlargement policy *practice*. This policy practice established adherence and the promotion of these principles as part of the EU's self-image, or, in other words, it increased the robustness of the behavioural norms through which this particular identity is enacted. Recent studies of norm construction emphasize the role of intentional and strategic norm construction by norm entrepreneurs. By contrast, the increased robustness of these norms – with regard to their communality and specificity – was primarily an unintended by-product of the EU's enlargement policy practice.

The EU's enlargement policy practice and role formation

There are a number of links between the EU's eastern enlargement policy and its broader role as a promoter of democracy and human rights. One more general link is the presentation of the promotion of human rights and democracy as a distinct and central *rationale* for the EU's enlargement. This particular justification of policy reflects back on the role and self-image that policy-makers ascribe to the EU.[2] EU policy-makers referred not only to (collective) security and economic interests or to an EU identity that prescribed integration of the CEECs. European Council declarations regularly asserted the promotion of democracy and human rights as a distinct goal to be served (indirectly) through enlargement (in addition to initiatives that were designed to promote this goal directly, such as the PHARE democracy programme). Two elements of the EU's enlargement practice stand out as key sources of the EU's role formation: *accession conditionality* and *changes in the founding treaties* in anticipation of enlargement. Both elements explicitly articulated respect for democracy and human rights as a key characteristic of the EU and thus increased the robustness of the behavioural norms that this role entails.

Political conditionality

Only in the context of eastern enlargement did the EU make adherence to human rights and democratic principles an increasingly explicit and central condition of its offers of aid, trade and eventual membership (see e.g. Smith 2001; Williams 2000; Vachudova 2001). The formulation of the political conditionality attached to the EU's enlargement policy conditionality is a crucial aspect of role formation. By defining and spelling out the criteria for membership, the EU explicitly articulated the fundamental characteristics that it ascribed to itself. The EU articulated the democratic requirements for associate status most explicitly in the Europe Agreements (EAs) signed in 1993 with Romania and Bulgaria. The preamble of the EAs and Article 6 spell out these principles:

> Considering the firm commitment of the Community and its member states and of [the associated country] to the rule of law and human rights, including those of persons belonging to minorities, and to the full implementation of all other principles and provisions contained in the Final Act of the Conference on Security and Co-operation in Europe (CSCE), the concluding documents of Vienna and Madrid, the Charter of Paris for a New Europe. . . . Respect for the democratic principles and human rights established by the Helsinki Final Act and the Charter of Paris for a New Europe . . . inspire the domestic and external policies of the Parties and constitute the essential elements of the present association.

In particular the concerns about the political situation in Romania led the member states to agree on the inclusion of a suspension clause, a measure that the majority of governments had still rejected in the earlier EAs. However, in order to point the finger less directly at the Romanian government, the EU decided to make such a suspension clause a general feature of *all* agreements between the EU and third countries from that date onwards (*Bulletin of the EC* 5–1992; see also Riedel and Will 1999). This spill-over of democratic conditionality from enlargement policy to the EU's external relations more generally was thus largely an unintended consequence of the particular case of Romania. Crucially, however, this step established the general significance of these principles for the EU's external relations. Furthermore, the EU not only insisted on the adherence of the associated countries to these principles, but also articulated them as values to which itself was committed.

The Copenhagen European Council of June 1993, which for the first time clearly acknowledged the eventual membership of the CEECs, made the political conditionality for accession explicit. In addition to economic conditions, these 'Copenhagen criteria' specified that '[m]embership requires that the candidate country has achieved stability of institutions guaranteeing democracy, the rule of law, human rights and respect for and protection of minorities ... ' (*Bulletin of the EC* 6–1993). These political conditions subsequently became a central part of the Commission's assessment of the candidates' accession prospects. The Commission's opinions on the CEECs' applications for membership insisted on further progress concerning the actual practice of democratic principles and the respect for human rights and minorities (European Commission 1997a), and the Commission continued to monitor these developments in its regular reports on the candidates' progress.

Crucially, the EU's policy practice validated the discourse underpinning its conditionality through strict and consistent application. The key example was the EU's critical position towards Slovakia under the Meciar government (see e.g. Henderson 1999; Pridham 2002). After repeated expressions of the EU's concern about respect for human rights, democracy and freedom of the press (*Agence Europe*, 27 October 1995, 4–5; *Agence Europe*, 8 February 1996, 4; European Commission 1997b: 9–18), the Luxembourg European Council in December 1997 followed the Commission's recommendation not to open accession negotiations, even though the economic record might have allowed doing so. After the election of the new government in September 1998, the Commission suggested that the new situation allowed the prospect of opening accession negotiations 'on condition that the regular stable and democratic functioning of its institutions are confirmed' (European Commission 1998: 29). In December 1999, the Helsinki European Council decided to open accession negotiations, after the Commission's positive assessment of the political reform process (European Commission 1999).

Treaty changes induced by eastern enlargement

The emphasis on respect for democracy and human rights as a condition of membership did not remain limited to the EU's external policies, but also reverberated inside the EU. In part, the conditionality practice stimulated a debate on whether the EU should 'take these basic constitutional values more seriously by entrenching them more firmly in its own legal order' (De Witte 2003: 210). In part, member states and EU institutions were keen to have treaty-based leverage over new members that might revert to authoritarian practices. Subsequent amendments of the founding treaties thus codified adherence to these principles as crucial characteristics of its members. They were thus not merely conditions to be met by applicants, but part of the member states' collective self-image.

The link between enlargement and expressions of the importance of democratic principles for EU members has a historical precedent. In the enlargements of the 1980s, the incumbents were similarly concerned about instruments and safeguards to guarantee the continued adherence of the new members to the fundamental democratic principles after accession has been granted. The result was the 'Declaration on Democracy' at the Copenhagen European Council in 1978. The official reason for this declaration was the decision to hold the first direct elections to the European Parliament in 1979. At the same time, however, the declaration was prompted by the impending accession of Greece, Spain and Portugal and 'was intended to strengthen the Community's leverage against any future member which might slip towards authoritarian rule' (Wallace 1996: 16).

In the case of eastern enlargement, these concerns were institutionalized in formal treaty changes. The shadow of eventual eastern enlargement led the negotiators of the Maastricht Treaty to insert Article F into the treaty, which stated in paragraphs 1 and 2 that:

> [t]he Union shall respect that national identities of its Member States, *whose system of government are founded on the principles of democracy* (my emphasis). The Union shall respect fundamental rights, as guaranteed by the European Convention for the Protection of Human Rights and Fundamental Freedoms signed in Rome on 4 November 1950 and as they result from the constitutional traditions common to the Member States, as general principles of Community law.

Concern about leverage against breaches of democracy and human rights in the prospective members after accession also influenced the drafting of the Amsterdam Treaty in 1996/97. The treaty explicitly made a strong commitment to democratic principles and human rights one of the principal characteristics of the EU. The new Article 6 proclaims that '[t]he Union is founded on the principles of liberty, democracy, respect for human rights and fundamental freedoms, and the rule of law. . . .' Article 7 furthermore provides the means to suspend a member state's rights under the treaty if it breaches these principles in a 'serious and persistent' way. In sum, these treaty changes codified the adherence to basic democratic principles not only as a precondition for accession, but also as a key characteristic of membership.

At the same time, however, by acknowledging these principles as constitutive values of its members, the EU's enlargement practice did not only feed back into the internal practices of the EU and its member states. This acknowledgement also creates expectations about the behaviour of the EU and its member states in European foreign policy, namely to protect and to promote these principles internationally.

Role formation through collective discursive practices

The discourse underpinning the EU's policy practice – in particular its conditionality and the membership obligations institutionalized in treaty amendments – thus formulated a broader role for the EU in the promotion of democracy and human rights. It did so through increasing the robustness of the behavioural norms this role entails. Norms are collective understandings of the proper behaviour for actors with a given identity or role. Constructivist analyses suggest that their impact on identity formation, actors' behaviour and collective practices depends on the robustness of the norm in question (Legro 1997: 33). The formation of a particular role conception for the EU and the likelihood of role performance or role-consistent behaviour thus depend on the robustness of the regulative norms through which it is enacted.

The EU's enlargement policy affected primarily two components of norm 'robustness': their commonality (or 'concordance') and their specificity (see Boekle *et al.* 2001: 109–10; Legro 1997: 34–5). 'Commonality' refers to how widely accepted rules and prescriptions are among the actors within a given system or community and 'specificity' relates to the extent to which a norm establishes precise and simple standards of appropriate behaviour. The EU's enlargement policy increased both the specificity and the commonality of a commitment to the international promotion of human rights and democracy within the EU. ✓

Role specificity

Enlargement practice increased the specificity of the EU's role in the international promotion of human rights and democracy by first articulating, and then concretizing, not only the importance of these principles for its members, but also for the EU to promote them internationally. By making the discourse about the promotion of human rights and democracy a distinct and central element of its eastern enlargement policy practice, EU policy-makers affirmed a self-image of the EU as an actor whose role prescribes the promotion and protection of these principles. The articulation and institutionalization of these principles as membership conditions made explicit that the type of community the EU forms is based on these principles.

For what reasons the EU initially established this conditionality and whether the resulting role conception was intentional or an unintended effect of its policy practice are less significant. Arguably, the EU promoted democracy, human and minority rights in the CEECs – at least partly – instrumentally and strategically to achieve material objectives, namely stability in neighbouring countries. However, the EU presented the promotion of these principles not merely as a means to achieve the ulterior goal of stability (as for the recognition of borders or good neighbourly relations), but also as an end in itself. This characteristic of the discourse makes an important difference for the EU's role conception. The emphasis on democracy and human rights as central membership conditions reveals something about the self-image and role that the EU attributes to itself. Once this particular justification is given, it provides a reference point that attests to the significance of these principles for the goals that the EU pursues and creates expectations about future conduct.

Role commonality

Just as the explicit articulation of such objectives and of principled justifications increases the specificity of the EU's role, the act of doing so in collective statements at the EU level also increases its *commonality*. Significantly, this process also can be the result of unintended consequences. For example, a member state government might be generally opposed to the transfer of competences in the area of fundamental rights to EU institutions and it might object to allowing considerations of a country's human rights record constrain its foreign policy if other material objectives are at stake. It might none the less agree to a common European Council declaration that emphasizes certain norms, as a result either of compromises, or neglect of semantic details and the possible consequences that these might have in the future. However, once such statements of policy goals or justifications for particular actions are made, they present expressions of *collective* commitments and understandings, even if the member states do not equally share such commitments, let alone agree on the extent to which ethical considerations should influence policy in specific situations.

This argument has affinities with the distinction that Jepperson *et al.* (1996: 54–5) draw between 'collective' and 'shared' norms:

> Norms may be 'shared', or commonly held, across some distribution of actors in a system. Alternatively, however, norms may not be widely held by actors but may nevertheless be collective features of the system – either by being institutionalized . . . or by being prominent in public discourse of a system. . . . [A] distinction between collectively 'prominent' or institutionalized norms and commonly 'internalized' ones, with various 'intersubjective' admixtures in between, is crucial for distinguishing between different types of norms and different types of normative effects.

Thus, by explicitly articulating elements of the EU 'collective' role, such common EU statements and discourse can none the less have a regulative effect on the behaviour of those actors who would otherwise prefer fewer constraints on the pursuit of material objectives in European foreign policy. While they do not 'share' this element of role to the same extent, they find themselves 'rhetorically entrapped' in these collective statements (Risse and Sikkink 1999: 28; Schimmelfennig 2001: 73). In a similar vein, we can interpret the argument by Karen Smith (2002: 16) that it makes an important difference for both the specificity and the communality of EU role conceptions if normative objectives become explicitly articulated, embedded and specified at the EU level:

> Once the objectives [to promote certain norms] are adopted at the EU level, the member states become involved in a process in which their initial preferences are reshaped and in which they must make compromises over how these objectives will be achieved. It also makes it very difficult to roll back rhetorical commitments to pursue the objectives. Through this process, the EU's international identity thus gradually acquires more substance.

Path-dependence and unintended consequences of discursive practices

The strengthening of regulative norms through the EU's enlargement policy differs from the processes emphasized in recent studies of the 'life cycle' through which international norms evolve. Finnemore and Sikkink (1998) underline the importance of intentional and strategic advocacy and persuasion by 'norm entrepreneurs' that pushes norms over the 'tipping' point at which a critical mass adopts the norm. By contrast, the increased specificity and commonality of the EU's commitment to the international promotion of human rights and democracy has a strong element of unintended consequences.

The EU's enlargement policy practice contributed to this role conception primarily through inducing a certain path-dependence into European foreign policy. In the discourse underpinning the EU's accession conditionality and related treaty changes, the member states and EU institutions explicitly and collectively ascribed a certain role to the EU. These discursive practices make it increasingly difficult to oppose policy options that can be legitimized with adherence to the EU's role and thus establish a 'critical juncture' in European foreign policy. They thus push this role conception towards the 'tipping point', even in the absence of an equally internalized consensus among the member states on whether certain norms should be prioritized in situations in which they might collide with material interests or countervailing norms.

In sum, new role conceptions for the EU in international politics are not only the result of design and of successful advocacy by 'role entrepreneurs'. To some extent, they can be also unintended consequences of policy practices in specific issue areas. However, the particular nature of this source of role conception has implications for role performance and its impact on European foreign policy.

Role performance: opportunities for role entrepreneurs

The importance of role entrepreneurs

Thus, it could be argued that the EU's enlargement policy practice has contributed to the formation of an EU role in the international protection and promotion of human rights and democracy. But how does the particular source of this role conception affect role performance, in the sense of behaviour that is consistent with this role conception? Clearly, the impact of these discursively created role-specific prescriptions on European foreign-policy choices is fragile, as reflected, e.g. in the inconsistencies of the EU's human rights conditionality with regard to Pakistan or Russia (see e.g. Smith 2001). Then how does this role conception affect European foreign policy? While the EU's enlargement policy practice increased both the specificity and commonality of this role conception, its particular origin also suggests that both these aspects of 'norm robustness' are still problematic.

First, the problem with the commonality of the role conception remains that it relies to a considerable extent on its characteristic as a collective property of the member states, rather than one that is shared and equally internalized. Second, despite the increased specificity of this role conception, its behavioural obligations are still rather diffuse. It establishes clear expectation about appropriate behaviour for the internal practices of members and would-be members, as well as for a consistent application of political conditionality in the EU's external relations. Yet it is much less clear what behavioural standards it prescribes for European foreign policy more generally. For example, does it prescribe any particular course of action in cases in which these norms are breached in non-member states, such as additional punishments other than suspending conditional rewards that might be in place?

These deficiencies concerning the robustness of the EU's role conception point at a key precondition for it to have none the less an impact on European foreign policy. Its policy impact depends on 'role entrepreneurs' who advocate particular policy options that conform to the EU's role. Constructivists or sociological institutionalists predominantly emphasize a 'logic of appropriateness' as the key logic of action through which actors enact a given role or identity. Actors determine 'what the situation is, what role is being fulfilled, and what the obligations of that role in that situation are' (March and Olsen 1989: 160). Role-guided behaviour thus requires that such situation-specific obligations are clearly identifiable. Conversely, role conceptions that are not sufficiently specific to prescribe a clear course of action in a particular situation are unlikely to lead to coherent role performance by the EU if the situation is also characterized by countervailing norms, uncertainty over whether a certain action (or inaction) is most conducive to producing norm-conforming behaviour in other states; and when certain member states face countervailing material incentives. Policy advocates can overcome problems with the specificity of behavioural prescriptions by framing specific policy options in concrete situations as 'appropriate behaviour'.

Norm entrepreneurs articulate and call attention to norms and collective role conceptions by making the case that in a particular situation the EU's role is at stake, justify particular policy options with references to the

EU's role, or point out potential discrepancies between behaviour and a collectively professed role. Thus, for the EU's role conception to have such an impact on EFP, policy entrepreneurs have to be successful in defining a certain situation in such a way that at least certain behavioural options are ruled out as inappropriate. Moreover, policy advocates might even exploit their diffuse nature of the EU's role by presenting more far-reaching interpretations of this role as appropriate.

Role entrepreneurs and communicative processes in European foreign policy

The need for policy entrepreneurs to identify, and promote, certain policy adoptions as 'appropriate behaviour' for a somewhat diffuse role conception means that communicative processes among EU foreign-policy-makers are key for role performance. We can distinguish two analytically different processes through which role entrepreneurs can connect specific situations and behavioural options with the EU's role conception. The first communicative process follows a 'logic of arguing' (Risse 2000: 7):

> Actors try to challenge the validity claims inherent in any causal or normative statement and to seek a communicative consensus about their understanding of a situation as well as justifications for the principles and norms guiding their action. Argumentative rationality also implies that the participants in a discourse are open to being persuaded by the better argument and that relationships of power and social hierarchies recede in the background.

According to this logic, role entrepreneurs in European foreign policy seek a reasoned consensus that a particular course of action is the appropriate enactment of their collective role as promoters of human rights and democracy in a given situation. Agreement on a particular foreign-policy action reflects that all participants are persuaded of the normative validity of the arguments presented. Such advocacy is attributed to principled norm entrepreneurs, who are motivated by ideational commitment. They generate a consensus among EU policy-makers not only about the general importance of certain role-specific norms, but also about the extent to which they have to be prioritized over competing concerns in a given (foreign-policy) situation. The precedents created through collective policy and discursive practices provide resources for policy advocates (see also Wiener 1998) by strengthening the legitimacy of their arguments.

However, certain actors might also advocate norm-conforming behaviour instrumentally, in order to further their material self-interest. They engage their counterparts in a communicative process which is characterized by 'rhetorical action' (Schimmelfennig 2001). This process assumes 'weakly socialized actors [that] ... belong to a community whose constitutive values and norms they share', but 'it is not expected that collective identity shapes concrete preferences' (2001: 62). An institutional environment – or a community's collective role identity – thus provides a resource for actors that can justify their selfish goals with reference to institutional norms or the collective identity, as the legitimacy that these bestow on their goals increases their bargaining power. Actors engaging in such rhetorical action do not aim to persuade other actors of the normative validity of their arguments, but rather to silence possible opposition. They exercise 'social influence' through social rewards and punishments (Johnston 2001). The addressees acquiesce in initiatives promoted through rhetorical action in order to avoid the (social and reputational) costs of non-compliance with professed community norms.

Alternatively, their acquiescence might not result from reputational cost–benefit calculations, but because they have internalized the norms in question and therefore cannot conceive of opposing an initiative when opposition is presented – or successfully framed – as rejection of the norm at stake (Sedelmeier 2005: 37–8). Indeed, a degree of intersubjective acceptance of such norms as standards of appropriate behaviour is a precondition for successful rhetorical action and 'social influence' (see also Johnston 2001: 501–2; Müller 2004: 406; Risse 2000: 9).

According to this logic, the EU's collective role conception provides an institutional environment for European foreign policy, which the actors involved take – to a certain extent – for granted. It increases the bargaining power of actors that can present a certain course of action as the defence of human rights and democracy. Other governments might be reluctant about such action, either because they are not convinced about the normative validity of the arguments presented, or because this course of action might compete with their material interests or countervailing norms. However, they feel inhibited to oppose such action if this is interpreted as failure to act in accordance with their professed role conception. The diffuse nature of the EU's role conception even increases the scope for rhetorical action (but not necessarily its success). The range of policy options that policy-makers might attempt to justify with references to the EU's role is larger than if it was more specific, and hence more narrowly defined.

Types of advocacy and their impact on European foreign policy

'Rhetorical action' presumes self-interested policy advocates, but principled role entrepreneurs might use a similar strategy. They might aim not only to persuade other actors, but to exploit their 'rhetorical entrapment' in collective discourse to shame them into acquiescing in an 'ethical' foreign policy. We can thus distinguish three different types of policy advocacy, depending on whether the advocates are principled or self-interested and whether principled advocates engage in persuasion or shaming. The different characteristics of such advocacy can be expected to affect its impact on role performance.

When principled role entrepreneurs engage in persuasion, they are likely to achieve policy impact only in the longer term. But, once successful, such impact is most likely to be sustainable. An example is the EU's international pursuit of the abolition of the death penalty (see Manners 2002; Lerch and Schwellnus 2003). The EU's collective endeavour in this area can be seen as an element of an 'ethical foreign policy', which was adopted despite material disincentives. There are few rewards from domestic audiences; it creates tensions in relations with countries with capital punishment (most notably the US), not least with regard to extradition. Furthermore, as late as 1994, five member states (the UK, Belgium, Spain, Italy, Greece) had not yet abolished the death penalty. Yet by 1998 all member states had not only abolished the death penalty but also collectively embarked on the pursuit of its international abolition. Policy advocates in the EU – including the European Parliament, the Commission's Directorate General of External Relations and a number of member state governments (as well as the international human rights movement) were able to persuade the more reluctant member governments to change their policies and to support an international abolitionist role of the EU. The EU's role conception and enlargement policy practice which set the abolition of the death penalty as a membership condition increased the legitimacy of their arguments and enabled them to argue for a more far-reaching international role of the EU. While the persuasion process took time, the consensus it generated made this policy sustainable.

Advocacy by instrumentally motivated actors engaging in 'rhetorical action' can lead directly to foreign-policy actions that can be framed as role-conforming, but it can also feed back into a further strengthening of the EU's role conception. If the member states collectively endorse such an initiative, this endorsement validates the salience of these arguments, even if the policy advocates were insincere in presenting them. Foreign-policy actions that are justified with reference to the EU's role can serve as precedents that facilitate, albeit as an unintended consequence, arguing for similar role-conforming behaviour at a later stage.

A key example of such policy advocacy with – at least – mixed motives is the case of the bilateral diplomatic sanctions against the Austrian government in February 2000. Note that the strong reaction of the EU XIV to the inclusion of the far-right Freedom Party into the Austrian government coalition concerns member state foreign policies, rather than common EU foreign policy. Yet this case is difficult to explain fully without appreciating the EU's role conception as a defender of democracy and human rights. The governments that initiated the sanctions of the EU XIV arguably had instrumental motives, as their initiative was aimed not only at Haider but at domestic party politics, in an attempt to discredit far-right parties or those within their own centre-right parties pondering co-operation with the far right (see Merlingen *et al.* 2001).

Such instrumental motives notwithstanding, it is very difficult to understand the participation of all other member governments in this strong measure without taking into account the EU's role on human rights and democracy. The EU's self-proclaimed role gave a strong legitimacy to the initiative. While it is far from obvious that the EU's role would have required such a strong reaction, it was difficult to object to once this particular action had been proposed. Opposition to participation could have been perceived as a refusal to act according to the EU's role. It thus made it difficult to voice scepticism about the proposed measures, either on the grounds that their effect might be counterproductive, or that such a measure might violate competing norms, such as not to isolate a member state. Thus, although references to the EU's role might have been used instrumentally, this worked only because the EU's role has become so much taken for granted.

Furthermore, this case illustrates that instrumental role entrepreneurs, motivated by domestic party political struggles, can contribute to a strengthening of the EU's role conception. It both set a precedent for involvement in other member states' domestic politics and – as a result of the ensuing dispute over the appropriateness of these measures – led to the specification of a procedural mechanism for doing so in an amendment of Article 7 of the Nice Treaty.

Finally, an example of the use of shaming by principled policy advocates is the strong initial reactions of the EU to Russian policy in Chechnya. The Nordic member states in particular argued that the EU should take a firm line in explicitly condemning what they considered the excessive use of force against civilians and human rights abuses by the Russian forces. By contrast, some of the big member states, namely the German, French and UK governments, were concerned that a too critical position would jeopardize good relations and a strategic partnership with Russia. However, despite such opposition and the intergovernmental character of the CFSP, the CFSP declarations of January 1995 were characterized by very critical normative language. The EU expressed its 'greatest concern' about the fighting in Chechnya, it noted 'serious violations of human rights and international humanitarian law' and deplored 'the large number of victims and the suffering being inflicted on the civilian population' (*European Foreign Policy Bulletin*, Statement 95/018). Despite strong initial reservations by a majority of governments, the strong pressure from the then new member states Sweden and Finland in particular forged an agreement, as the reluctant governments could not dispute the normative validity of the arguments.[3]

However, this case also demonstrates that the success of such shaming strategies alone might be rather short term. Exposing individual member states and criticizing them publicly for not conforming to the EU's normative standards is in itself behaviour that is deemed inappropriate for member states. Thus, such a strategy can be used only sparingly. Indeed, the EU's position during the second Russian military campaign of 1999/2000 was much less critical than its approach during the first Chechnya conflict. In turn, just as the feedback of 'positive' precedents of successful advocacy with references to the EU's role can strengthen its role conception and hence generate more consistent role performance, such emerging inconsistencies in role performance can start to undermine earlier role conceptions.

Conclusion

This chapter has pinpointed one distinct source of new roles of the EU in international politics: policy practice in apparently discrete policy areas of its external relations. The EU's policy practice with regard to eastern enlargement was an important focal point for the formation of the EU's role in the international promotion of human rights and democracy. The collective discourse justified policy practices – such as the accession conditionality – with reference to the intrinsic importance of these norms, rather than just material foreign-policy goals. The presentation of these norms as fundamental aspects of the EU did not only feed back into the internal codification of fundamental rights in the EU, but also into a broader role conception in international politics.

These discursive practices increased the robustness of this role conception, both with regard to its specificity and commonality. However, remaining shortcomings in both dimensions make 'role entrepreneurs', who present certain foreign-policy behaviour as appropriate for the EU's role, a crucial precondition for consistent role performance. The EU's role conception strengthens the argumentative power of such role entrepreneurs by increasing the legitimacy of foreign-policy options that can be justified with reference to the promotion and protection of human rights and democracy. It thus creates the scope to advance, at least incrementally, policy initiatives that can be presented as enactments of this role, sometimes even in the face of countervailing material interests.

As the EU's role conception and the behavioural obligations that it entails are still fairly diffuse, the role entrepreneurs can engage in two analytically distinct communicative processes: 'persuasion' and 'rhetorical action'. Principled role entrepreneurs might either rely on persuasion or shaming strategies, while instrumentally motivated actors might use references to the EU's role to pursue their self-interests in specific cases. In turn, role-conforming action that is collectively justified with reference to the EU's role, or directly resulting from advocacy with reference to the EU's role – even if this advocacy was instrumental and insincere – further increases the salience of role-based arguments for subsequent foreign-policy activities.

A common point in both mechanisms is their emphasis on accepted standards of legitimacy, based on the collective role and identity of a political community. Arguments that relate particular foreign-policy options and initiatives to the EU's role conception thus enjoy greater legitimacy than arguments referring merely to the expected utility for particular member states. The EU's role conception thus limits the realm of feasible policy options (including non-action) and reduces the ground for self-interested objection to particular policy initiatives. In this way, the EU's identity might create an opportunity structure that enables role entrepreneurs, who can claim to act in the name of the EU's role, to obtain approval for their policy initiatives.

For the EU's role in the international promotion of democracy and human rights, this means that the stronger the salience of these principles as constitutive of the EU and its external relations the harder it is to deny that the EU also has to play an active role in the defence and promotion of these norms. This does not imply that it is a sufficient condition for the EU to agree on a common, role-conforming action in specific cases. Nor does it imply that the EU's identity is a direct cause if the member states engage in such activities. However, it does create enabling conditions and an argumentative logic that are conducive to such courses of action. Argumentative consistency bestows legitimacy to calls for action to protect and defend these principles if they are at stake in the EU's external relations. At the same time, while this enhances the scope to advance policy initiatives aimed at defending democracy and human rights, it might also reduce the grounds for scrutinizing potential breaches of countervailing norms that specific policy options might entail.

Notes

I would like to thank the editors and the participants at the Uppsala workshop, and in particular Ian Manners, Karen Smith and Helene Sjursen, for comments on an earlier version of this chapter.

1 The term 'European' foreign policy usually includes the national foreign policies of the EU member states, as well as collective EU foreign policy and Community external policy (see e.g. White 2001).
2 See also Sjursen (2002) for a more general argument that the EU's particular justification of eastern enlargement reflects the EU's self-image as a particular type of international community.
3 Interview with official in the Council Secretariat, 15 October 1997.

References

Alston, P. and Weiler, J. (1999) 'An "Ever Closer Union" in Need of a Human Rights Policy: The European Union and Democracy', *Harvard Jean Monnet Working Papers* 1/99, New York: Jean Monnet Center for International Regional Economic Law and Justice, New York University School of Law.

Boekle, H., Rittberger, V. and Wagner, W. (2001) 'Constructivist Foreign Policy Theory', in V. Rittberger (ed.) *German Foreign Policy since Unification*, Manchester: Manchester University Press, 109–10.

De Witte, B. (2003) 'The Impact of Enlargement on the Constitution of the European Union', in M. Cremona (ed.) *Enlargement of the European Union*, Oxford: Oxford University Press, 209–52.

European Commission (1997a) 'The Opinions of the European Commission on the Applications for Accession', COM (97) 2000, 15 July.

European Commission (1997b) 'Commission Opinion on Slovakia's Application for Membership in the European Union', COM (97) 2004, 15 July.

European Commission (1998) 'Composite Paper. Reports on Progress Towards Accession by each of the Candidate Countries', COM (98) 700–12, 4 November.

European Commission (1999) 'Regular Report from the Commission on Progress towards Accession by each of the Candidate Countries', COM (99) 500–13, 13 October.

European Commission (2001) 'The European Union's Role in Promoting Human Rights and Democratisation in Third Countries', COM (2001) 252, 8 May.

Finnemore, M. and Sikkink, K. (1998) 'International Norm Dynamics and Political Change', *International Organization*, 52: 887–917.

Henderson, K. (1999) 'Slovakia and the Democratic Criteria for EU Accession', in K. Henderson (ed.) *Back to Europe*, London: UCL Press, 221–40.

Jepperson, R., Wendt, A. and Katzenstein, P. (1996) 'Norms, Identity, and Culture in National Security', in P. Katzenstein (ed.) *The Culture of National Security*, New York: Columbia University Press, 33–75.

Johnston, A. I. (2001) 'Treating Institutions as Social Environments', *International Studies Quarterly*, 45: 487–515.

Legro, J. (1997) 'Which Norms Matter? Revisiting the "Failure" of Internationalism', *International Organization*, 51 (1): 31–63.

Lerch, M. and Schwellnus, G. (2003) 'Europe's Role as a Promotor of International Human Rights: Modes and Dynamics of Justifying Supranational Foreign Policy', paper presented at the ECPR general conference, Marburg, 18–21 September.

Light, M. and Smith, K. (eds) (2001) *Ethics and Foreign Policy*, Cambridge: Cambridge University Press.

Manners, I. (2002) 'Normative Power Europe: A Contradiction in Terms?', *Journal of Common Market Studies*, 40 (2): 234–58.

March, J. and Olsen, J. (1989) *Rediscovering Institutions*, New York: Free Press.

Merlingen, M., Mudde, C. and Sedelmeier, U. (2001) 'The Right and the Righteous? European Norms, Domestic Politics and the Sanctions against Austria', *Journal of Common Market Studies*, 39 (1): 61–79.

Müller, H. (2004) 'Arguing, Bargaining and All That: Communicative Action, Rationalist Theory and the Logic of Appropriateness in International Relations', *European Journal of International Relations*, 10 (3): 395–435.

Pridham, G. (2002) 'The European Union's Democratic Conditionality and Domestic Politics in Slovakia: The Meciar and Dzurinda Governments Compared', *Europe-Asia Studies*, 54: 203–27.

Riedel, E. and Will, M. (1999) 'Human Rights Clauses in External Agreements of the EC', in P. Alston (ed.) *The EU and Human Rights*, Oxford: Oxford University Press, 723–54.

Risse, T. (2000) '"Let's Argue!" Communicative Action in World Politics', *International Organization*, 54 (1): 1–39.

Risse, T. and Sikkink, K. (1999) 'The Socialization of International Human Rights Norms into Domestic Practices: Introduction', in T. Risse, S. Ropp and K. Sikkink (eds) *The Power of Human Rights*, Cambridge: Cambridge University Press, 1–38.

Schimmelfennig, F. (2001) 'The Community Trap: Liberal Norms, Rhetorical Action, and the Eastern Enlargement of the European Union', *International Organization*, 55 (1): 47–80.

Schimmelfennig, F., Engert, S. and Knobel, H. (2003) 'Costs, Commitments, and Compliance: The Impact of EU Democratic Conditionality on Latvia, Slovakia, and Turkey', *Journal of Common Market Studies*, 41 (3): 495–517.

Sedelmeier, U. (2005) *Constructing the Path to Eastern Enlargement: The Uneven Policy Impact of EU Identity*, Manchester: Manchester University Press.

Sjursen, H. (2002) 'Why Expand? The Question of Legitimacy and Justification in the EU's Enlargement Policy', *Journal of Common Market Studies*, 40 (3): 491–513.

Smith, K. (1998) 'The Use of Political Conditionality in the EU's Relations with Third Countries: How Effective?', *European Foreign Affairs Review*, 3 (2): 253–74.

Smith, K. (2001) 'The EU, Human Rights and Relations with Third Countries: "Foreign Policy" with an Ethical Dimension?', in M. Light and K. Smith (eds) *Ethics and Foreign Policy*, Cambridge: Cambridge University Press, 185–203.

Smith, K. (2002) 'Conceptualising the EU's International Identity: *Sui Generis* or Following the Latest Trends?', paper presented at the ECPR European Union Politics Conference, Bordeaux.

Smith, K. (2003) *European Union Foreign Policy in a Changing World*, Cambridge: Polity Press.

Vachudova, M. (2001) 'The Leverage of International Institutions on Democratizing States: The European Union and Eastern Europe', RSCAS Working Paper 2001/33, Florence: European University Institute.

Wallace, W. (1996) *Opening the Door: The Enlargement of NATO and the European Union*, London: Centre for European Reform.

White, B. (2001) *Understanding European Foreign Policy*, Basingstoke: Palgrave.

Wiener, A. (1998) *'European' Citizenship Practice*, Boulder, CO: Westview Press.

Williams, A. (2000) 'Enlargement of the Union and Human Rights Conditionality: A Policy of Distinction?', *European Law Review*, 25 (6): 601–17.

8 The constraints on EU action as a 'norm exporter' in the Mediterranean

Stefania Panebianco

In asking what roles the European Union (EU) plays in international politics, this chapter explores the extent to which the EU can act as a norm exporter. In particular, the chapter asks whether the EU is able to promote the adoption of norms in defence of human rights and democracy (HRD) through regional co-operation. Is the EU so influential as to compel its partners to comply with EU HRD standards? The conceptualization of the EU's role as an exporter of norms to promote HRD in the Mediterranean, the performance of the EU's role within the framework of regional co-operation and the impact of the EU's role on Mediterranean non-member countries (henceforth Med countries) are the issues which will be addressed in this chapter.[1]

The conceptualization of the EU's role in international politics as HRD exporter is exemplified by the EU documents and treaty norms regulating EU foreign policy and relations with Med countries, where continued reference is made to the promotion of HRD. The EU assumes that the protection of HRD is a distinctive feature of EU external identity, and for this reason it has since the 1990s included the protection of human rights and the promotion of democratic procedures as a key component of EU foreign policy. The European Commission has contributed a lot to the creation of a linkage between economic development and political and social pluralism; in fact it assumes that a contagion effect can be produced through multidimensional co-operation and multilateral institution-building. However, in its relations with Med countries the EU acts as a 'gentle' power and its capacity to act as a normative power, to 'extend its norms into the international system' (Manners 2002: 241), is affected by a pragmatic approach which often prevails over a more idealistic desire to export principles and values through regional co-operation. Thus, the EU has an unimpressive performance as an 'external actor of democratization' (Huntington 1991) in the Mediterranean.

In the literature on EU international action, the EU has been regarded respectively as a 'civilian power' (Duchêne 1972), an 'actor' (Sjöstedt 1976), a 'presence' (Allen and Smith 1990, 1998), having a 'role' (Hill 1993, 1998), having an 'impact' (Ginsberg 2001) and as a 'normative power' (Manners 2002). This chapter enters into the debate about the nature of the EU as an international actor and provides some empirical evidence on EU relations with Med countries in order to explore the EU's ability to play the role of a norm exporter. The EU seeks to conduct an EU foreign policy aimed at exporting to other countries EU *principled* norms, that is, norms which derive from the principles which inspired the Union's creation: 'democracy, the rule of law, the universality and indivisibility of human rights and fundamental freedoms, respect for human dignity, equality and solidarity, and respect for the principles of the United Nations Charter and international law' (Article III-193 (1) of the Constitutional Treaty). Still, the EU's impact on Med countries' political systems and legislation has so far been meagre.

In this chapter, EU relations with Med countries will be revisited through analytical tools which combine the literature on the EU as an international actor with comparative analysis on democratization and regime transitions, in order to verify whether the EU is an international actor which pursues *principled* foreign action, and whether it can provide a regional co-operation framework able to promote democratization processes and improve human rights protection. A comparative analysis of respect for democracy and human rights in the Med countries (based on data from Freedom House surveys) suggests that the EU has not been able to produce any substantial diffusion of norms, values and principles to the Med Arab countries. In 10 years of co-operation within the Euro-Mediterranean Partnership (EMP) only small changes in the political systems of Med countries have been recorded. So far, local leaders of Med countries have allowed only minor political reforms and have tended to improve human rights standards and democratic practices only in so far as they believe it does not produce domestic instability.

Although HRD are repeatedly recalled in official documents and political discourses regulating both multilateral and bilateral co-operation, the EMP thus does not seem to be a regional co-operation framework suited to produce a 'contagion' effect (Whitehead 1996) and to bring Med countries to adopt EU norms in defence of HRD. The Med partners seem to adhere to the so-called Barcelona *acquis* – which relies largely upon the promotion of democratic principles and human rights via political declarations – but are reluctant to implement it. As the Turkish case reveals, the enlargement process (or just the promise of it) is a much more effective co-operation process through which to export EU norms and improve HRD standards. On the one hand, the adoption of the *acquis communautaire* (which can be regarded as the bulwark of the EU's complex of norms and principles) is an obligation for candidate members; on the other, the enlargement process provides candidate members with the necessary incentive to reform their political systems, to adopt democratic processes and to increase human rights standards. But this does not apply in the case of the Med countries, for which enlargement is excluded. Through the enlargement process the EU is able to impose on applicant countries domestic reforms to improve HRD;[2] the EMP, by contrast, is a less effective co-operation framework for the export of EU norms, since the EU has neither the political instruments nor the political will to impose political reforms on Med countries.

The hypothesis proposed here is that, despite EU claims to act as a 'norm exporter' in the Mediterranean, effective EU action is undermined by an EU institutional schizophrenia which derives from the different strategies followed by EU institutions to deal with other countries, and by the fact that the adoption of the Barcelona *acquis* is *de facto* based upon voluntary adherence, since non-adoption of norms agreed within the EMP framework is not sanctioned.

The EU's role in regional politics: EU relations with the Med countries

Since the early 1990s the EU has expressed its will to have a real Mediterranean policy.[3] With the launching of the Barcelona Process the EU tried to organize its relations with Med countries within a structured regional framework. In November 1995 the EU and 12 south Mediterranean countries[4] adopted the Barcelona Declaration and established the EMP, which is composed of the Political and Security Partnership, the Economic and Financial Partnership and the Partnership in Social, Cultural and Human Affairs. The ambitious goal set out in the Barcelona Declaration is 'to turn the Mediterranean basin into an area of dialogue, exchange and co-operation granting peace, stability and prosperity' (Barcelona Declaration 1995). To achieve this goal, the EMP institutional framework incorporates several levels of interaction: regular meetings at ministerial level, meetings of governments' experts, a Euro-Mediterranean Parliamentary Assembly and networks of civil society (Panebianco 2003: 6). This multi-layered system of regional co-operation was conceived to favour a contagion effect, as if a sort of 'learning' process could be produced through interaction and co-operation allowing the transfer of values and practices from the EU to partner countries.

The EMP is the result of a comprehensive approach to EU foreign policy which assumes as distinct but interrelated the following fundamental components: political and security co-operation, economic and financial co-operation, co-operation in social and human affairs. Following this threefold strategy of EU international action, the EU has adopted a Mediterranean policy that addresses not only the traditional trade and financial issues, but also a wide range of non-traditional political security issues such as migration, terrorism, social development, and cultural issues such as the inter-religious dialogue, racism, xenophobia. The change of nature of EU international action reflects broader systemic changes, which have expanded the concept of security to become comprehensive and multidimensional, a key feature of the global system where threats to security often have transnational origins and go beyond a purely military dimension. Viewed in this context, the EU has reacted to growing regional interdependence and strengthened its relations with the Med partners in order to find common solutions to common threats (Panebianco 2003: 4).

The basic assumption of the EMP is that economic development in EU partner countries cannot take place without taking into due account political instability and socio-economic disparities, deterioration of the environment, threats to security deriving from illegal migration, terrorism, organized crime and other such factors. The EMP reflects the linkage between political reforms, economic co-operation, the promotion of democracy and protection of human rights, which has been illustrated by the European Commission (2001a). In this approach there is an implicit presumption that poverty reduction can only be achieved with functioning democratic institutions and accountable governments, and that only democratic, pluralist governments respecting minority rights can lead to domestic stability.

How the EU portrays its role as norm exporter in the Mediterranean

EU political documents and treaty norms offer a useful means through which to conceptualize the EU's role in international politics. The EU depicts itself as a 'norm exporter', that is to say, an actor in international politics committed to promote norms in defence of HRD and defend values which are repeatedly emphasized as distinctive and constitutive elements of EU external identity. To express its commitment to conduct *principled* international action, the EU makes extensive use of 'declaratory measures' (Manners 2002: 248) to export EU norms, values and principles. A discourse and normative analysis reveals a strong EU political commitment to use regional co-operation as a means to transpose to Med countries the norms the EU itself has experienced in the political, economic and social fields of integration. Alongside economic liberalization and the rules of free markets, the Union's external action seeks to export to other countries the EU model of political development based upon democratic norms and practices, and human rights protection.

A useful starting point to illustrate how the EU constructs its international role as a norm exporter, and in particular HRD promoter, is the Laeken Declaration on the Future of Europe adopted by the European Council in December 2001. Here Europe's new role in a globalized world is defined as a 'stabilizing role worldwide', which has to be played by exporting the EU's 'humane values' including democracy, human rights and fundamental rights. A major step forward in the construction of the EU's international role is represented by the Constitutional Treaty, which despite its 'frozen' status since June 2005 – represents an explicit statement of such a role. First of all, HRD are recalled in the Preamble. Then, the Constitutional Treaty lists HRD among the Union's values (Article I-2). Finally, Title V on the Union's external action sets as the objectives of the EU common policies and actions to 'consolidate and support democracy, the rule of law, human rights and international law' (Article III-193/2b). Hence, democratic principles, minority rights, equal opportunities and solidarity – *inter alia* – are the values and principles the EU seeks to share with Third World countries.

The Barcelona Declaration, and the political documents which followed, contain explicit reference to democracy, human rights, fundamental freedoms, the rule of law, good governance, sustainable development and solidarity. It is very significant that Med countries subscribed to the Barcelona Declaration and formally signed up to the EU values and principles it contains. They also agreed to 'conduct a political dialogue to examine the most appropriate means and methods of implementing the principles adopted by the Barcelona Declaration' (Barcelona Declaration 1995). The Valencia Action Plan adopted by the Euro-Mediterranean Ministers of Foreign Affairs in April 2002 reaffirmed the commitment of the participants in the EMP to the institutional and value framework of the EMP.

In order to strengthen the principled approach to EU international relations, the European Commission in 2003 expressed the importance it attaches to HRD in relations with Med partners in a Communication to the Council and the European Parliament where it proposes the mainstreaming of human rights and democracy. The Commission reiterated the linkage between security, economic development, human rights and democracy, and stated that this linkage must be reflected in external policies because 'the promotion of democracy, the rule of law and the respect of Human Rights and fundamental freedoms constitutes one of the core objectives of the EU's external policies' (European Commission 2003: 2). The Commission recalled with satisfaction that all the documents adopted in the framework of the Barcelona Process (Presidency Conclusions to the Foreign Ministers' Meetings, Valencia Action Plan, EU Common Strategy on the Mediterranean, etc.) regularly reaffirm the joint commitment to promote human rights, fundamental freedoms and democracy.

However, the domestic political and socio-economic system which proved successful in Western Europe and which has been extended to Eastern Europe through the enlargement process cannot necessarily be easily exported to Med countries. The Med partners seem to express political adherence to principles which they do not translate into norms to be coherently implemented. And the EU cannot achieve its 'milieu goals'[5] if the inclusion of norms in support of HRD in the Euro-Mediterranean Association Agreements is not followed by close monitoring of norm implementation. This approach to EU international relations can be successfully applied only provided that third countries do not feel that 'a particular "model" of agreement [e.g. the Euro-Mediterranean Association Agreement], and regional links [e.g. the EMP], is imposed upon them from outside rather than emerging from their own priorities, choices and aims' (Cremona 2004: 561).

Moreover, EU partners have to be provided with attractive incentives to adopt EU norms. And the EMP does not seem to provide Med countries with such incentives. As it has been clearly stated in the European Neighbourhood Policy (ENP), the Arab countries can share with the EU *all but institutions* (Prodi 2002). Although EU membership is excluded, in the long run the EU can extend to the southern neighbours the four freedoms.

The ENP also stresses liberty, democracy, respect for human rights and fundamental freedoms as values the EU shares with its neighbours (Council *Conclusions*, 2003). However, the insistence on economic co-operation and the neighbours' participation in the EU internal market gives the impression that reference to political co-operation is destined to remain on the back burner. Economic liberalization and the establishment of free markets – which are also crucial EU values – seem to come before human rights and democratic principles. Another significant element of the newly adopted ENP is the fact that instead of offering substantial *new* funds, interoperability between the existing instruments (i.e. TACIS, MEDA) is envisaged. It is as if old wine had been poured into new bottles just to divert attention from the real problem of EU relations with the Med countries: the lack of EU resources to help enhance HRD in Med countries.

A critical evaluation of the EMP as a regional co-operation framework to promote human rights and democracy

In order to evaluate the performance of the EU's role as a norm exporter in the Mediterranean area, the following questions must be addressed. Is the EU able to influence regional norms? Is the EU able to transfer to its Mediterranean partners norms, principles and values which are depicted in the Constitutional Treaty as distinctly European? Does the EU have an impact on domestic legislation in Med countries? Empirical analysis shows that there is a big difference between the EU's political rhetoric and the reality of Med countries' political regimes, where HRD respect is improving very slowly (if at all). Before analysing in which Med countries political reforms have been adopted (see below), a critical evaluation of the EMP in general will help to clarify the disappointing performance of the EU as a HRD promoter.

Ten years have passed since the Barcelona Declaration was adopted (a lapse of time that can be termed the *Barcelona timeline*), but the achievements of the EMP so far seem quite controversial. Although the EU has offered a wide framework for co-operation within the EMP, co-operation has not progressed in all fields, and multilateral co-operation is lagging behind. In the Political and Security Partnership the adoption of the Charter on Peace and Stability in the Mediterranean has been frozen due to the critical political situation in the Middle East since the beginning of the second *intifada* in September 2000. The creation of a Euro-Mediterranean free trade area is proceeding slowly and the most recent documents refer to 2010 as a *target date*, almost implying that the 2010 deadline might not be met. On the other hand, the former Commissioner for External Relations, Chris Patten, welcomed the signing of the Agadir Agreement establishing a sub-regional free trade area between four Med countries only (Jordan, Egypt, Tunisia and Morocco) as a 'major step in the process of economic and social integration in the Arab Mediterranean world' (Patten 2004). As far as the promotion of HRD is concerned, data on the presence or absence of democratic institutions show that during the Barcelona timeline, Med countries have not progressed much with political and social reforms to meet EU HRD standards (see *infra* Table 8.2).

Bilateral co-operation is progressing with all Med countries, although at an uneven pace. New Euro-Mediterranean Association Agreements have been negotiated by all partners, demonstrating that economic and financial co-operation remains the primary incentive to regional co-operation (see Table 8.1). The negotiating process was quicker in the cases of Tunisia and Morocco, much longer for Algeria and Syria. But there is no empirical evidence that the implementation of the Euro-Mediterranean Agreements, which also include conditionality clauses, can improve HRD standards in Med countries. If we consider Tunisia, for instance, the Euro-Mediterranean Association Agreement has been in force since March 1998, but since 1995 no change has been registered as far as respect of political and civil liberties by the domestic regime is concerned (see Freedom House data in Table 8.2). The inclusion of the conditionality clause in the agreement seems to have had no deterrent effect on local political leaders, nor has the EU attempted to use conditionality so far.

Table 8.1 Pace of Euro-Mediterranean Association Agreement negotiations

Med countries	*Signature of the agreement*	*Agreement's entry into force*
Palestinian Authority	February 1997	July 1997
Tunisia	July 1995	March 1998
Morocco	February 1996	March 2000
Israel	November 1995	June 2000
Jordan	November 1997	May 2002
Egypt	June 2001	June 2004
Lebanon	June 2002	December 2004
Algeria	April 2002	–
Syria	October 2004	–

Explaining the limited impact of the EU as a norm exporter in the Mediterranean

The EU's difficulties in acting as a norm exporter in the Mediterranean are threefold. First of all, the adherence to the Barcelona *acquis* seems to rest upon a voluntary basis. The Barcelona Declaration is a politically binding document, not a juridical one. This leaves the contracting parties free to adhere to co-operation projects when and if they are interested in the single issue at stake. The EU seems to limit itself to a certain rhetoric in favour of political and democratic reforms and respect of human rights rather than directly sanctioning violations of democratic norms and human rights. Since the 1990s all EU agreements with third countries include 'human rights clauses', but so far there is no evidence of CFSP provisions adopted to react to cases of lack of good governance, democratic practices and values, and poor respect for human rights, which are still evident in Med countries.[6] Despite the political rhetoric, the EU avoids directly tackling the most controversial issues such as restrictions on the media, repression of dissent, unfair trials, etc., as if political change towards democratization might be potentially destabilizing (Youngs 2002).

Second, the effectiveness of EU democratization policies is weakened by the paucity of the funds allocated to these objectives. In the years 2002–04, the MEDA regional support envelope certainly did not privilege co-operation to strengthen democratization, good governance and the rule of law. Examining the financial breakdown by priority,[7] one finds that only €6 million (out of a total of €93 million) were devoted to enhancing the rule of law and good governance. The 'more advantaged' priority areas were instead: bringing the partnership closer to the people (€25 million); the sustainability of Euro-Mediterranean integration (environment, equal opportunities, education and training for employment: €20 million); regional infrastructures (€17 million); the EuroMed free-trade zone (€10 million). If one compares the emphasis the EU puts on initiatives to strengthen HRD with the amounts contained in these financial chapters, one gets a revealing picture of the EU aid offered to Med partners in these fields. Needless to say, these are puny allocations to cover such a wide range of initiatives. The mainstreaming of democracy and human rights envisaged by the Presidency Conclusions to the Euro-Mediterranean Conference of Ministers of Foreign Affairs (Naples, 2–3 December 2003) implies a need for much more extensive financial support.

Third, a comparison of EU institutions' attitudes shows a sort of institutional schizophrenia. Each institution has a different approach to Arab countries' (non)compliance with EU standards. The European Commission plays the role of a *policy entrepreneur*: it has a creative vision of external relations and seeks to elaborate innovative regional frameworks of co-operation which can produce a diffusion of EU HRD norms. The

European Commission not only frames new policies (e.g. the ENP), but also tries to reinvigorate them when progress is lacking (as the Commission did in 2000 when it adopted the Communication 'Reinvigorating the Barcelona Process') and indicates priorities. Moreover, the Commission favours a bottom-up approach and considers representatives of civil society as privileged actors of co-operation;[8] civil society has been singled out by the Commission as the best channel to implement EMP regional co-operation programmes (EuroMed Heritage, EuroMed Youth, EuroMed Audiovisual), or to set up networks such as Archimedes (Panebianco 2003: 17). The European Parliament, on the other hand, acts as a critical watchdog to denounce Med countries' violations of human rights and restrictions on individual freedoms, in particular through the adoption of the Annual Report on Human Rights in the World. In its 2003 report, the Parliament urged the Council to sanction human rights violations by Med partners and to act more coherently (European Parliament 2003). Finally, the Council follows a different strategy. It opts for a pragmatic approach, which is led primarily by political considerations; this implies acceptance of EU partners' weaknesses in the implementation of democratic reforms or of low human rights standards in EU partners. Despite EU official declarations, human rights violations and restrictions on fundamental rights are not sanctioned, as if EU member states did not want to destabilize Arab countries' governments.

Although the EU has expressed the desire to create a 'democratic regional community' (Whitehead 1996) which includes the south Mediterranean countries, there is a gap between EU declared objectives and the operational policies to achieve HRD promotion. Moreover, different strategies are envisaged at bilateral or regional level. The instrument which is included in the Euro-Mediterranean Agreements to promote democracy is conditionality, although it has never been practised. Within the EMP the EU has opted instead for a contagion effect produced within specialized networks or regional multi-level co-operation programmes. This ambivalence between the bilateral and the multilateral strategy weakens the coherence of the EU as a norm exporter.

The EU – perhaps naïvely – seems to assume that it is sufficient to create regional networks connecting specific sectors of society for democracy to spread, almost regardless of governmental approval or legislative reforms. This strategy is unlikely to prove successful, and Philippe Schmitter reminds us that the empirical research on regime transition indicates that 'these external efforts to penetrate civil society (and even to create a regional or global civil society) may have begun when the regime was still autocratic, but they rarely – if ever – seem to have contributed much to its demise' (Schmitter 1996: 41). Communication flows and regional networks are important ways to bring people together, but their impact upon democratization cannot be exaggerated, since local political leaders are the key actors in launching political reforms aimed at improving HRD standards. It seems that the EU does not possess the political leverage (or the political interest) to play a role in regional politics and export HRD at any costs by pressing political leaderships to proceed with reforms. Unfortunately, the result of this inconsistent institutional attitude is a low-profile EMP, which implements only a minor part of the goals originally set in Barcelona.

Liberalization without democratization in some Arab Med countries

Some conceptual clarification is required at this point to distinguish the reference to democracy, which is embedded in the political rhetoric of the EU, from more precise conceptual usages in political science. The EU reference to a 'democratization' policy clashes in fact with the widely accepted definition used by the democratization literature, which neatly distinguishes the initial liberalization process (the opening process of authoritarian regimes which usually starts with the granting of partial individual rights and freedoms) from the democratization process which can follow liberalization (the creation of substantial democratic institutions and real democratic processes requires the granting of full political and civil rights). Moreover, for the democratization process to be accomplished, the consolidation of the newly created democratic institutions and procedures is required. The transition process marks the passage from an authoritarian to a democratic regime and implies the creation of the political institutions required for democracy, but, without democratic consolidation, the newly created democratic institutions might collapse and lead to the installation of another authoritarian regime; only functioning democratic institutions, structures and norms can lead to a stable democratic regime. But this is not a linear process, because there is not an automatic progression from one phase to the other. The picture, then, is much more complicated than the Brussels discourse implies.

Since the early 1990s most Arab regimes have undergone important political changes: elections, multi-party systems, political and socio-economic pluralism (Brynen *et al.* 1998: 267). These political changes usually characterize the transition process, which in most cases allows for the passage from an authoritarian regime to democracy. However, this process seems to be much more advanced at the procedural than at the substantive level (Korany and Noble 1998: 7). The transition process from authoritarianism to democracy is not a linear process, and in Arab Med countries it has been subject to a stop–go pattern or even reversal. The limited reforms which have been adopted by some Arab Med countries are thus producing liberalization but not democratization. Elections are regularly held and human rights conventions are signed, but this is short of a real democratization process which implies also effective participation, party competition, pluralism and accountability. Despite the continuous reference to HRD, which features equally in EU and Arab political discourses, the Arab Med countries do not fulfil yet the minimum requirements of democracy, that is to say, to grant to their citizens (no longer subjects) at the same time universal suffrage; free, competitive, recurrent and correct elections; more than one political party; and alternative sources of information (Morlino 2003: 25). In most Arab countries the liberalization process has started, since some democratic institutions have been created. But elections, for instance, are far from being free, competitive, recurrent *and* correct. This has not yet produced genuine democratization and the EU emphasis on support to HRD has not favoured a real democratization process.

When assessing political change in the Arab world, the key issue is that in most cases 'these are changes *within* the authoritarian regime which fall short of bringing about a change *of* regime ... which thus ceases to be authoritarian and becomes democratic' (Hamladji 2002: 3). The overall picture is rather undemocratic: in the early 2000s Jordan experienced a deliberalization phase (Lucas 2003); in Egypt and Tunisia non-competitive presidential elections deprive this typical institution of democracy of its democratic essence; the Tunisian multi-party system dominated by a single party falls short of political pluralism; elections are not always procedurally correct (for example, the 2002 municipal election in Egypt). In some countries a certain degree of socio-economic and political pluralism exists, but meaningful political participation and accountability remain absent from the policy process. Governments fully accountable to the electorate are still missing even in Morocco and Jordan (the only two Arab Med countries which are regarded as 'partly free' by Freedom House), where the influence of the monarchy over the political and religious spheres remains overwhelming.

All these contradictions of the liberalization process have produced 'non-competitive electoral authoritarian regimes' as in Egypt (Levitsky and Way 2002: 52) and 'blocked transitions' as in Jordan. In sum, 'hybrid regimes' (Diamond 2002: 21) are more common than democratic regimes. Hybrid regimes have some formal aspects of democratic regimes such as elections, constitutions granting fundamental freedoms and political rights, but even then there are no real guarantees, for effective participation is limited, censorship prevents real freedom of expression (therefore dissent cannot be expressed), elections are not free and competitive, and multi-party systems are just a façade to defend the prerogatives of a dominant party. Hybrid regimes can thus be placed in the grey zone between authoritarian and democratic regimes (as in Figure 8.1). This suggests that the 'third wave' of democracy that has opened up so much of the world over the past 30 years (Huntington 1991) seems to have left the Arab Med countries untouched. Despite some ferment and some important instances of democratic opening, countries in the Middle East and North Africa have been resistant to democratization and human rights have stagnated (Karatnycky 2003: 101).

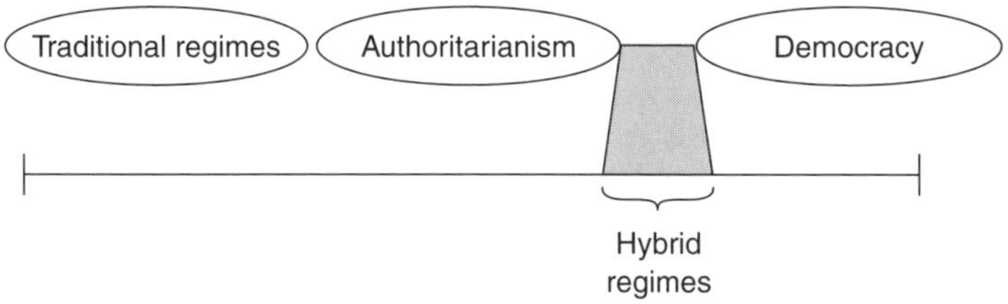

Figure 8.1 Hybrid regimes: between authoritarianism and democracy.

Moreover, the literature on democracy stresses something which is neglected by the EU approach: the EU impact upon the *timing* and the *nature* of the varied transitions from autocracy can be only marginal. It was limited in the 1970s for the change of regime in Spain, Portugal and Greece (Schmitter 1996: 33), and again in the 1990s in Central and East European countries, where governments reacted more to the collapse of the Soviet Union than to genuine democratic contagion from the EU. Notwithstanding the influence of the international context upon democratization processes (Whitehead 1996), the *timing, type* and *outcome* of democratization cannot be dictated or determined by the international political context, because the beginning of democratization is 'a domestic affair *par excellence*' (Schmitter 1996: 27). Domestic factors play a predominant role in the transition process. Once the transition starts, led by local actors, the EU can provide a co-operation framework helping the democratization process to succeed. But the EU cannot promote HRD in Med countries if the partners' domestic context is not receptive. This means that the EU cannot act as a 'prime mover' of regime change (Schmitter 1996: 27), since the change from one political regime to another is primarily an 'autochthonous political act' (Schmitter 1996: 26). Thus, the local political actors (be they newly emerged or existing 'enlightened' ones) must take the lead.

A comparative analysis of the presence or absence of democratic institutions in the Med countries[9]

The comparative analysis of change (or absence of change) in the political regimes of the Med countries summarized in Table 8.2 shows that the only Med country that experienced a consistent movement towards a democratic regime during the Barcelona timeline is Turkey, while the other Med countries have not significantly improved their HRD standards. This indicates that the EU's impact upon the constitutional reforms adopted in Turkey to comply with the requirements for enlargement has been consistent, while the EMP does not provide the EU with legal or political instruments to act as a norm exporter. Since the EMP does not

Table 8.2 Presence/absence of democratic institutions in the Med countries

Country	*Polity*	*Status*	*Political rights*		*Civil liberties*	
			2005	*Barcelona timeline*	*2005*	*Barcelona timeline*
Algeria	Dominant party	Not free	6	▲	5	▲
Egypt	Presidential dominant party	Not free	6	–	5	▲
Israel	Parliamentary democracy	Free	1	–	3	–
Jordan	Traditional monarchy and limited parliament	Partly free	5	▼	4	–
Lebanon	Presidential parliamentary	Not free	6	–	5	–
Libya	One-party presidential dictatorship	Not free	7	–	7	–
Morocco	Traditional monarchy and limited parliament	Partly free	5	–	4	▲
Syria	Dominant party	Not free	7	–	7	–
Tunisia	Presidential dominant party	Not free	6	–	5	–
Turkey	Presidential parliamentary democracy	Partly free	3	▲	3	▲
West Bank/Gaza	Military administered	Not free	5	–[a]	6	–[a]

Source: Freedom House data on freedom in the world in 2005 are available at www.freedomhouse.org.

Note
a Since 1997.

provide a framework for compliance with EU standards, it logically cannot be an effective instrument to promote HRD.

For many years the EU adopted a 'wait and see' position towards Turkey. Several European Councils had promised Turkey entry into the EU, but the enlargement process was repeatedly postponed because Turkish HRD standards were considered unsatisfactory. In the late 1990s Turkish political leaders launched a constitutional reform process to 'please' the EU and meet the Copenhagen criteria which have to be achieved in order to enter the EU. Lastly, in December 2004, the European Council accorded Turkey the status of candidate member and the accession negotiations started on 3 October 2005. The Turkish political system has been reformed via an elite-led gradual process of liberalization, which has involved all key institutions (the government, the parliament, the court of justice and the administration). In 1995 Turkey was scored five for both political rights and civil liberties on the Freedom House scale; in 2004 it was scored three for both political rights and civil liberties and can be regarded as a 'partly free' country. This reform process can be regarded as a result of the EU's insistence on democratic practices and human rights protection as minimum HRD standards to join the EU.

Jordan and Morocco can also be regarded as 'partly free' countries. But there is a big difference between their transition process, which is only experiencing its initial opening phase (they are both scored five in respect of political rights and four in respect of civil liberties), and the democratic transition which is almost accomplished in Turkey (scored 3/3). Since transition has stopped for a while (in Jordan), or is progressing slowly (in Morocco), they remain hybrid regimes in between authoritarianism and democracy. These countries experienced a transition process during which authoritarian regimes lost authoritarian characteristics and acquired democratic ones, but they are not yet democracies because they do not fulfil all the requirements of democracy as defined above. Moreover, the Jordanian experience proves that liberalization is not a straightforward process; on the contrary, it can be subject to reverse tendencies of deliberalization. During the Barcelona timeline Jordan experienced a reverse trend, and today (according to Freedom House) respect for political rights is still lower than in 1995. In the late 1980s Jordan experienced extraordinary steps towards political opening which at that time put the country in the forefront of liberalization in the Arab world (Lucas 2003: 137), but within one decade this liberalization trend had reversed. King Abdallah shifted to an authoritarian repressive policy to deal with the mass dissatisfaction of the late 1990s provoked by the domestic economic crisis, and by a Jordanian foreign policy regarded as too pro-Western. Following the eruption of the second *intifada* in 2000 and the US-led wars in Afghanistan and Iraq, public protests criticized the pro-Western stance of the Jordanian government and demanded the annulment of the 1994 Peace Treaty with Israel. The regime showed little tolerance of public opposition and reacted with a ban on demonstrations. In June 2001 the king dissolved the parliament and has repeatedly postponed parliamentary elections; for almost two years he governed by decrees and temporary laws, and freedom of expression and freedom of assembly were greatly restricted. Since 2003 the situation is improving.

Algeria, Egypt and Tunisia are 'not free' countries (all scored 6/5 respectively for political rights and civil liberties). These regimes can been regarded as 'electoral authoritarian regimes' (Levitsky and Way 2002), because they make use of some institutions of democracy (such as elections) to give the regime an appearance of democratic processes that in practice do not exist. Egypt and Tunisia remain two authoritarian regimes with strong Presidents, weak parliaments, a façade of multi-party elections and party rule, and elections that are not procedurally correct (irregularities remain systematic) nor competitive. The Tunisian case is probably the most interesting one. Although no domestic change has been registered in these ten years, Tunisia has always claimed to be in the forefront of co-operation with the EU both bilaterally (it was the first partner to sign a Euro-Mediterranean Agreement) and regionally within the EMP framework. But the political rhetoric of being close to Europe is not supported by reality.

Elsewhere in Arab Med countries no change at all is registered, and we also find in the Med two countries which are included by Freedom House among the eight countries with the lowest rating in the world. At the left extreme of the continuum illustrated in Figure 8.1, we can place one EMP member (Syria) and the EMP 'observer' Libya, 'not free' countries that scored seven on both political rights and civil rights.

To summarize, a decade of EMP co-operation has resulted in only limited changes in human rights standards and democracy practices in some Med countries. This comparative analysis therefore suggests that the EU has not succeeded in producing any major spread of EU values and principles to these states.

Conclusion

This chapter has analysed the EU's role as a norm exporter, and has particularly explored the EU's role as HRD promoter in relations with Med countries. The empirical analysis showed that, although the EU tends to consider HRD as distinct elements of its international identity and HRD promotion permeates the EU political rhetoric, the EU's promotion of HRD seems more part of political discourse than a priority of international action. The impact the EU has on Med countries in terms of normative influence remains weaker than might be expected.

The empirical analysis also indicates that, despite the suggestive idea of a linkage between political, economic and human dimensions allowing for sustainable development respectful of human rights and democratic processes, within the EMP the promotion of HRD seems a faded frame for economic co-operation. The Barcelona Process is not suited to the transfer of norms to other countries. As far as the transmission of norms is concerned, the difference between the enlargement process and the Barcelona Process is enormous. EU candidate countries have to adopt and implement *in toto* the *acquis communautaire* to join the EU, while the Barcelona Process is a completely different scheme of regional co-operation. The Turkish case is rather emblematic in this regard. The EU offered Turkey the 'carrot' of joining the EU, and at the same time it repeatedly used the 'stick' and sanctioned the Turks in respect of the Copenhagen principles. It thus appears that the enlargement process (or just the promise of it) induced Turkey to launch important reforms to adopt EU HRD standards before the accession process could start.

The Barcelona Declaration, the Euro-Mediterranean Association Agreements and political declarations adopted within the EMP express the support of all the Barcelona partners for HRD. Democratic principles and human rights protection have become part of the Barcelona *acquis* and no Arab government officially denies these principles. However, there is a big hiatus between official declarations by the governments (political rhetoric) and the way that democratic practices and human rights are implemented (domestic *Realpolitik*).

Ten years after the adoption of the Barcelona Declaration, the Med Arab countries seem to be interested in bilateral and economic co-operation but half-hearted in other areas of co-operation. The real interest of Med Arab countries is to proceed with economic co-operation; they have adhered formally to EU principles of democracy and human rights because the EU attaches so much importance to HRD, but they are far from implementing those principles at the domestic level. The political rhetoric and propaganda which are still so widespread on both sides of the Mediterranean are thus a challenge not only for political analysts, but also for politicians and practitioners. The EU cannot in the long run blindly accept that the leaders of Med countries adhere to common political documents and treaties and officially plead for democratic institutions which are only formally recognized or partially implemented. It could thus be argued that the EU should react to the disparity between political rhetoric and reality by strengthening the financial instruments to implement EU democratization policy and by setting up control instruments to verify compliance with the Barcelona *acquis*. The European Parliament has singled out sanctions as the instrument to be adopted to defend EU credibility. This might be a starting point for more effective EU support to democratic practices and human rights protection in non-member countries.

So far, in order to act as an HRD promoter the EU has preferred civil society to political leaders, but the bottom-up approach – if not supported by a top-down strategy led by domestic political actors – has proved to be an ineffective means of promoting political reforms leading to democracy.

The European Commission rightly seeks to strengthen pluralism, which is still limited in Med countries, as pluralism is a key element of democracy. The ultimate aim of the Commission's support for issue networks is to induce 'contagion', to help the process of 'learning' democratic practices and to allow democratization from below. Indeed, it is important to involve socio-economic actors in the process of democracy learning, but the political elites must also participate in the creation of the fundamentals of democracy.

Political reforms require – as in the Turkish case – a synergy of key political institutions. The involvement of political leaders is fundamental to create an individualistic society (or we might say a secular society) where the individual, not the state, is at the centre of politics (where society is the product of individuals and not vice versa), to offer citizens continuous information on governmental action, to guarantee transparency of the bureaucracy (instead of state secrecy), to allow the effective accountability of governments to the electorate. For these fundamental changes, a top-down strategy is essential. This implies that the role of civil society should be complemented by a comprehensive process of democracy-building favoured by all political actors, since democratic practices must be practised at all levels to produce real democratic change.

Notes

1 The definitions of 'role conceptions', 'role performances' and 'role impact' are drawn from Chapter 1 in this volume.

2 For more on the promotion of HRD through enlargement see Chapter 7 in this volume. See also the role of the EU as a 'magnet' for neighbour countries in Cremona (2004: 564).

3 On the EU emphasis on regional linkages and policies as an aspect of the Union's role as a 'stabilizer' in the neighbouring countries see Cremona (2004: 560).

4 The 12 south Mediterranean countries which adopted the Barcelona Declaration in 1995 are Morocco, Algeria, Tunisia, Egypt, Israel, Gaza/West Bank, Jordan, Lebanon, Syria, Malta, Cyprus and Turkey. The EMP has since changed towards a stronger Arab component of non-EU member countries. Following the 2004 enlargement, Cyprus and Malta have become EU members; in December 2004 Turkey acquired the status of accession candidate; Libya is an EMP observer partner and is also involved in the European Neighbourhood Policy adopted by the European Council in 2003. This group of Arab countries plus Israel has been identified as the 'southern neighbours', which are the recipient group of the EU actions on Human Rights and Democratization with Mediterranean partners (European Commission 2003: 3).

5 See the Introduction to this volume for the definition of EU 'milieu goals' as goals aiming to shape the environment in which the EU operates.

6 Negative CFSP provisions have been adopted by the Union against only one Med country: Libya (http://ue.eu.int/pesc/default.asp).

7 Cf. Euro-Med Partnership, *The Regional Strategy Paper 2002–2006 and Regional Indicative Programme.*

8 In the financial year 2000, 80 per cent of EIDHR funds were used through civil

society representatives (NGOs, professional associations, foundations, etc.) (European Commission 2001b: 25).

9 The Freedom House dataset has been reviewed to assess the presence/absence of democratic institutions in the Med countries. Freedom House monitors political rights and civil liberties around the world and publishes *The Annual Survey on Freedom in the World*, which is based upon two indicators of democracy: political rights (i.e. political parties can be formed freely, voters can choose among more than one party, party leaders can compete for positions of power in government) and civil liberties (respect for religious, ethnic, economic, linguistic, gender and family rights; personal freedoms; freedoms of the press, belief and association). The Freedom House Survey uses a seven-point scale ranging from 1 (the most free) to 7 (the least free). The country 'status' combines political rights and civil liberties scores as follows: countries whose ratings average 1–2.5 are regarded as *free*, countries whose ratings average 3–5.0 are *partly free*, countries whose ratings average 5.5–7 are *not free*. 'Partly free' countries display a limited respect for political rights and civil liberties; they often suffer from environments of corruption, a weak rule of law, single-party dominance. In 'not free' countries basic political rights are absent and basic civil liberties are widely and systematically denied.

References

Allen, D. and Smith, M. (1990) 'Western Europe's Presence in the International Contemporary Arena', *Review of International Studies*, 16 (1): 19–37.

Allen, D. and Smith, M. (1998) 'The European Union's Presence in the New European Security Order: Barrier, Facilitator or Manager?', in C. Rhodes (ed.) *The European Union in the World Community*, Boulder, CO: Lynne Rienner, 45–63.

Brynen, R., Korany, B. and Noble, P. (1998) 'Conclusion: Liberalization, Democratization, and Arab Experiences', in B. Korany, R. Brynen and P. Noble (eds) *Political Liberalization and Democratization in the Arab World*. II, *Comparative Experiences*, Boulder, CO: Lynne Rienner, 267–78.

Council of the European Union (2003) *Conclusions on Wider Europe–New Neighbourhood*, 18 June.

Cremona, M. (2004) 'The Union as Global Actor: Roles, Models and Identity', *Common Market Law Review*, 41 (2): 553–73.

Diamond, L. (2002) 'Thinking about Hybrid Regimes', *Journal of Democracy*, 13 (2): 21–35.

Duchêne, F. (1972) 'Europe's Role in World Peace', in R. Mayne (ed.) *Europe Tomorrow: Sixteen Europeans Look Ahead*, London: Fontana.

European Commission (2001a) *The European Union's Role in Promoting Human Rights and Democratization in Third Countries*, Communication from the Commission to the Council and the European Parliament, 8 May, COM (2001) 252 final.

European Commission (2001b) *European Initiative for Democracy and Human Rights Programming Document 2002–2004*, Commission Staff Working Document, Rev. 1 final, 20 December.

European Commission (2003) *Communication on Reinvigorating EU Actions on Human Rights and Democratisation with Mediterranean Partners*, COM (2003) 294 final, Brussels, 21 May.

European Parliament (2003) *Annual Report on Human Rights in the World in 2002*, Final Resolution, P5–TA(2003)0375.

Ginsberg, R. (2001) *The European Union in International Politics: Baptism by Fire*, Boulder, CO: Rowman & Littlefield.

Hamladji, N. (2002) *Do Political Dynamics Travel? Political Liberalization in the Arab World*, EUI Working Papers SPS 2002/11, Florence: European University Institute.

Hill, C. (1993) 'The Capability–Expectations Gap, or Conceptualizing Europe's International Role', *Journal of Common Market Studies*, 31 (3): 305–28.

Hill, C. (1998) 'Closing the Capabilities–Expectations Gap?', in J. Peterson and H. Sjursen (eds) *A Common Foreign Policy for Europe? Competing Visions of the CFSP*, London: Routledge, 18–38.

Huntington, S. (1991) *The Third Wave: Democratization in the Late Twentieth Century*, Norman, OK: University of Oklahoma Press.

Karatnycky, A. (2003) 'Liberty's Advances in a Troubled World', *Journal of Democracy*, 14 (1): 100–13.

Korany, B. and Noble, P. (1998) 'Introduction: Arab Liberalization and Democratization: The Dialectics of the General and the Specific', in B. Korany, R. Brynen and P. Noble (eds) *Political Liberalization and Democratization in the Arab World*. II, *Comparative Experiences*, Boulder, CO: Lynne Rienner, 1–10.

Levitsky, S. and Way, L. (2002) 'The Rise of Competitive Authoritarianism', *Journal of Democracy*, 13 (2): 51–65.

Lucas, R. (2003) 'Deliberalization in Jordan', *Journal of Democracy*, 14 (1): 137–44.

Manners, I. (2002) 'Normative Power Europe: A Contradiction in Terms?', *Journal of Common Market Studies*, 40 (2): 235–58.

Morlino, L. (2003) *Democrazie e democratizzazioni*, Bologna: Il Mulino.

Panebianco, S. (2003) 'The EuroMediterranean Partnership in Perspective: The Political and Institutional Context', in S. Panebianco (ed.) *A New Euro-Mediterranean Cultural Identity*, London: Frank Cass, 1–20.

Patten, C. (2004) *Speech on the Occasion of the Signature of the Agadir Agreement*, Speech/04/101, 25 February.

Prodi, R. (2002) *A Wider Europe: A Proximity Policy as the Key to Stability*, speech 02/619 delivered at Sixth ECSA World Conference, Brussels, 5–6 December.

Schmitter, P. (1996) 'The Influence of the International Context upon the Choice of National Institutions and Policies in Neo-democracies', in L. Whitehead (ed.) *The International Dimensions of Democratization*, Oxford: Oxford University Press, 26–54.

Sjöstedt, G. (1976) *The External Role of the European Community*, London: Saxon House.

Whitehead, L. (1996) 'The International Dimensions of Democratization', in L. Whitehead (ed.) *The International Dimensions of Democratization*, Oxford: Oxford University Press, 3–25.

Youngs, R. (2002) 'The European Union and Democracy Promotion in the Mediterranean: A New or Disingenuous Strategy?', in R. Gillespie and R. Youngs, *European Union and Democracy Promotion: The Case of North Africa*. Special issue of *Democratization*, 9 (1): 40–62.

9 The limits of proactive cosmopolitanism

The EU and Burma, Cuba and Zimbabwe

Karen E. Smith

A striking development in the European Union's foreign policy over the last decade or so is its growing role as a 'proactive cosmopolitan': the EU is attempting to create a consensus about liberal values and behaviour among diverse communities around the world. Until the end of the Cold War, the European Community took a much quieter approach to promoting political change, a function both of the tentative nature of foreign-policy co-operation at the time, and of a desire by member states not to emulate superpower and/or colonial politics. Now it is actively trying to export certain norms by, for example, promoting human rights and democracy in other countries.

This chapter analyses the EU's attempts to promote such norms in three geographically distant countries: Burma (Myanmar), Cuba and Zimbabwe. In distant countries, the EU's most powerful policy instrument – the conditional promise of membership – is of little use, although small developing countries can be quite dependent on the EU, so it can presumably wield considerable leverage. The three cases analysed here are all high-profile examples of EU proactive cosmopolitan activity; few other countries have been targeted as much. The EU has mostly used negative measures vis-à-vis all three countries (less so with Cuba) to try to force them to reform. Yet Burma, Cuba and Zimbabwe are still led by governments that are quite deliberately resisting this pressure. The EU has also tried to convince other international actors to back its policies, but again with little success.

The literature on international human rights pressure on third countries concentrates on explaining why third countries comply with human rights norms, rather than on why they violate those norms in spite of pressure (Cardenas 2004: 213–31). There are, however, several possible explanations for such violations. Realists argue that despite the fact that Northern/Western countries proclaim their rhetorical commitment to human rights, they do not consider it in their material interest to force compliance with human rights norms, so violators do not face damaging sanctions. Constructivists point out that countervailing norms – such as those of non-intervention – can 'protect' norm violators from international pressure. Domestic explanations include perceptions by violators that threats to national security require them to ignore human rights, or the dominance of pro-violation constituencies (Cardenas 2004: 219–26).

The last two reasons fit at least partially the three countries considered here (think, for example, of the threat Cuba perceives from the US), but given their relative weakness it is still surprising that pressure from outsiders such as the EU has had apparently little influence. This chapter thus considers how useful the realist and constructivist arguments are for explaining the limits of EU policy in these cases. The first section describes the development of the EU's role as a proactive cosmopolitan. The second analyses the EU's policies towards the three countries, and highlights the difficulties the EU has had in maintaining a consistent stance and the compromises that have resulted in weak lowest-common-denominator policies towards each of the three countries. The third section recounts the EU's attempts to convince other international actors to back its policies. Here again, the effort put into this varies. In addition, the extent to which third countries hold to the non-intervention norm has significantly limited the EU's proactive cosmopolitanism. Both realist and constructivist arguments are helpful here.

The EU as a proactive cosmopolitan

Since the end of the Cold War, the EU has been practising what Paul Taylor calls 'proactive cosmopolitanism', which is 'a deliberate attempt to create a consensus about values and behaviour – a cosmopolitan community – among diverse communities'. The EU – and other actors, such as the UN and individual states – have increasingly pushed 'the civil and political values of Western liberal states in other parts of the world' (Taylor 1999: 540). One example of this is the EU's promotion of human rights and democracy in third countries, which is considered an 'essential component' of the EU's foreign relations (European Union 1998).

The EU's role as a proactive cosmopolitan is new. During the Cold War, the European Community maintained a 'neutral' stance vis-à-vis the human rights and democracy records of third countries; development aid was supposed to be non-political, relations with the 'Third World' free of the vestiges of colonialism and distinct from the superpowers (Grilli 1993: 102). With the end of the Cold War, the Community (soon the EU) became much more assertive about exporting certain values and fostering political and economic change. The rhetorical commitment to human rights is strong, and is backed up with substantive, though not necessarily consistent, policies. The EU uses political conditionality alongside policy instruments of engagement such as dialogue and targeted aid. The EU has increasingly made 'benefits' – aid, trade concessions, political dialogue – conditional on the recipient protecting human rights and democratic principles, and threatened to cut them off if the conditions are violated.

The EU's role is partly the result of thinking that promoting human rights and democracy is a long-term security strategy: violations of human rights threaten security and stability within countries and between them, and democracies do not go to war with each other (Cremona 2004: 558–9). But it also reflects the belief, shared by the member states and EU institutions, that human rights and democracy *must* be promoted internationally, for their own sake. While the security rationale may loom large in policies to promote human rights and democracy in countries that are geographically close to the EU, it is less of a motivation in policies towards distant countries, though there is an increasing tendency to link all sorts of security concerns (from terrorism to organized crime to illegal immigration) to failed/failing states and norm violators – no matter how far away. But proactive cosmopolitanism in distant cases seems likely to stem mostly from a perceived responsibility to promote liberal values abroad, to foster a liberal international system. The EU's human rights policy would lose credibility and legitimacy if it ignored gross violations in distant countries. Its 2004 annual human rights report stated that the main objective of EU human rights policy is 'raising the level of human rights protection and promotion around the world' (Council of the European Union 2004b: 8).

But the EU's role is contested by third countries because it is seen as imperialist and self-serving rather than ethical and enlightened. The EU's practice of proactive cosmopolitanism clashes with the traditional norm of non-intervention, and 'interference' is still controversial in the developing world (Clapham 1999). The use of political conditionality is particularly contentious: while some governments and political activists appreciate the support it gives reformers, others resent it as an imposition of foreign values. The critics are aided by the inconsistent use of conditionality – which opens the EU to charges that it imposes conditionality only when its interests are not adversely affected.

For violations in some distant countries *are* ignored by the EU: the three countries here have attracted much EU attention, but other violators have not. Burma, Cuba and Zimbabwe have been targeted for two reasons: (1) their respect for human rights and democracy is indeed poor; (2) some member states have pushed for EU action. The last reason is crucial: EU action depends on member states' agreement; without it, some countries will not be targeted – though expecting the EU (or any actor) to act *everywhere* there are human rights violations is unrealistic. In addition, EU policy towards the three countries has been an uneasy compromise between condemning the violations and protecting national political and commercial interests. Its role as a proactive cosmopolitan is not translated into consistent and credible policy.

The EU's policies towards Burma, Cuba and Zimbabwe

None of the three countries has been subjected to full sanctions; instead, negative measures have been 'smart', targeted at the regime. This reflects doubts about the utility of full sanctions, but also allows member states to protect their commercial and/or political interests in the three countries. Not surprisingly, all three regimes have condemned the EU's negative measures; opposition leaders and dissidents have been far more welcoming of EU sanctions and have called for even tougher measures.

Burma/Myanmar

The EU first imposed limited sanctions on Burma in 1990, following the refusal of the military regime to honour the results of elections in 1990, which were won overwhelmingly by the democratic opposition led by Aung San Suu Kyi, the National League for Democracy (NLD). An arms embargo was imposed in 1990, defence co-operation was suspended in 1991, and all bilateral aid (except for humanitarian aid) was suspended the same year.[1] In 1996, a CFSP common position confirmed the existing sanctions, imposed a visa ban on members of the military and government, and suspended high-level governmental visits to the country (Council of the European Union 1996a). In March 1997, the Council suspended the Generalized System of Preferences (GSP) for Burma, because of the use of forced labour there. The CFSP common position was periodically renewed, and the negative measures were strengthened (for example, by freezing the assets of people subjected to the visa ban). The Council did not, however, impose trade sanctions or an investment ban on the country, despite such pressure from northern EU member states, Denmark, Ireland and the Netherlands (Youngs 2001: 139).

In April 2003, the Council consolidated all previous measures and expanded the list of people affected by the visa ban and asset freeze. In an attempt to mix carrots and sticks, it suspended the new measures until 29 October, but threatened to impose them on that date if there was no 'substantive progress towards national reconciliation, the restoration of a democratic order and greater respect for human rights' (Council of the European Union 2003b). When a convoy carrying Aung San Suu Kyi was attacked and she was detained again on 30 May, the Council imposed the measures early.

In September 2004, just before an Asia–Europe Meeting (ASEM) summit (see p. 165 below), the EU allowed Burma to attend the summit, but also threatened to tighten sanctions if certain demands, including Suu Kyi's release, were not met beforehand. They were not, and EU foreign ministers imposed more sanctions on 11 October. Those sanctions, for the first time, prohibit European companies from investing in some (not all) state-owned firms in Burma, but, after French pressure, do not apply to existing investments, which could be extended or prolonged (Dombey and Kazmin 2004).

The EU's negative measures have not had much impact on respect for human rights and democratic principles in Burma. In August 2003, the military regime issued a seven-step roadmap for political change and promised to hold a constitutional convention. But the NLD has not been allowed to take part in the convention, and Suu Kyi remains under house arrest. In October 2004, the junta replaced the prime minister with Lieutenant General Soe Win, a hard-liner who opposes freeing Suu Kyi and compromising with the NLD. Since then, there has been some reconsideration of EU strategy. In March 2005, External Relations Commissioner Benita Ferrero-Waldner stated that the EU would engage in a critical dialogue with the regime, to try to push it to reform (Kubosova 2005b). This does risk signalling, however, that a worsening of the political situation is 'rewarded' by the EU with an opening to dialogue, although it also illustrates EU frustration with the ineffectiveness of its negative measures.

Cuba

Of the three countries, Cuba has suffered the least from EU negative measures. It receives EU humanitarian and development aid (about €20 million in 2001; Roy 2003: 18) and is included in the GSP, and there are no barriers to trade between EU member states and Cuba, but it is the only Latin American country not to have concluded a co-operation agreement with the EU. Having lost its Soviet patron, Cuba has become more dependent on Europe: in 2001, two-thirds of its imports from developed countries came from the EU; almost 70 per cent of its development aid came from Europe; and European direct investment accounted for over 50 per cent of total foreign investment (Roy 2003: 2). In theory, then, the EU could exercise much leverage.

The EU's position – little official engagement but no limits to member state engagement – contrasts with that of the US, which has maintained an embargo on Cuba ever since Fidel Castro assumed power. In the mid-1990s, a US attempt to extend its sanctions extraterritorially, the Helms–Burton law, was opposed vigorously by the EU. Largely in response to the law but also at the behest of the conservative Spanish Prime Minister José Maria Aznar (whose attitude towards Cuba was more hard-line than the previous government's), the EU issued a CFSP Common Position on Cuba in December 1996. It declared 'that full co-operation with Cuba will depend upon improvements in human rights and political freedom', but noted that 'it is not European Union policy to try to bring about change by coercive measures with the effect of increasing the economic hardship of the Cuban people' (Council of the European Union 1996b).

EU policy has since been a mixture of engagement and light coercive measures. Cuba was invited to the first EU–Latin American summit in

June 1999 (and subsequent summits). But European support for a UN Commission on Human Rights resolution condemning Cuban human rights violations in April 2000 led Cuba to freeze its relations with the EU. Over the next two years, the EU periodically tried to reopen dialogue, succeeding by the end of 2002. At the same time, the Council encouraged development co-operation with Cuba, to promote reform and improve standards of living in the country (Roy 2003: 17). In March 2003, the European Commission opened an office in Havana.

EU member states were divided over whether Cuba should be allowed to join the Cotonou Agreement between the EU and African, Caribbean and Pacific (ACP) countries: some member states (Spain, France) argued that it would increase the EU's leverage over Cuba – because of Cotonou's provisions for political conditionality – while others (the UK, Sweden) opposed Cuban accession (*The Economist* 2003a). As Roy (2003: 3) notes, there was a north–south split here too, between 'blockers' (Finland, the Netherlands, Sweden and the UK) and 'openers' (France, Italy, Portugal and Spain).

In March 2003, Cuba arrested journalists and dissidents, and then executed three men who had tried to hi-jack a ferry to escape Cuba. This united the member states in opposition to the regime, though they did not take the drastic step of imposing economic sanctions. On 1 May, the EU froze Cuba's application to join Cotonou; in June, it imposed light diplomatic sanctions: it would limit bilateral high-level governmental visits; reduce the profile of member states' participation in cultural events; invite dissidents to national day celebrations; and re-evaluate the Common Position (Council of the European Union 2003c).

Castro reacted aggressively, leading protests outside the Spanish and Italian embassies in Havana (Spain had pushed for the sanctions; Italy had cut off some aid to Cuba), and imposing similar restrictions on cultural and diplomatic exchanges with EU countries (*The Economist* 2003b). He described the EU as a 'group of old colonial powers historically responsible for slave trafficking, looting and even the extermination of entire peoples' (*BBC News online* 2003a). In July, the EU condemned Cuba, but reaffirmed that 'constructive engagement remains the basis of the European Union's policy towards Cuba', and that political dialogue should be continued and development co-operation strengthened (General Affairs and External Relations Council 2003).

Over a year later, and after a socialist government won elections in Spain, the EU's position softened still further. In October 2004, Spain argued for resuming dialogue with the Cuban government. In January 2005, after months of debate, the foreign ministers suspended the diplomatic sanctions, and called for dialogue with both the government and the opposition. The EU's new position was not greeted warmly by dissidents (Beatty 2004a), and even within the EU, the Czech Republic and Poland resented the policy change (Kubosova 2005a): Cuba had not reformed enough to justify lifting the sanctions, although it had released some dissidents before the decision.

Zimbabwe

Zimbabwe's slide into autocratic rule became an issue for the EU only from the late 1990s, even though during that decade human rights and democracy became ever more important in the EU's relations with the ACP countries, which include Zimbabwe. But until 2001, the EU only expressed concern at developments, and took no action against Robert Mugabe's government.

Anticipating problems with the 2002 presidential elections, the UK led attempts to harden the EU's policy, and in June 2001 the EU Council pressed Zimbabwe to improve its human rights and democracy record and threatened 'appropriate measures' if it did not (Taylor and Williams 2002: 554–5; General Affairs Council 2001a). In October, the Council launched consultation procedures under Article 96 of the Cotonou Agreement.[2] The consultations, held in early January 2002, did not go well, but the EU member states were divided, with some southern member states favouring engagement, and northern states pushing for the imposition of tough measures (Council of the EU ACP Working Party 2002).

On 28 January, the Council threatened to implement targeted sanctions if Zimbabwe did not take immediate measures such as allowing the deployment of EU observers (General Affairs Council 2002). Zimbabwe still insisted that it would not allow in monitors from Sweden, Denmark, Finland, Germany, the Netherlands or the UK, whom it accused of favouring the opposition. Pierre Schori, the Swedish head of the election observation mission, was refused accreditation; when he entered the country anyway on a tourist visa, he was expelled on 16 February. This forced the EU's hand, and on 18 February the EU imposed sanctions and withdrew its electoral observers.

The EU suspended financial aid, imposed an arms embargo, banned 20 Zimbabwean officials, including Robert Mugabe, from entering or transiting through the territories of the EU member states, and froze their financial assets (Council of the European Union 2002b, c, d). The Zimbabwean government lambasted the EU, accusing it of imposing the observation mission on Zimbabwe (*BBC News online* 2002a). In July 2002, the EU extended its sanctions to cover more Zimbabwean officials.

The EU's rhetorically tough stance, however, was difficult to implement in practice. By late 2003, only £500,000 of Zimbabwean officials' assets had been found and frozen (Eaglesham 2003). The member states could grant exemptions to the travel ban, for example for officials attending international meetings. Mugabe himself attended a World Food Summit in Rome in June 2002, and Pope John Paul's funeral in Rome in April 2005. But above all the French invitation to Mugabe to attend a Franco-African summit in Paris on 19 February 2003 illustrated the limits of EU proactive cosmopolitanism. The EU's sanctions were due to be renewed on 18 February, and France threatened to veto their renewal if the other member states did not allow Mugabe into France. France claimed that the summit would discuss human rights and democracy, and was therefore a permissible exemption to the travel ban, but it seemed instead to be a French attempt to expand its influence in Africa.[3] Other member states – including Greece, Italy and Portugal – preferred engagement to isolation and argued that the sanctions only further entrenched the Mugabe regime (Perkins *et al.* 2003).

In the end, the Council renewed the sanctions and granted the travel exemption, but member states have even more leeway to grant exemptions, and if a member state objects to an exemption, then the Council may act by qualified majority to grant it anyway (Council of the European Union 2003a). Since 2003, the EU's attention has drifted away; sanctions have been renewed, but not strengthened or extended. None the less, the opposition Movement for Democratic Change has welcomed the renewal of the sanctions (*BBC News online* 2004). But Mugabe's government has taken further steps towards autocracy; in September 2004 it banned international human rights groups from working in Zimbabwe, and prohibited foreign funding to local democracy groups. In March 2005, the ruling party Zanu-PF 'won' clearly unfair parliamentary elections.

EU policies towards Burma, Cuba and Zimbabwe: a comparison

The EU's policies towards the three countries reveal several internal tensions: between southern and northern member states, between those in favour of engagement and those for exercising leverage, between member states balancing national commercial and political interests with concern for human rights and member states trying to uphold a more consistent proactive cosmopolitanism. The fault lines do not depend on the specifics of the case: 'engagers' want engagement with all three countries, though even their patience can be exhausted (as it was with Castro in 2003); 'leveragers' urge a harder stance towards all three. And engagers are not always the member states with the most at stake commercially: although France, Italy and Spain are often among the top EU traders with the three countries, so are Germany, the Netherlands and the UK.

The tensions are resolved in an uneasy and sometimes shifting compromise, and, inevitably, inconsistent policy-making as well as rather weak 'lowest common denominator' agreements. Because the 'old EU' is so divided, EU enlargement is not likely either to heal the tensions or to exacerbate them.

As realists would argue, the EU has not attached a high cost to non-compliance with human rights and democratic norms. Now, we may question whether stronger measures would effectively promote change within these distant countries,[4] but that is not the only reason why the EU has taken measures against them: they form part of the EU's objective of creating an international community based on the rule of law and respect for human rights. Ignoring the situation in these three countries is simply incompatible with that objective; even the engagers do not argue for that. Yet the very failure to stick to principled positions in these particular cases calls into question the EU's credibility as a proactive cosmopolitan in general.

The EU's multilateral approach

To an extent, the EU has also taken a multilateral approach, trying to convince other states and regional groupings to follow its policies. This is classic proactive cosmopolitanism, and in line with the EU's multilateral instincts. It is also wise, since although the EU is an important commercial and political reference point for the three countries, with the support of other actors, and especially the neighbours, its measures are likely to be considerably more effective.

One of the key outside actors is the US, whose policies towards all three countries are more coercive than the EU's. The US banned all imports from Burma in July 2003 (in addition to a visa ban on regime members), and had already banned new investment by US companies in 1997 (Bowers 2004). The US initially followed the EU's lead on Zimbabwe: it imposed visa restrictions on Zimbabwean officials in March 2002, and a year later strengthened economic sanctions on the country. In 2005, it signalled a tougher approach, labelling the country an 'outpost of tyranny'. On Cuba, there are obvious differences between US and EU policy, and the US has persistently pressed the EU to harden its policy towards Cuba. Cornered, the EU has little scope to influence US policy.

Building wider support for measures against the three countries is difficult. Action at the United Nations is hamstrung by the need for the Security Council's agreement (sanctions on Burma without Chinese concurrence are impossible), and by the support that developing countries have given to the three countries in the General Assembly and other fora, such as the Commission on Human Rights with respect to Zimbabwe. While UN executive organs (the Secretary General) or agencies (such as the International Labour Organization) may condemn the three countries, there is no consensus within the UN as a whole.

Then there are the countries' neighbours: with respect to Burma and Zimbabwe, the EU has tried to convince them to back its policy. The situation vis-à-vis Cuba is more complex: Latin American countries have been divided in their positions on Cuba, though resolutely opposed to the US embargo, which rules out a multilateral approach.

Cuba's neighbours

Declarations from various ministerial meetings and summits between the EU and Latin American groupings, such as Mercosur or the Andean Pact, do not mention Cuba at all. Nor do EU–Latin America summit declarations. But they do all prominently refer to human rights and democracy (see, for example, Declaration of Guadalajara 2004). In fact, arguably Latin America is the one developing region that most closely shares the liberal values promoted by the EU – at least since the spread of democracy (albeit shaky in some parts) there in the 1980s.

Latin American countries differ in their approaches to Cuba, but all oppose the US embargo. As a result, many are wary of appearing to 'side with' the US, and singling out Cuba for condemnation is thus problematic: Castro will often accuse his foreign critics – including the EU – of endorsing US policy. US policy thus limits EU (and Latin American) proactive cosmopolitanism in this case.

Burma's neighbours

The EU has not (yet) convinced Burma's neighbours to isolate the regime. Although the Association of South East Asian Nations (ASEAN) and its member states have occasionally expressed soft criticism of the regime, the EU has not been able to build a durable consensus about values and behaviour with South East Asian countries.

The EU's relationship with ASEAN (which dates from 1978) hit trouble in the 1990s over the Indonesian occupation of East Timor and ASEAN's decision to expand to include Burma (as well as Cambodia and Laos) in 1997. The EU refused to allow Burma to accede to an EC–ASEAN co-operation agreement, and in November 1997 it called off a senior officials' meeting because ASEAN insisted that Burma be a full observer at the meeting. Dialogue remained suspended for the next two years. In the meantime, in 1996, the Union launched the Asia–Europe meeting (ASEM) with most ASEAN member states (but not Burma, Cambodia and Laos), Japan, China and South Korea. ASEM was a convenient way to get around the tricky issue of dialogue with South East Asian states, since it excluded Burma.

With agreement on East Timorese autonomy in 1999, one of the major stumbling blocks in EU–ASEAN relations was removed. So the EU minimized the Burmese problem: it agreed to resume meetings with ASEAN even if they included Burma. In May 1999 senior officials met in Thailand; Burma attended but could not talk during formal sessions. In July 2000 the EU said that high-level talks with ASEAN would resume, and in January 2003 the Burmese foreign minister participated in an EU–ASEAN meeting on European territory. Richard Youngs argues that the opening to Burma was the result of an intra-EU deal: in return for southern EU member states agreeing to strengthen sanctions, northern states accepted a Burmese presence in EU meetings with ASEAN ministers (Youngs 2001: 139).

The issue of human rights and democracy in relations with South East Asia has long been a difficult one, illustrated in the 'Asian values' response to Western claims that 'universal' human rights should be respected. The EU has hesitated to counter Asian governments' resistance to protect human rights, and has assumed that economic development will have positive consequences for human rights (Crawford 2000: 106–7). In contrast to the African Union (see below), ASEAN has never made respect for human rights and democratic principles a key objective or norm of the organization. The fundamental principles – most notably that of non-interference – that are to be followed in relations between ASEAN member states prevent such 'domestic concerns' from being an issue. The international reaction to the renewed detention of Aung San Suu Kyi in 2003, however, forced ASEAN to respond. In June, ASEAN foreign ministers 'looked forward to the early lifting of restrictions placed on Daw Aung San Suu Kyi and the NLD members' (ASEAN 2003a: paragraph 18).

But there are few indications that ASEAN will back the EU's negative measures. In July 2003, Malaysia threatened to expel Burma from ASEAN, a proposal immediately rejected by Thailand. The same month, ASEM foreign ministers called for Suu Kyi's immediate release (ASEM 2003). In October 2003, at the ASEAN summit in Bali, Cambodia wanted to repeat the call (*BBC News online* 2003b), but the final statement did not criticize her detention, and even 'welcomed the recent positive developments in Myanmar . . . *The Leaders also agree that sanctions are not helpful in promoting peace and stability essential for democracy to take root*' (ASEAN 2003b: paragraph 25; emphasis added).

ASEAN has since backtracked from its limited criticism of Burma, and throughout 2004 relations between the EU and ASEAN have been rocky. Two meetings of ASEM finance ministers were cancelled because Asian countries insisted that Burma should participate in them and the EU refused. Controversy then swirled around the biannual ASEM summit, scheduled for 8–9 October 2004 in Hanoi. The EU sought to include its ten new member states in the meeting; ASEAN refused to allow this unless the EU allowed its three new members to participate. In September, EU foreign ministers agreed that Burma could attend the summit, but at a lower level than the other delegations (Council of the European Union 2004a). At the same time, it imposed additional sanctions on Burma (see above). Astonishingly, however, the chairman's statement on the ASEM summit mentioned human rights only once and democracy not at all, welcomed Burma's admission to ASEM, and, with respect to that country, declared only that the leaders encouraged the national reconciliation process and 'looked forward to the early lifting of restrictions places (*sic*) on political parties in accordance with the assurances given by Myanmar'

(Council of the European Union 2004c: paragraph 4.7). It did not even mention Suu Kyi, much less call for her release.

At ASEAN's annual summit in November 2004, there was no mention at all of Burma in the final declaration. Apparently officials admitted that ASEAN could not take effective action against Burma without Chinese support (Kazmin and Mallet 2004). China is indeed an important player, and the chances of convincing it to back human rights sanctions on Burma are slim. But ASEAN support for sanctions would, none the less, be extremely significant, since Asian countries *and* China are Burma's main trading partners.

As Amitav Acharya notes, the non-interference norm still enjoys considerable legitimacy in South East Asia, and there is no regional tradition of promoting human rights and democracy: 'ASEAN was founded as a grouping of illiberal regimes with no record of collectively promoting human rights and democratic governance.... The campaign by human rights activists against Burma failed because advocacy of human rights and democratic governance had no place in ASEAN, which did not specify a democratic political system as a criterion for membership' (Acharya 2004: 262–3). There have been cracks in this position, so that the non-interference norm may not be as robust in the future, but there is still considerable resistance to the EU's stance on Burma. Yet the EU has also not pressed ASEAN very hard for support, to try to widen those cracks: instead ASEAN is succeeding in softening the EU's stance. The EU caved in to ASEAN pressure on Burmese participation in ASEM and to Asian reluctance to criticize Suu Kyi's continued detention, and in 2005 moved towards opening dialogue directly with the Burmese regime.

Zimbabwe's neighbours

In contrast to ASEAN, African countries have paid at least lip service to liberal values. The constitutive act of the African Union, agreed in July 2000, declares that its objectives include the promotion of democratic principles and institutions, and of human rights (African Union: Article 3). Governments which come to power through unconstitutional means will not be allowed to participate in AU activities (Article 30). In July 2001, African countries approved a 'New Partnership for Africa's Development' (NEPAD). NEPAD is essentially a trade-off: to attract foreign investment and aid, African countries will implement principles of democracy and good political, economic and corporate governance, and protect human rights. A voluntary peer review mechanism will promote adherence to NEPAD principles. The EU thus had good reason to believe that African countries would support its measures against a country that was manifestly not adhering to NEPAD principles. In practice, however, they have not been convinced to do so.

The EU has been keen to co-operate with the Southern African Development Community (SADC) on Zimbabwe (see General Affairs Council 2001b). And in October 2001, it began an informal dialogue with Nigeria, South Africa and Malawi on the Zimbabwe crisis (Council of the EU, ACP Working Party 2001). But the EU's imposition of sanctions in 2002 was not welcomed in the region. African countries, including South Africa and Nigeria, criticized the move, and Nigerian President Olusegun Obasanjo even declared that Mugabe was not abusing democratic principles (*BBC News online* 2002b). In March 2002, the EU introduced a draft resolution expressing concern about Zimbabwe to the UN Commission on Human Rights (CHR). Nigeria, on behalf of the Africa Group, tabled a no-action motion on the resolution, which was carried by the CHR. Nigeria argued that human rights could be resolved in Zimbabwe only if the land question was solved; other developing countries – including China, Cuba and Algeria – pointed to the legacy of colonialism as the root cause of human rights problems in the country (European Commission 2002: 62). A year later, they again blocked an EU-sponsored resolution on Zimbabwe at the CHR. An EU–Africa summit, scheduled for April 2003, has been postponed indefinitely because several EU member states (led by the UK) refuse to allow Mugabe to attend, while several African leaders will not attend if Mugabe does not (Black 2003).

According to the 2003 Greek presidency, the EU seeks to encourage 'African solutions to African problems' (Beatty 2003). Yet in fall 2004, Morgan Tzvangerai, the leader of the opposition Movement for Democratic Change, urged the EU to tighten its measures on Zimbabwe, and to press South Africa and Nigeria to do more to isolate Zimbabwe (Beatty 2004b). There have been cracks in the position on non-interference: in August 2004, SADC agreed to new electoral standards and pressed for Zimbabwe to comply with them in the March 2005 parliamentary elections (Muleya 2004); South Africa's ANC party publicly called for Zimbabwe to adhere to the standards. But in March 2004, African countries again allied with Asian countries to stymie the EU's resolution condemning Zimbabwe in the CHR; in the face of such opposition, in March 2005 the EU dropped the resolution, sending an unfortunate signal in the wake of the rigged parliamentary elections. South African President Thabo Mbeki tolerates Mugabe, and South Africa (and SADC) even welcomed the results of those parliamentary elections and declared them to be free and fair.

The EU's proactive cosmopolitanism extends beyond its attempts to enforce respect for human rights and democracy in particular target countries; it has been trying to garner wider support for its policies, though with varying degrees of effort. Paradoxically, Latin America largely shares the EU's values yet the issue of Cuba is kept off of the collective diplomatic agenda principally because no one wants to appear to back the US embargo. With Africa and Asia, the values that the EU are exporting are not fully accepted, even though there may be rhetoric which indicates otherwise. There is norm collision here: the non-intervention norm is strongly held, and regional groupings (ASEAN, SADC, AU) allow countries to better contest EU interference. But the EU has also not actively challenged the attachment to this countervailing norm – apparently preferring to devolve some of this task to regional actors, who may or may not take it up.

Conclusion

It is of course unreasonable to attribute the non-respect of democracy and human rights in Burma, Cuba and Zimbabwe to EU failings alone, and even to expect that 'better' EU policy would generate fundamental political change on the ground. Outsiders, after all, have considerably less influence on events within a country than do domestic actors. None the less, they can have *some* influence, particularly given the realities of interdependence. The three cases here illustrate the limits of the EU's role as a proactive cosmopolitan, and realist and, to a more limited extent, constructivist arguments help explain why. The EU's bilateral relations with each of the three show a tendency to formulate lowest-common-denominator and rather inconsistent policies, indicating that the EU member states cannot agree to impose far-reaching sanctions that might damage their own material interests (be they commercial or political). The EU's multilateral policies vis-à-vis the neighbours show similar inconsistencies, though US policy has had a constraining effect on EU and Latin American policies towards Cuba. But, as the constructivists point out, the clash of norms has limited EU influence in Africa and Asia.

If the EU is to be serious about playing the role of proactive cosmopolitan, then it must address these problems, but of inconsistency above all: taking a principled stance and then backtracking on it fundamentally damages the credibility and legitimacy of its role. As R. J. Vincent noted:

> finding its place in the empire of circumstance is more damaging to human rights policy than it might be to other items of foreign policy, because it can be argued that it is on the substance and appearance of even-handedness that a successful human rights policy depends.
>
> (Vincent 1989: 58)

Even-handedness is simply not apparent in these three cases. Quite possibly, if it were, the EU might find it easier to build a broader consensus about how to deal with violators of human rights and democratic principles. As it stands now, the EU's role as a proactive cosmopolitan is clearly not an all-encompassing one or consistent with EU foreign policy in practice.

Notes

1 Since 1995 the EU has also sponsored a resolution on Myanmar at the UN Commission on Human Rights (CHR), which has always been passed by the CHR.
2 Under Article 96, a party can call for consultations if it considers that the other party has failed to fulfil an obligation with respect to human rights, democratic principles and the rule of law. If consultations do not result in progress on these obligations, then appropriate measures can be taken.
3 French officials admitted that if Mugabe had not been allowed to come, several other African leaders would not have attended, and that would have been a failure for French policy towards Africa (Graham 2003).
4 We could also ask whether policies based mostly on engagement/dialogue would be more effective. Yet the EU's 'critical human rights dialogues' with China and Iran have so far not produced much domestic change in those countries either.

References

Acharya, A. (2004) 'How Ideas Spread: Whose Norms Matter? Norm Localization and Institutional Change in Asian Regionalism', *International Organization*, 58 (2).

African Union, 'The Constitutive Act', http://www.africa-union.org/About_AU/AbConstitutive-Act.htm.

ASEAN (2003a) 'Joint Communique of the Thirty-sixth ASEAN Ministerial Meeting', Phnom Penh, 16–17 June, http://www.aseansec.org/14834.htm.

ASEAN (2003b) 'Press Statement by the Chairperson of the Ninth ASEAN Summit and the Seventh ASEAN + 3 Summit, Bali, Indonesia, 7 October 2003', http://www.aseansec.org/15260.htm.

ASEM (2003) 'The Fifth ASEM Foreign Ministers' Meeting, Bali, Indonesia, 22–24 July 2003, Chair's Statement', issued 24 July.

BBC News online (2002a) 'EU Agrees Zimbabwe Sanctions', 18 February (news.bbc.co.uk).

BBC News online (2002b) 'EU Sanctions Move "Baffles" African Nations', 19 February.

BBC News online (2003a) 'EU Unfazed by Castro Rebuff', 28 July.

BBC News online (2003b) 'Burma in for Rough Ride at Summit', 6 October.

BBC News online (2004) 'Zimbabwe Sanctions Extended by EU', 23 February.

Beatty, A. (2003) 'Anger at "Non-action" on Zimbabwe', *EUObserver.com*, 5 June.

Beatty, A. (2004a) 'Diplomats Asked to Revise Ties with Cuban Opposition', *EUObserver.com*, 17 November.

Beatty, A. (2004b) 'Zimbabwe Opposition Urges EU Pressure ahead of Elections', *EUObserver.com*, 23 November.

Black, I. (2003) 'Disarray over Mugabe Forces EU to Delay Summit', *Guardian*, 15 February.

Bowers, P. (2004) *Burma*, House of Commons Research Paper 04/16, 23 February.

Cardenas, S. (2004) 'Norm Collision: Explaining the Effects of International Human Rights Pressure on State Behaviour', *International Studies Review*, 6 (2).

Clapham, C. (1999) 'Sovereignty and the Third World State', *Political Studies*, 47 (3).

Council of the European Union (1996a) 'Common Position 96/635/CFSP of 28 October 1996 on Burma/Myanmar', *Official Journal of the European Communities* (hereinafter OJ) L 287, 8 November.

Council of the European Union (1996b) 'Common Position 96/697/CFSP of 2 December 1996 on Cuba', OJ L 322, 12 December.

Council of the European Union (2002a) 'Consultations with the ACP Side concerning Zimbabwe pursuant to Article 96 of the Cotonou Agreement', press release 5243/02 (Presse 4), 11 January.

Council of the European Union (2002b) 'Council Decision of 18 February 2002 concluding Consultations with Zimbabwe under Article 96 of the ACP–EC Partnership Agreement (2002/148/EC)', OJ L 50, 21 February.

Council of the European Union (2002c) 'Council Common Position of 18 February 2002 concerning Restrictive Measures against Zimbabwe (2002/145/CFSP)', OJ L 50, 21 February.

Council of the European Union (2002d) 'Council Regulation (EC) No. 310/2002 of 18 February 2002 concerning certain Restrictive Measures in respect of Zimbabwe', OJ L 50, 21 February.

Council of the European Union (2003a) 'Council Common Position 2003/115/CFSP of 18 February 2003 amending and extending Common Position 2002/145/CFSP concerning Restrictive Measures against Zimbabwe', OJ L 46, 20 February.

Council of the European Union (2003b) 'Council Common Position 2003/297/CFSP of 28 April 2003 on Burma/Myanmar', OJ L 106, 29 April.

Council of the European Union (2003c) 'Declaration by the Presidency, on behalf of the European Union, on Cuba', press release 9961/03 (Presse 157), 5 June.

Council of the European Union (2004a) 'ASEM – Council Conclusions', press release 12068/04 (Presse 251), 13 September.

Council of the European Union (2004b) 'EU Annual Report on Human Rights 2004', 13 September (Luxembourg: OOPEC, 2004).

Council of the European Union (2004c) 'Chairman's Statement of the fifth Asia–Europe Meeting, Hanoi, 8–9 October 2004', document 12895/04 (Presse 280), 10 October.

Council of the European Union, ACP Working Party (2001) 'Letter to Representatives of SADC and Abuja Partners concerning Zimbabwe', document 14602/01, 28 November.

Council of the European Union, ACP Working Party (2002) 'Zimbabwe: Consultations under Article 96 of the Cotonou Agreement', document 5533/02, 21 January.

Crawford, G. (2000) 'European Union Development Co-operation and the Promotion of Democracy', in P. Burnell (ed.) *Democracy Assistance: International Co-operation for Democratization*, London: Frank Cass.

Cremona, M. (2004) 'The Union as a Global Actor: Roles, Models and Identity', *Common Market Law Review*, 41 (2).

Declaration of Guadalajara (2004) Third EU–Latin American and Caribbean Summit, Guadalajara, Mexico, 29 May.

Dombey, D. and Kazmin, A. (2004) 'EU Dilutes Sanctions Plan on Burma', *Financial Times*, 9–10 October.

Eaglesham, J. (2003) 'Blair Seeks Tougher Measures on Zimbabwe', *Financial Times*, 10 December.

The Economist (2003a) 'Cuba and the EU: Wary Partners', 15 March.

The Economist (2003b) 'Cuba's Cocktail-party War: no eating my canapés any more', 21 June.

European Commission (2002) 'Overview of the Fifty-eighth Session of the United Nations Commission on Human Rights, 18 March–26 April 2002', available at http://www.europa.eu.int/comm/external_relations/human_rights/doc/uncom 58.pdf.

European Union (1998) 'European Union Statement on Human Rights', *EU Bulletin*, No. 12.

General Affairs Council (2001a) 'Conclusions on Zimbabwe', press release 10228/01 (Presse 250), 25 June.

General Affairs Council (2001b) 'Conclusions on Zimbabwe', press release 12391/01 (Presse 390), 29–30 October.

General Affairs Council (2002) 'Council Conclusions – Zimbabwe', press release 5636/02 (Presse 16–G), 28 January.

General Affairs and External Relations Council (2003) 'Re-evaluation of the EU Common Position on Cuba – Council Conclusions', press release 11439/1/03/REV 1 (Presse 209), 21 July.

Graham, R. (2003) 'Chirac seeks to widen French role in Africa', *Financial Times*, 20 February.

Grilli, E. (1993) *The European Community and the Developing Countries*, Cambridge: Cambridge University Press.

Kazmin, A. and Mallet, V. (2004) 'Asean abandons move to censure Burma over human rights abuses', *Financial Times*, 30 November.

Kubosova, L. (2005a) 'EU lifts sanctions on Cuba', *EUObserver.com*, 1 February 2005.

Kubosova, L. (2005b) 'EU shifts its strategy towards Burma', *EUObserver.com*, 11 March 2005.

Muleya, D. (2004) 'SADC Corners Mugabe', *Zimbabwe Independent*, 20 August, www.allAfrica.com.

Perkins, A., Black, I., Henley, J. and Meldrum, A. (2003) 'UK moves to limit damage over invitation to Mugabe', *Guardian*, 24 January.

Roy, J. (2003) 'The European Union Perception of Cuba: From Frustration to Irritation', Institut Universitari d'Estudis Europeus, Observatori de Política Exterior Europea, Working Paper 47, Barcelona, May.

Taylor, I. and Williams, P. (2002) 'The Limits of Engagement: British Foreign Policy and the Crisis in Zimbabwe', *International Affairs*, 78 (3).

Taylor, P. (1999) 'The United Nations in the 1990s: Proactive Cosmopolitanism and the Issue of Sovereignty', *Political Studies*, 47 (3).

Vincent, R. J. (1989) 'Human Rights in Foreign Policy', in D. Hill (ed.) *Human Rights and Foreign Policy: Principles and Practice*, Basingstoke: Macmillan.

Youngs, R. (2001) *The European Union and the Promotion of Democracy: Europe's Mediterranean and Asian Policies*, Oxford: Oxford University Press.

10 Proactive policy entrepreneur or risk minimizer?

A principal–agent interpretation of the EU's role in the WTO

Bart Kerremans

As is well known, the European Union (EU) forms an important trading bloc – with potentially an impressive amount of market power – in the world trading system and *a fortiori* in the World Trade Organization.[1] Its ability to transform this potential market power into effective power depends on its ability to cope with its internal diversity. In itself, this is not a remarkable observation, as every member of the WTO has to cope with internal diversity one way or the other. In the EU, however, this internal diversity translates itself into internal institutional fragmentation and this in both a horizontal and a vertical way.

The former – horizontal fragmentation – concerns the interaction among a number of EU institutions, each with its own powers and resources. The resulting system of checks and balances potentially weakens the EU's capacity to play a proactive role in the WTO, as, by definition, the hands of the one who represents the EU in the WTO will be tied. Those hands can be loosely or tightly tied, but tied they always are to a certain extent. Still, this characteristic does not distinguish the EU from other players in the WTO. Plenty of them operate with a system of internal checks and balances. What distinguishes the EU (and a limited number of its WTO counterparts) is its internal vertical fragmentation. Two government levels – each with substantial resources and substantial powers – coexist. Ultimately, the lower (i.e. national) level needs to approve what the higher level (the EU) agrees to in the WTO. WTO agreements negotiated by the Commission need to be approved by the member states (either through the Council, or through a combination of member states' and Council approval). What the Commission can do, or cannot do, is thus affected by the transfer of instructions from the domestic political systems of the member states, via their representatives in the Council, to the Commission. Derivatively, the same holds for the role the EU is able to play in the WTO, be it proactive or reactive. It is in this way that the EU's potential role in the WTO is affected by the multi-level nature of its political system.

This way of analysing the EU's role in the WTO is far from complete, however. One important dimension is missing. Instructions may be relative in significance. Representatives may exploit the opportunities of their representational role and the resulting informational asymmetries. It is here that principal–agent analysis enters the picture. Indeed, the agents may be able (and even eager) not to closely abide by the instructions of their principals (i.e. those they are supposed to represent), and thus to engage in autonomous action. They may have different reasons to do so, and divergent abilities too.

Some of these reasons and abilities may be related to the internal characteristics of the agent, including his/her preferences, and resources. Others may be due to the external negotiating context, which may create its own imperatives and opportunities for autonomous action. The Commission cannot determine what happens in the WTO. It needs to operate in a context where rules and counterparts affect its room for manoeuvre. But opportunities and constraints for autonomous action may emerge because of that. In this chapter, the focus will be on the abilities and constraints of the Commission in the WTO, as these may tell us a lot about the role the EU is able to play through the Commission, the institution that negotiates on its behalf. The following elements will be used to analyse this: the principal–agent relationship between the Commission and the member states, and the constraints and opportunities provided by the WTO. An illustration of the dynamics of these elements will be provided by the way in which the Commission approached the on-going negotiations on the Doha Development Agenda (DDA) in the WTO, at least until the Cancun Ministerial in September 2003.

Principal–agent analysis and the EU's decision-making on external trade

As has been indicated above, principal–agent analysis highlights the reasons why an agent who is supposed to represent a principal (or a range of principals) may wish to act autonomously on the one hand, and may be able to do so, on the other hand. Central in the relationship between the principal and the agent is the act of delegation by which the principal enables the agent to act on its behalf. This act is closely related to an act of control by which the principal wants to increase the probability that the agent will act in a way that warrants the former's interests. In this sense, both the act of delegation and the act(s) of control are intended to enable the principal to achieve benefits that are larger than the benefits it would reap by acting itself and on its own, given the cost that delegation entails (cf. Epstein and O'Halloran 1999: 7; Majone 2001: 103). What is warranted then is a theory of delegation that explains why principals delegate in the first place, and a theory of control. The latter needs to explain why principals engage in control, and the way in which they do so. Both theories need to be applicable in the context of the EU's external trade policy, as the purpose is to explain delegation and control in the context of WTO negotiations.

A theory of delegation

Several reasons have been put forward to explain delegation by principals. Among them are enabling credible regulation, overcoming incomplete contracting, enabling compliance monitoring, and avoiding cycling problems in coalition-formation on policies (Pollack 2003: 20–5). In the area of the EU's external trade policy, two of them stand out as possible building blocks for a theory of delegation, be it in a slightly adapted way: enabling credible representation on the one hand, and dealing with incomplete contracting on the other hand.

The first building block consists of credible representation, which is the strongest factor explaining delegation here. By delegating a number of trade negotiating powers to an agent like the European Commission, the member states provide not only for their representation in international trade negotiations but for the credibility of that representation too. This credibility pressurizes the EU's negotiating partners to recognize it as a single actor in the international trading system, and thus to take the EU's joint market power seriously (cf. Jupille and Caporaso 1998: 215–16).

The second building block consists of incomplete contracting. It refers here to the fact that the member states, when creating the EU and when deciding about its policies, could not take all the external consequences of their actions into account. They needed to provide for a system, then, that enabled them to deal with these in a more or less efficient way on the one hand, and in a way that preserves the benefits of the original endeavour, i.e. the commonality of the *acquis communautaire* and the EU's legal order, on the other hand. There are two elements here. The first concerns the fact that the EU's internal *acquis* often requires it to deal with third countries too, often (but not only) in response to demands from countries affected by the *acquis*. Second, the fact that the EU as it exists today legally incapacitates the member states to conduct an external trade policy on their own, or at least to a large extent.

The latter element refers to the exclusive nature of a large part of the EU's competences on external trade, be it either as a consequence of explicitly attributed powers or of implied powers derived from internal competences. It is important to notice, however – as Young (2000, 2003) does – that variation exists in the extent to which the EC enjoys exclusive powers on trade and that this has serious ramifications for the games that are being played in this area (two-level or three-level games). From the perspective of delegation, it means that variation exists in the relationship between delegation and the ability to negotiate externally. In the absence of exclusive competences (thus in the presence of shared competences), member states can still act separately, and do not need to take the decision to act jointly and thus to delegate negotiating power to the Commission. They may feel the need to do so whenever the benefits of cooperation through delegation exceed their costs, but they don't have to.

In the case of exclusive competences, be they explicit or implied, the member states have no alternative. For all issues covered by these competences, each of them is legally incapacitated to negotiate separately with third countries. Together, they need to act through the community system if they want to negotiate with third countries on such issues. The stronger the need to negotiate externally, the higher the probability that delegation to the Commission will take place and thus, the higher the chance that agency losses will be incurred.

Agency losses refer to the fact that principals who delegate authority may not be able to act against an agent that is either not pursuing their interests to the extent that they want it to, or that even acts against their interests. A distinction can be made between slippage and shirking. The former refers to a situation where an agent is confronted with a delegation that is structured in such a way that it contains incentives to engage in agency slack. The latter stresses the opportunism of the agent. Without being incited to engage in agency slack, the agent does so. The distinction between these two is not always sharp. What is the definition of a situation in which the Commission exceeds the negotiating directives that the Council may have defined? It could be slippage, as a narrow negotiating mandate may make it impossible for the Commission to really negotiate with the EU's external partners. This may be seen as an incentive to slip into concessions not permitted by the directives. But it could also be interpreted as shirking, as the Commission could have been expected to convince its external partners to agree with an agreement that falls within the limits of the Council's negotiating directives. If that is the interpretation, the Commission could be blamed for opportunistically exceeding the negotiating directives.

The agent's preferences

In trying to distinguish between slippage and shirking, the question of the agent's motives to engage in agency slack shows up. This certainly needs to be questioned in cases of shirking. In such cases, only the agent's own motives matter and these may be based on substantive policy interests, moral convictions or competence maximization. And even then, different policy outcomes may result from each of these motives. Competence maximization may, for instance, result in both market liberalization policies, or in policies aimed at (re)regulation at the EU level (Pollack 2003: 39). In addition, when focusing on competence maximization one needs to take into account the time horizon used by the agent, and the possible disincentives for it to discount the future. Such disincentives may consist of the time frame of the delegation itself, as Pollack (2003) has stressed. If the agent's authority has been delegated indeterminately, the agent can afford to discount the future. If the authority has been delegated for a limited period of time, a preference for competence maximization requires the agent to be concerned about the preparedness of its principals to delegate in the future too.

In the case of the EU's external trade policy, such a concern must be paramount, as it concerns an area where delegation occurs at regular intervals, and where the Commission's delegated negotiating ability expires with the conclusion of the negotiations to which the delegation applied in the first place. Indeed, the Commission can start a negotiation only if the Council authorizes it to do so. If the Commission wants to conduct another negotiation, it needs a new delegation decision from the EU's Council of Ministers, and thus the approval by at least a qualified majority of the member states.

In the EU's external trade negotiations, it may thus be plausible to assume that the Commission's preference for the maximization of its *future* negotiating competences entails a preference for more negotiating autonomy *today*. Such autonomy would allow the Commission to negotiate in a way that maximizes its own substantive interests on trade, but to do so within the limits of what the member states have allowed it to do. At the same time, however, it may be equally plausible to assume that the Commission's preference for the maximization of its *future* negotiating competences reduces the probability that it will engage in shirking and that it will avoid slippage. The narrower the confines within which the Council allows the Commission to negotiate, the more difficult it will be for the Commission to avoid slippage, especially if the preference distance between the Council and the EU's external partners is relatively large. The larger that distance the more difficult slippage avoidance will become.

In addition, the smaller the preference distance between the Commission and the EU's external partners – given a large preference distance between these partners and the Council – the stronger the incentives for the Commission to engage in shirking too. In that case, a real dilemma emerges between the Commission's *current* substantial interests, and its concerns about its *future* delegated negotiating abilities.

If we translate this conclusion to the question of the role that the EU can play in an organization like the WTO, the above suggests that as far as the Commission is concerned part of the answer lays in the way in which it deals with the incentives and disincentives of slippage and shirking to which it is exposed. In terms of probabilities, the more reluctant the member states are in relation to trade liberalization, and the more this reluctance translates itself in restricted mandates for the Commission, the stronger the impact of the Commission's assessment of the costs and benefits of slippage and shirking on the extent to which the EU will be able to play a proactive role in the WTO. The role of the Commission's assessment is thus of central importance. And in that assessment, the member states' ability to control its external negotiating behaviour will be an important component. This brings us to the question of control.

A theory of control

Indeed, whatever the propensity of agents such as the Commission to engage in slippage or shirking, it can occur only because the principals are not able to identify such behaviour, and consequently, to check it. Agency losses – and the related costs – are rooted, therefore, in information asymmetries. As Pollack observes:

> In *any* principal–agent relationship, information about the agent and its activities is *likely* to be asymmetrically distributed in favour of the agent, making control or even evaluation by the principal difficult.
> (Pollack 2003: 26, emphasis added)

Indeed, the principal has to take into account that the agent will use the policy room provided by the information asymmetry to pursue its self-interests, or at least to balance that self-interest against the interests of the principal and the latter's ability to sanction shirking (Sloof 2000: 248–9). To limit or to avoid agency losses, principals need to invest in control. Indeed, the preparedness to delegate is even strongly affected by the ability to control.

Seen from the perspective of the EU's external trade policy, three control devices are available to the member states with regard to the Commission's external negotiating behaviour: an *ex ante*, an *at locum* and an *ex post* device. The first refers to the negotiating directives, the second to monitoring, and the third to non-ratification. The basis of these three is provided by Articles 133 and 300 of the EC Treaty.

Negotiating directives (the *ex ante* device) are not required by the EC Treaty. That means that the Treaty provides for the possibility that the Commission negotiates with third countries without a negotiating mandate from the Council. What the Treaty does require, however, is Council authorization for such negotiations. Whether strings will be attached to it is a matter for the Council to decide. The member states need to make an assessment of the costs and benefits of doing so. Indeed, defining negotiating directives may have benefits in terms of control; it also has pitfalls. By adopting negotiating directives, member states create not only benchmarks on which to assess the Commission's negotiating work, but also benchmarks to assess each other's behaviour vis-à-vis the negotiations and vis-à-vis the possible concessions made in them. A mandate – whenever issued – is a text that not only reflects the limits within which the Commission is supposed to negotiate externally, it also reflects the maximum concessions the member states are prepared to agree to vis-à-vis each other at the start of the external negotiations. Especially in cases where the Council cannot refuse to authorize the Commission to negotiate because of external constraints, or can only do so at a prohibitively high political cost, the most conservative (or most reluctant) member states cannot exploit a possible refusal to authorize a negotiation as a bargaining chip to enhance their leverage in the internal EU negotiations on a possible mandate. In such situations, a dilemma emerges for them: either to agree to a mandate that reflects a compromise with the other member states but that commits them later in the process, or to relinquish the opportunity to define a mandate while authorizing the Commission to negotiate. For the member states that hope to achieve trade liberalization or regulation in the WTO, agreeing to a mandate early in the negotiating process may be counterproductive unless it pins the Commission down to the kinds of regulation or liberalization that they prefer. The outcome is often, then, that no mandates (or no mandates that substantively limit the Commission's room for manoeuvre) are being defined and that the member states have to rely on the other control devices.

One of these is the *at locum* device. It consists of the activities of a committee of member states' representatives – Committee 133 – whose function it is to closely control the Commission during the external negotiations (Johnson 1998: 22–3). It largely fulfils three functions: an aggregation function, a watchdog function and a sounding-board function.

The aggregation function refers to the Committee's job to try to come up with one instruction on behalf of all the member states if it wants to maximize its impact on the Commission. The watchdog function (Somerset 2002: 63) refers to the monitoring role that the committee fulfils. Through the Committee 133 the member states get direct access to the external negotiating process itself even if they cannot take over the negotiating role from the Commission. The sounding-board function stresses the fact that the Committee 133 provides the framework within which the member states can individually express their concerns and demands on specific negotiating issues. This enables the Commission to anticipate member state reactions to concessions or demands it intends to make (Somerset 2002: 66), and to act pre-emptively in this regard. This brings us to the *ex post* control device of non-ratification.

Non-ratification is indeed an ultimate control device for the member states. Depending on the required majority in the Council – once again when it concerns exclusive EU competences – member states will be able to wield this device individually (in the case of unanimity), or in collaboration with the number of member states needed to reach a blocking minority (in the case of QMV). It is a control device, because as long as the Commission wants to avoid non-ratification, it needs to anticipate such an eventuality when it is negotiating externally. Member states can (and often do) send signals in this regard, either directly (in Committee 133, through their permanent representations in Brussels or otherwise) or indirectly (through their domestic media, speeches in their national parliament, etc.), and may thus have an indirect impact on what the Commission is doing. This impact will of course depend on the majority requirement in the Council, on the voting weight and preference of each of the member states, and on the expected distance between what the Commission intends to negotiate and what is acceptable for each of the member states.

What conclusion can be drawn about the relationship between member state control and the Commission's ability to play a proactive role in external trade negotiations?

It is plausible to assume that the smaller the preference distances between the Commission and the member states are, the larger the potential for the EU to play a proactive role. Smaller preference distances increase the probability of less strict control by the member states, and thus more leeway for the Commission to engage in autonomous action. Ultimately, the Commission's preferences in relation to such action will determine, then, the extent to which the EU will take a proactive role. In cases where it is more conservative than its external negotiating partners, it will act as a risk-minimizer. In cases where it is more trade liberal-minded than its external partners, proactive action will ensue.

The larger the preference distances between the Commission and the member states – assuming that the Commission would be less conservative – the more the latter will engage in control on the former, and thus the less leeway the Commission will have to engage in proactive action. In such cases, the Commission is not powerless, however. It still has the prerogatives of the external negotiator and can use these to enhance its capacity to act proactively. It even may find it to be in the EU's interest to do so, for instance when it believes the costs of non-participation in external negotiations to be higher for the EU than the benefits. The Doha Development Round provides an example of such a situation. It provides the basis to explain the Commission's relentless efforts to convince the EU's WTO partners to engage in a new round of multilateral trade negotiations. That was far from evident, as many of them had lost confidence in the added value of such large rounds due to the seven years that it took to conclude the Uruguay Round negotiations (1986–93). As a matter of fact, the Commission engaged in a proactive strategy in order to minimize the risk for itself as a negotiator. In doing so, it acted in a way that pre-empted the risks that were created with the built-in agenda of the Uruguay Round.

Anticipation by pre-emption: the Commission and the DDA

A central component in the Commission's efforts to launch a new round consisted of the built-in agenda of the Uruguay Round (Patterson 1997; Coleman and Tangermann 1999). This agenda provided for on-going negotiations on a number of topics. On some of these, the built-in agenda provided an important element of the compromises reached in the Uruguay Round. In exchange for concessions received on the reduction or dismantling of trade barriers, countries had to accept to reopen negotiations on such issues within a predetermined time span. Article 20 of the Uruguay Round Agreement on Agriculture (AoA), for instance, provided for such a reopening on agriculture by 2000. In addition, the agreement also contained a provision in which the members would lose their protection against dispute settlement cases on agricultural subsidies after a period of nine years. That protection shielded the members from complaints about subsidies allowed by the agreement (Steinberg and Josling 2003). Upon the expiry of that clause by the end of 2003, members risked being exposed to numerous cases on such subsidies. There were thus two sources of pressure on the EU as far as its agricultural subsidies were concerned.

There was thus no escape from new negotiations on agricultural trade and, thus, from the acrimonious internal EU debates and painful concessions that they could be expected to entail. This was very problematic for the Commission. It would have to negotiate under the close and suspicious scrutiny of several member states, and the pressure of its external negotiating partners. Whatever the outcome, it would be blamed, either by one or the other. There was thus a serious reason for the Commission to be concerned. In addition, however, compared with the Uruguay Round negotiations, the problem was compounded by the fact that agricultural negotiations would be conducted on their own, as stand-alone negotiations, not as part of a large and broad negotiating agenda. This would make it impossible to link painful agricultural concessions and their concomitant costs to the benefits of concessions granted by other countries in other sectors, so as to soften the pain and to make the agricultural concessions politically more acceptable. Likewise, it would make it impossible to limit the agricultural concessions by offering the EU's negotiating partners concessions (and thus benefits) in other sectors. In other words, the stand-alone nature of the agricultural negotiations would make it impossible to construct a broad cross-sectoral package deal, something the Commission considered to be a condition sine qua non for the conclusion of an agricultural agreement and, more important, for its ability to pre-empt the inevitable member states' attacks on the way in which it wields its negotiating authority.

Two elements were thus important for the Commission. First, it needed to expand the WTO's negotiating agenda beyond agriculture to sectors attractive to member states that would suffer from agricultural concessions, or where such member states would be prepared to make concessions in exchange for a softer treatment on agriculture. Such sectors needed to be sufficiently appealing to attract wider support among the WTO membership as well. Second, it needed to get the WTO members to accept the principle of a single undertaking on those issues. Only a single undertaking would provide the ability to engage in broad package deals. Allowing the unravelling of such an undertaking by accepting so-called early harvests would be out of the question, or at least be severely restricted.

Getting the member states on board

On the first element, the fact that service negotiations were planned to take place parallel to the agricultural negotiations helped a lot. It provided a first, but important, opportunity for the Commission to propose a linkage between agriculture and a range of sectors more important for EU employment. In addition, it concerned sectors with a high (partly underused) export potential due to EU competitiveness and to the fact that the GATS agreement had provided only for a first modest step in the direction of trade liberalization.

In addition, the Commission hoped to trigger pressure in favour of a new negotiating round in the WTO – because that was ultimately the objective – by including issues in the negotiating agenda that would mobilize domestic business support within the member states in favour of a new round. The inclusion of non-agricultural market access, investment and trade facilitation are cases in mind as well as competition and, as a first step, transparency in government procurement.

Ultimately, most member states accepted the idea of a new round in March 1998 because they realized how problematic stand-alone negotiations on agriculture would be, not only for the Commission, but for the EU, and in some cases for themselves. For some of them, the consideration certainly played a role in that, by agreeing to a new round, the pressure on the EU would increase to further reform the CAP and to reduce its cost, especially in the perspective of the EU's new southern and eastern enlargements.

Getting the WTO on board

Convincing the other WTO members to accept a new round of multilateral trade negotiations (MTNs) was far from easy, however. Two major problems consisted of convincing a US government suspicious of the EU's intentions and a US Congress faced with increasing opposition to trade liberalization on the one hand, and convincing the developing countries that a new round would benefit them too on the other hand. The latter was not easy as most developing countries concluded that as the Uruguay Round negotiations had not brought them the promised benefits, it was no use starting a new one, rather the contrary (cf. Panagariya 2002: 1219–23). Resistance from the US and many developing countries – or at least their ambivalence on a new round – in combination with the pressure engendered by street manifestations in Seattle culminated in the collapse of the first attempt to launch one at the Seattle Ministerial Conference of November–December 1999.

After Seattle, the Commission was quickly in the driver's seat again to push forward the idea of a new attempt to launch a round. To appease the developing countries, the Commission intensified the internal EU decision-making on Everything but Arms (EBA) – thereby implementing a commitment that was made at the WTO Ministerial in Singapore in December 1996 with regard to market access for the least developed countries. Everything but Arms – a decision adopted on 28 February 2001 – provided for the tariff- and quota-free import into the EU of all products except weapons and ammunition,[2] originating in (at that time) 49 least developed countries, with transitional periods provided for bananas, rice and sugar.[3] The EU equally started to show more support for the demand of the developing countries to adopt an implementation agenda in which deficiencies of the Uruguay Round agreements for these countries, including their implementation, would be dealt with. One of the politically most visible parts of this consisted of the compulsory licensing for trade in generic medicines, an issue that was especially important for countries that did not benefit from the EBA or were even hurt by it (Oxfam International 2000; Page and Hewitt 2002), but that have a strong production capacity of generic medicines (such as India and Brazil).

On the US side, two important changes took place that facilitated the Commission's efforts. First, the fact that the Bush administration's – that entered into office in January 2001 – assessment of the Commission's strategy on a new round resulted in the conclusion that the probability of agricultural concessions by the EU – extremely important for President Bush in electoral terms – would be higher with a new round than with standalone negotiations. At the same time, the US Congress engaged in the process that would result in the Farm Act,[4] thereby changing US interests on agricultural subsidies somewhat (cf. below). Still, the Bush administration had to walk a narrow line as congressional resistance to WTO negotiations on anti-dumping and countervailing measures (the so-called trade remedies) increased tremendously, and as the President was looking for congressional delegation of trade negotiating authority to him knowing that his predecessor had failed in this endeavour and that resistance to trade liberalization and regulation was running high in Congress (largely the House) and beyond (Kerremans 2003). The result was a persisting US ambivalence on the need to launch a new round and on the agenda to be pursued in it. This was especially the case with the so-called Singapore issues: investment, competition, trade facilitation and transparency in government procurement. Whereas the US was originally not enthusiastic about the first, it none the less pushed for negotiations as broad in scope as possible (including portfolio investment). About the second, the US never really supported the EU's attempts to launch negotiations here. The third and the fourth certainly interested the US even if it accepted to drop the latter surprisingly quickly at the 2003 WTO Ministerial in Cancún (cf. below).

The reluctance, even resistance, of most developing countries to a new round, combined with lukewarm US support, made it necessary for the EU, especially the Commission, to remain in the driver's seat in the WTO, so as to keep the agenda of the negotiations as large and integrated as possible. This meant that the Commission wanted to safeguard the single undertaking throughout the negotiations, both before and after the Doha Ministerial of November 2001.

Preserving the single undertaking before and after Doha

The biggest challenge for the Commission was to preserve the single undertaking vis-à-vis scepticism from both some member states, and some of its WTO partners. The Commission's handling of the negotiations between November 2001 (the Doha Ministerial) and September 2003 (the Cancun Ministerial) provides plenty of evidence of such efforts. At the Doha Ministerial itself, the Commission made a large effort to include the Singapore issues in the negotiating agenda even if several member states were not convinced of the need to include issues such as investment and competition. In addition, up to the last minute of the Ministerial, the Commission attempted to include eco-labelling, the precautionary principle, and the relationship between the WTO and multilateral environmental agreements (MEAs) in the agenda as well. At the end of the day, a decision on the launching of negotiations on the Singapore issues was postponed until 2003, whereas eco-labelling was being referred – without any commitment to negotiations – to the WTO Committee on Trade and Environment (CTE). For the remainder, however, a large negotiating agenda – the Doha Development Agenda (DDA) – was being adopted with the objective of concluding a comprehensive agreement by the end of 2004. That outcome was largely reached because of the use of vague and equivocal language in the Ministerial Declaration so that everybody could be satisfied. The price of this way of working was, however, that many problems were being postponed and would show up later, sometimes more intensely.

From the perspective of the Commission, an important concern about the outcome of Doha was to maintain the linkages between the different parts of that agenda with the objective of enlarging its scope with the inclusion of the Singapore issues by September 2003. This concern manifested itself on two elements: the question of the modalities' deadlines, and the linkage between the agricultural negotiating process and the other issues.

The modalities' deadline question – a highly technical issue the political importance of which was not immediately obvious to everyone involved in the DDA – was basically – at least from the perspective of the Commission – a question of linking the deadlines (moments against which sensitive concessions needed to be negotiated) for the agricultural negotiations with those of the other issues. In Doha, no deadline on non-agricultural market access had been agreed to. So the Commission's objective was to put one on the same date as the deadline for the agricultural modalities negotiations: 31 March 2003. This would enable it to trade concessions on agricultural modalities against concessions made by others in other areas, or vice versa. The point was, however, that some developing countries favoured a non-agricultural modalities' deadline a couple of weeks later than the one for agriculture, namely on 31 May 2003. This would enable them to carefully assess the EU's (and other WTO members') agricultural concessions and to see whether such concessions warranted non-agricultural concessions in return. The Commission adamantly opposed such an approach, as it feared that it would undermine its ability to make concessions in the first place. The idea was indeed that, with a similar deadline, the Commission would be able to present agricultural and non-agricultural modalities' concessions as one package to the member states, thereby reducing the probability of internal EU gridlock on the agricultural part of the negotiations. It took the Commission a while to convince its WTO partners, up to the point where it indicated it would be prepared to block the whole negotiating process because of the modalities' deadline. Ultimately, a Solomon's judgement of working with an informal and a formal deadline enabled an agreement. By 31 March 2003 – the agricultural modalities deadline – the WTO members committed to reach a 'common understanding on a possible outline on modalities with a view to reaching agreement on modalities by May 31, 2003'. In the event, both deadlines were missed.

The linkage between agriculture and the other issues became a real concern after the failure to respect the modalities deadline. It seems that, from then on, the Commission's strategy consisted of working towards the final negotiation of a package containing all issues at the Cancún Ministerial in September 2003, including the modalities on agriculture and non-agricultural market access, the inclusion of the Singapore issues in the DDA, and the inclusion of geographical indications (GIs) in the talks. It must be added, however, that the Commission's work was being facilitated by three developments. First, by the internal EU deals on agricultural spending between 2007 and 2013, and the concomitant question of the decoupling between subsidization and production (Koester and Brümmer 2003: 247); second, by the resistance of farm constituencies in the US to any possible unravelling of the subsidy benefits granted them by the 2002 Farm Act; third, by the conviction of an increasing number of WTO members that the US and the EU needed to reach an agricultural deal between themselves before the DDA could proceed on agriculture, and on the other issues as several developing countries had refused to allow any progress on the other issues before the agriculture modalities gridlock had been resolved.

The agricultural deals reached by the EU member states certainly helped the Commission in pursuing its linkages approach in the WTO. On the one hand, the deals provided the Commission with some breathing space in the agricultural negotiations on domestic support (much less, or even not on export subsidies) in the WTO. On the other hand, however, they required the Commission to watch its back even more than before, as some member states believed that all the necessary concessions had now been made, and consequently that no new concessions should be accepted or negotiated by the Commission in the WTO.

The US Farm Act opened a window of opportunity for the Commission. Because of it, the US had an interest in being more forthcoming on the question of domestic support in the WTO, which increased the probability that it would agree with at least the preservation of the so-called blue box. This is a category of domestic support created by the Uruguay Round Agreement on Agriculture (AoA), that allows for support measures on the assumption that they have a limited impact on productivity levels. It is a box specifically created for the EU, as it contains only EU direct payments to farmers, a support measure that emerged as a consequence of the 1992 CAP reform (Tangermann 1999). In the course of 1999–2002 the US had made no secret of its intention to dismantle the blue box. But due to the 2002 Farm Act, the US suddenly started to show interest in its preservation on the condition that it would become a tool to shield US domestic support from reduction commitments as well.

As several developing countries refused to accept any progress on the other negotiating issues before the agriculture modalities gridlock had been resolved, pressure started to build on the EU and the US to unblock the negotiations by an agreement between themselves. The combination of US interest in the blue box's preservation with the Commission's newly found self-confidence as a consequence of the EU internal deal on agricultural subsidies paved the way to a US–EU agreement that would not run the risk of becoming a Blair House scenario for the Commission. Rather than pinning down the Commission to major concessions – as the 1992 Blair House agreement had done – this agreement was believed to smooth the US' approach to the agricultural negotiations, something the Commission hoped to benefit from in the final marathon negotiating session in Cancún to which it aspired.

The problem was, however, that the agreement – the EC–EU Joint Text of 13 August 2003 – made matters worse, rather than facilitating the WTO negotiating process. One part of the agreement played a particularly large role in this: the expansion of the definition of the blue box so as to allow the inclusion of US counter-cyclical payments. It triggered a developing-country response that proved to become of paramount importance for the outcome in Cancun: the creation of what became the G-20. It came in addition to developing-country irritation about the lack of significant progress – including three missed deadlines – on the issue of their Special and Differential Treatment (SDT) in the WTO, and on the lack of responsiveness – especially but not exclusively from the US – to the request by four least developing countries to dismantle domestic support and export subsidies for cotton.[5]

Despite the fact that, right before the start of the Cancún Ministerial, agreement was being reached on the issue of the export and import of generic medicines (compulsory licensing), the atmosphere in Cancún was poisoned from the start. There was a heavy agenda (largely due to the fact that many issues were not ripe for a deal). There were unclear objectives as the ambitions for the Ministerial had been downgraded to such an extent that it became unclear what kinds of modalities agreements would be aimed at, something that made the negotiators keep their cards up their sleeves, rather than putting them on the table in a game of concession and counter-concession. In sum, the context of Cancún was certainly not conducive to allow a situation that would serve the Commission's interests best: a large final but feasible marathon negotiating session in which a large modalities package would be negotiated and finalized. In addition, the Commission's strategy of trying to do so was being unravelled by the decision, taken by the chairman of the Ministerial, to end the negotiations before such a final session had started. Particularly painful for the Commission was the fact that this decision was being taken midcourse in its attempts to convince recalcitrant developing countries – especially the G-20 – that such a final session could serve their interests. It was painful because the Commission had started to make a number of concessions – on the question of the Singapore issues – and had to return to the member states now before it had been able to reap the benefits of doing so, something that would have been possible in the event of a final package agreement being agreed to. But now the Commission had conceded on dropping investment and competition (at least from the multilateral negotiations) in the hope of adding trade facilitation and government procurement transparency to the single undertaking, and of enabling an agreement on the different modalities too, preferably including the geographical indications on more than wines and spirits. Because the negotiating process was being interrupted, it had made the concessions without getting something in return, and this was being exposed to the member states. This partly explains the irritation, even the bitterness, inside the Commission about the way in which the Mexican foreign minister had handled the Cancún Ministerial. Indeed, the single undertaking approach – the central component in the Commission's strategy – had been unravelled.

Conclusion

The Commission's handling of the Doha Development Agenda negotiations up to the Cancún Ministerial shows how proactiveness in external negotiations may be essential for risk minimization in the EU itself. By deliberately expanding the WTO agenda, the Commission tried to enhance the EU's ability to deal with the agricultural question in the WTO. The scope of the external negotiations became an essential part of the Commission's strategy to manage the relationship with its principals. It also made the Commission's strategy vulnerable to the vagaries of the WTO negotiating process itself, as the Cancún Ministerial showed. None the less, for the WTO this meant that the Commission – and as a derivative the EU as a whole – took the driving seat in the launching of a broad agenda of multilateral trade negotiations and thus, that the characteristics of the WTO negotiating process needed to cushion what was essentially a problem between the Commission-as-agent and some of the member states as principals. As such, internal risk minimization by the Commission required a proactive EU role externally. This doesn't mean, however, that internal risk minimization is always by definition linked to the EU's proactiveness in the international arena. But it does show that sometimes it may have that effect.

Notes

1 Note that even if we will be referring to the European Union in the remainder of this chapter, legally, whenever it concerns trade policy-making, reference should be made to the EC, as, unlike the EU, the EC has a legal personality (cf. Article 281, EC Treaty) and thus the legal capacity to negotiate externally.
2 CN chapter 93.
3 *EC Official Journal*, L 60, 1 March 2001. The 49 countries are listed in annex IV of regulation 2820/98, see *EC Official Journal*, L 357, 31 December 1998, p. 82.
4 Officially the Farm Security and Rural Investment Act of 2002, Public Law 107–71.
5 Chad, Burkina Faso, Mali and Benin.

References

Coleman, W. D. and Tangermann, S. (1999) 'The 1992 CAP Reform, the Uruguay Round and the Commission: Conceptualizing Linked Policy Games', *Journal of Common Market Studies*, 37: 385–405.

Epstein, D. and O'Halloran, S. (1999) *Delegating Powers: A Transaction Cost Politics Approach under Separate Powers*, Cambridge: Cambridge University Press.

Johnson, M. (1998) *European Community Trade Policy and the Article 113 Committee*, London: Royal Institute of International Affairs.

Jupille, J. and Caporaso, J. A. (1998) 'States, Agency, and Rules: The European Union in Global Environmental Politics', in C. Rhodes (ed.) *The European Union in the World Community*, Boulder, CO: Lynne Rienner.

Kerremans, B. (2003) 'Coping with the Nettlesome Dilemma: The Long Road to the U.S. Trade Act of 2002', *Journal of World Investment*, 4: 517–51.

Koester, U. and Brümmer, B. (2003) 'How Relevant is the Failure of Cancún for World Agriculture?', *Intereconomics*, 38: 245–9.

Majone, G. (2001) 'Two Logics of Delegation. Agency and Fiduciary Relations in EU Governance', *European Union Politics*, 2: 103–22.

Oxfam (2000) 'EU Trade Concession to the Least Developed Countries, Everything but Arms Proposal: Possible Impacts on the Agricultural Sector' (unpublished).

Page, S. and Hewitt, A. (2002) 'The New European Trade Preferences: Does

"Everything but Arms" (EBA) Help the Poor?', *Development Policy Review*, 20: 91–102.

Panagariya, A. (2002) 'Developing Countries at Doha: A Political Economy Analysis', *The World Economy*, 25: 1205–33.

Patterson, L. A. (1997) 'Agricultural Policy Reform in the European Community: A Three-level Game Analysis', *International Organization*, 51: 135–65.

Pollack, M. A. (2003) *The Engines of European Integration: Delegation, Agency, and Agenda Setting in the EU*, Oxford: Oxford University Press.

Sloof, R. (2000) 'Interest Group Lobbying and the Delegation of Policy Authority', *Economics and Politics*, 12: 247–74.

Somerset, K. (2002) 'When the European Union is a Lobbyist: The European Commission and External Trade', in A. Warleigh and J. Fairbrass (eds) *Influence and Interests in the European Union: The New Politics of Persuasion and Advocacy*, London: Europa Publications.

Steinberg, R. H. and Josling, T. (2003) 'When the Peace Ends: The Vulnerability of EC and US Agricultural Subsidies to WTO Legal Challenge', Research Paper 03-10, Public Law and Legal Theory Research Paper Series, University of California, Los Angeles, School of Law.

Tangermann, S. (1999) 'Europe's Agricultural Policies and the Millennium Round', *The World Economy*, 22: 1155–76.

Woolcock, S. (2003) 'The Singapore Issues in Cancún: A Failed Negotiation Ploy or a Litmus Test for Global Governance?', *Intereconomics*, 38: 249–55.

Young, A. R. (2000) 'The Adaptation of European Foreign Economic Policy: From Rome to Seattle', *Journal of Common Market Studies*, 38: 93–116.

Young, A. R. (2003) 'What Game? By Which Rules? Adaptation and Flexibility in the EC's Foreign Economic Policy', in M. Knodt and S. Princen (eds) *Understanding the European Union's External Relations*, London: Routledge.

11 Punching its weight?

The EU's use of WTO dispute resolution

Alasdair R. Young

The European Union's role in trade policy is commonly (and rightly) regarded as one of its most clearly defined and effective international roles. The creation of the World Trade Organization (WTO) and the establishment of binding multilateral dispute resolution, by shifting from a more diplomatic to a more confrontational and legalistic process, however, challenged the EU's existing trade role. By analysing how the EU has responded to that challenge, this chapter sheds light on how the EU's role in international trade is conceived, as well as on its role performance and role impact.

In particular, in the wake of the Uruguay Round, there was some concern that the EU's character as an international organization would adversely affect its ability to participate effectively in the WTO's new dispute resolution process. First, there was some legal uncertainty about whether the EU or its member states were the appropriate actor (a question of role conception). Second, even if the EU were the appropriate actor, there was concern that the EU's then 15, now 25, member governments would have trouble agreeing to act aggressively (a question of role performance).

In practice, however, these concerns have proved unfounded. The idea that the EU, in the shape of the Commission, would represent all of the member states in WTO dispute resolution has not been problematic. Further, the EU's role performance has been broadly comparable to that of the United States (US), another major player in world trade and the EU's most obvious comparator, which suggests that there are no particular problems stemming from the EU's character as an international organization. This chapter aims to explain the effectiveness of the EU's role performance despite the apparent obstacles stemming from its character as an international organization.

I argue that the EU's role performance in WTO dispute resolution is facilitated by the member governments' acceptance of the EU's role in the WTO, by the politics of trade disputes, by a high degree of delegation to the European Commission, and by the member governments' tendency not to challenge each other's trade policy preferences unless they have strong countervailing interests. This chapter, therefore, identifies the EU's role in WTO dispute resolution, examines how that role emerged and has been institutionalized, and analyses how well the EU has performed it.

I begin by examining different aspects of the EU's role conception in WTO dispute resolution, and their origins, before setting up the central puzzle of the chapter by contrasting academic concern about the EU's role performance with its actual performance. I then explain how the EU has managed to overcome the obstacles to effective role performance. This discussion focuses separately on the initiation of trade disputes and the imposition of sanctions. I also engage with whether the EU has delivered concrete results (role impact). I conclude by reflecting on the EU's role as a proactive player in WTO dispute resolution.

Role conception

Which actor?

One consequence of the EU being an international organization is that it is not always apparent whether it or its individual member states is the appropriate actor. This is reflected in the EU and all of its member states being members of the WTO. Thus under WTO rules any one of the EU's member states has the right to initiate a trade dispute. Further, prior to the 2001 Treaty of Nice a number of important policy areas – most notably trade in services and intellectual property protection – that fell within the ambit of the WTO did not fall within the exclusive authority of the EU. Even after Nice a number of important issues – including non-service foreign direct investment and audio-visual services – remain outside the EU's exclusive competence (Bronkers and McNelis 2001: 427; Young 2002: 47). These two inverse legal situations – multiple memberships of the WTO and incomplete EU competence – raise questions about whether the EU and only the EU may perform the role of engaging in WTO dispute resolution.

Legal scholars, in particular, anticipated that the absence of exclusive EU competence would present two potential problems. First, the member governments might be more critical of Commission investigations of trade barriers affecting matters of mixed competence (Bronkers and McNelis 2001: 427; MacLean 1999: 95). Second, agreeing retaliation against a measure that fell outside EU competence would be extremely difficult because it would not be obvious that the EU was the appropriate actor (Kuijper 1995: 59–60).

That it was not obvious that the EU would be the actor is illustrated by others not automatically treating it as such. As of the end of 2004 the US had initiated more complaints against individual EU member states – Ireland (four), Belgium (three), France (two), Greece (two), Denmark (one), Netherlands (one), Portugal (one), Sweden (one) and the UK (one) – than against the EU *qua* the EU (15). By contrast, other WTO members have named the EU as the respondent in disputes about purely national measures.[1] Thus there is no clear, common external conception of the EU's role.

Internally, however, that the EU, and only the EU, should participate in disputes has not been problematic. This has been the case even for those supposedly awkward issues of mixed competence – which were most salient between the conclusion of the Uruguay Round in December 1993 and the signing of the Treaty of Nice in February 2001 (Bronkers and McNelis 2001; Chatháin 1999).[2] During the first ten years of the WTO the EU initiated six WTO complaints concerning the protection of intellectual property rights,[3] five concerning foreign direct investment,[4] and one concerning services.[5] Mixed competence did not even present an obstacle to the EU's vigorous response to the extraterritorial implications of the US's Helms–Burton law, despite the location of competence for foreign direct investment being extremely politically charged at the time (Young 2002: 95–6). Further, although individual member governments pursue trade disputes bilaterally through diplomatic channels, no member state of the EU has initiated a WTO complaint.

The EU's role in WTO dispute resolution reflects the EU's member governments' general willingness to co-operate in international negotiations in areas beyond the formal scope of the EU's competence (Woolcock 2000; Young 2002: 36–42). This practice of co-operation is particularly highly developed with regard to the multilateral trading system, where co-operation has long been an established norm and the EU's role is particularly well established (Young 2002). Thus, in practice, it has been accepted that the EU is the appropriate actor when it comes to initiating WTO complaints.

Which role?

Although the EU is a single actor in WTO dispute resolution, it does not play a one-dimensional role. The EU's, or, more accurately, the Commission's (as I shall explain below), role has three facets:

- Advocate for particular economic interests.
- Champion of multilateral trade rules.
- Defender of the *acquis communautaire.*

Each of the three facets is relevant to any given issue, although with varying intensities.

The first facet is the most explicitly articulated. The first 'key objective' of the EU's market access strategy is to 'Serve Europe's exporters through practical operational measures'.[6] The Commission's Market Access Database and the EU's Trade Barrier Regulation (TBR) were explicitly created in order to make it easier for firms to seek the Commission's help in addressing foreign trade barriers.

The second facet of the Commission's role concerns championing the multilateral trading system. With regard to trade policy, self-interest reinforces any general preference for multilateralism (see Jørgensen in Chapter 2 of this volume). Legally binding multilateral rules are considered the most efficient way to ensure compliance by one's trading partners, and thus to open foreign markets to one's producers (Abbott *et al.* 2000; Smith 2000). Enforcing multilateral rules through prosecuting trade disputes is perceived to enhance compliance in the future. This reasoning is evident in the EU's market access strategy, which has as its third 'key objective' to 'Eliminate trade barriers and ensure that our partners comply with their international commitments'.[7] The section of the Directorate General for Trade's webpage dealing with WTO dispute resolution is entitled 'Respecting the rules'.[8] Thus enforcing multilateral rules in specific instances is compatible with promoting economic interests, albeit in a more abstract sense.

While under this framing any WTO complaint could be classified as championing multilateral rules, the Commission sometimes initiates complaints that do not benefit any particular economic interest (Shaffer 2003). Through 2004 the EU had initiated nine complaints (13 per cent of all EU complaints)[9] that sought to establish or enforce important principles about how the multilateral trading system functions. These complaints have overwhelmingly targeted the US. This is not surprising, as a key reason for the EU's support of the legalization of multilateral dispute settlement was to curb US unilateralism (Goldstein 2000: 267).

As both of the first two roles involve getting others to change their policies, thereby situating the 'losers' outside the EU, they are extremely unlikely to come into conflict. The Commission's role as defender of the *acquis*, however, is less compatible with the first two roles. As normally understood, the Commission's role as defender of the *acquis* is to ensure that the member governments live up to their commitments. In the context of WTO dispute resolution, the Commission defends the EU's rules against external obligations. The benefit of increased compliance by others comes at the price of a decrease in one's own policy autonomy (Smith 2000).

The Commission's role as defender of the *acquis* is most explicit when the EU is a respondent in a complaint. Then the Commission quite literally defends the EU before the WTO. This role, however, also matters when the EU initiates a complaint. Because precedent matters in WTO dispute resolution, governments, including the Commission, are reluctant to initiate complaints that risk setting precedents that might apply equally to their own rules (Shaffer 2003). The Commission's role as defender of the *acquis*, therefore, may contradict its role as advocate of economic interests or champion of multilateralism.

Assessing role performance

Given that the collective representation of the EU in initiating WTO complaints is not contested, the key question becomes how effective it is in performing the roles described above.

Before examining the EU's role performance, however, it is necessary to draw a distinction between role performance and role impact. In this context role performance concerns the action taken by the EU, while an assessment of role impact concerns whether the trade barrier is actually removed. The ultimate success of EU action depends on a number of factors beyond the EU's control. The escalation of disputes and the prospects of compliance reflect the interaction between the complainant and respondent, and particularly on whether the domestic politics of the respondent make it susceptible to external pressures (Conybeare 1987; Guzman and Simmons 2002; Schoppa 1993; Zeng 2002). Further, whether a country complies with a WTO ruling also in part reflects the impact of the WTO as an institution (Busch and Reinhardt 2000). As a consequence, this chapter focuses on the EU's role performance – its ability to initiate complaints and to push for enforcement through the imposition of sanctions – although it considers role impact later.

The central concern about the EU's ability to perform its role effectively was the expectation that it would be difficult to get 15 (now 25) governments to agree to act. Sophie Meunier (1998) has argued that the EU's 'strength in weakness' – that problems of internal agreement make the EU's negotiating positions stronger – applies only when the EU is on the defensive. When the EU is on the offensive, as is the case in dispute settlement, the challenge of internal agreement is expected to hamper effective action (Bronkers and McNelis 2001; Meunier 1998; Molyneux 2001). The imposition of sanctions is expected to be particularly difficult because of the contentious issue of the distribution of the costs associated with enforcing compliance through the imposition of sanctions (Kuijper 1995: 56).

Against the odds: effective role performance

In practice, however, the EU has been the second most prolific user of the WTO's dispute settlement system, only slightly behind the US and in line with its share of world exports (see Table 11.1).[10] With the exception of Japan, however, the EU makes relatively less use of the system than any of the other major users. This relative underperformance, however, seems to be due to factors other than impeded political capacity. In particular, European firms tend to be less inclined than their US counterparts to demand political action to address trade barriers (Shaffer 2003). Further, a recent survey of European firms found that only 10 per cent of respondents made direct contact with government when they encountered a barrier to trading in a foreign market.[11]

Table 11.1 The principal users of WTO dispute resolution, 1 January 1995–31 December 2004

Rank	*Complainant*	*No. of complaints*	*Share of complaints (%)*	*Share of world merchandise exports 2002 (%)*	*Ratio of share of complaints to share of exports*
1	US	79	22.4	14.0	1.60
2	**EU**	**68**	**19.3**	**19.0**	**1.02**
3	Canada	26	7.4	5.1	1.45
4	Brazil	22	6.3	1.2	5.12
5	India	16	4.5	1.0	4.56
6	Mexico	14	4.0	3.2	1.22
=7	Japan	12	3.4	8.4	0.40
=7	Korea	12	3.4	3.2	1.04
9	Thailand	11	3.1	1.4	2.21
=10	Argentina	9	2.6	0.5	5.20
=10	Chile	9	2.6	0.4	6.50
	Other complainants (29)	74	21.0	29.0	0.72
	Total	352	100		

Source: Own calculations based on the WTO's dispute settlement database and *World Trade Statistics 2003*.

Notes

As of 31 December 2004, there had been 324 WTO complaints, but some involved multiple complainants. Counting each complainant individually yields 352 complaints.

Shares of world exports exclude intra-EU trade.

Most of the EU's complaints, as with those of other complainants, do not proceed all the way to formal panel hearings before the WTO (see Table 11.2). Most complaints are settled in one form or another, or are not considered worth pursuing for various reasons. The US, which initiates the most complaints, pursues a lower than average proportion of them to adjudication. This may reflect the ability of the US to secure concessions prior to adjudication, but its relatively low success rate in panels suggests that it may initiate more weaker cases than other governments.

By contrast, the EU has a better than average success rate in panels, significantly better than the average of the 11 most frequent complainants. As a result of the EU's higher proportion of complaints leading to panels and higher success rate in panels, the EU has won more panels than the US (24 to 19), even though it has initiated fewer complaints. The EU's high success rate suggests that its relatively low number of complaints may be due to it being more selective in those that it chooses to pursue, rather than suffering from problems of capacity.

The EU has also been vigorous in seeking to enforce the rulings that it has won. It has sought, threatened or imposed sanctions on four occasions, all involving the US, more than any other WTO member (see Table 11.3). Brazil and Canada have each done so on three occasions, but in two of those (US steel safeguards and the Byrd Amendment) the EU took the lead. The US has sought and imposed sanctions on two occasions. To date the EU has actually imposed traditional sanctions on only one occasion – Foreign Sales Corporations – but the value of those sanctions is by far the highest thus far. In addition, it has adopted Council Regulation 2238/2003, which prohibits the recognition and enforcement of decisions based on the Antidumping Act of 1916 and allows EU companies to sue the US plaintiff to recover costs and damages caused by a complaint under the 1916 Act. The EU is also the only WTO member to date to have reached an agreement on compensation for non-compliance.[12] The EU is thus clearly willing and able to impose sanctions.

Explaining the EU's role performance

The reality of the EU's use of the WTO's dispute settlement mechanism belies the academic hand-wringing about its ability to perform its role. The following sections set out the different dynamics that I argue explain its effectiveness with regard to *dispute initiation* and the *imposition of sanctions.*

Dispute initiation

The literature's understanding of EU dispute initiation is misguided for three reinforcing reasons. First, it largely discounts the implications of the exceptional degree of delegation to the Commission. Second, it neglects

Table 11.2 EU performance in panels, 1 January 1995–31 December 2004 (%)

Complainant	*% of complaints going to panel (excludes complaints since 1 January 2004)*	*% of completed panels won*
EU	**43**	**96**
All	44	91
Eleven most frequent complainants	45	89
US	36	79

Notes
'Winning' is defined as any aspect of the respondent's measure being found incompatible with WTO rules in any way (see Davey 2001; Holmes *et al.* 2003).
The US's win percentage is slightly distorted because it lost three closely related complaints. Treating these as one complaint yields a success rate of 86%.

the non-reciprocal character of dispute initiation. Third, it overlooks the positive implications for co-operation of the member governments' intense, iterated interaction.

A high degree of delegation

Institutionally, trade disputes are characterized by a particularly high degree of delegation to the Commission, which is higher even than that in EU trade policy generally, itself one of the policy areas in which delegation is particularly pronounced (Pollack 2003). The degree of delegation differs somewhat between the EU's two mechanisms for deciding whether to initiate a formal trade dispute – the Trade Barriers Regulation[13] (TBR) and the 'non-procedure' of the 133 Committee of member government trade officials – but in both cases the Commission enjoys a significant degree of autonomy.

Delegation is formal and explicit under the TBR,[14] which provides an avenue for European firms and trade associations to initiate action. It puts the Commission clearly and firmly in the driving seat. The Commission takes all the important decisions – whether to initiate an investigation, what course of action to take and how to follow through, including whether to initiate a WTO complaint – although it consults the member governments through the TBR Committee of government officials.

Although the TBR Committee is only advisory, any member can appeal the Commission's decision to the Council of Ministers. The Council can then overrule the Commission, but crucially only by a qualified majority vote. Consequently, there is a high hurdle for rejecting a Commission decision, which gives the Commission significant policy autonomy (Pollack 2003).

As there is no formal procedure for the 133 route there is some uncertainty about where authority lies. The Commission contends that on the

Table 11.3 WTO sanctions sought, threatened and imposed as of 31 December 2004

Complaint	*Complainant*	*Respondent*	*Measure*	*Sanctions status*	*Value (US$)*
DS108	**EU**	**US**	**Foreign sales corporations**	***Suspended*** **Policy change being checked for compliance**	**4043 million**
DS248	**EU, Brazil, China, Japan, Korea, New Zealand, Norway, Switzerland**	**US**	**Safeguards on steel**	**Threatened Subsequent compliance**	**358 million (EU only)**
DS136	**EU**	**US**	**Antidumping Act of 1916**	***Imposed*** Counter-regulation	**Variable**
DS217	**EU, Australia, Brazil, Chile, India, Indonesia, Japan, Korea, Thailand**	**US**	**Byrd Amendment**	**Authorized**	**Disbursement in previous year × 0.72 (up to $150 million)**
DS27	US	EU	Banana trade regime	*Imposed* Subsequent compliance	191.4 million
DS26	US	EU	Ban on hormone-treated beef	*Imposed*	116.8 million
DS48	Canada	EU	Ban on hormone-treated beef	Imposed	7.6 million
DS46	Canada	Brazil	Measures affecting export of civilian aircraft	Authorized	231.7 million
DS234	Canada, Mexico	US	Antidumping Act of 1916	Authorized	Disbursement in previous year × 0.72
DS222	Brazil	Canada	Measures affecting export of civilian aircraft	Authorized	247.8 million
DS27	Ecuador	EU	Banana trade regime	Authorized Subsequent compliance	201.6 million

Source: Values are from the relevant WTO arbitration report, except for DS248 which is from *Financial Times*, 20 July 2002, p. 8.

Notes
DS248 was not subject to arbitration over the value of sanctions. DS46, DS48 and DS248 sanction values were converted into US$ at the Federal Reserve Bank's exchange rate for the year in which the arbitration decision was taken.

basis of the 1957 Treaty of Rome it has the authority to launch a complaint without the Council's approval (Bronkers and McNelis 2001; Shaffer 2003).[15] The Legal Service of the Council's General Secretariat, however, contends that the Council should give its explicit approval, although this does not happen in practice (Woolcock 2000).[16] Whatever the situation might be legally, in practice the Commission always consults the 133 Committee.[17]

There are two pragmatic reasons for this. First, if the Commission were to act against the wishes of the member governments too often, the member governments might be moved to adopt secondary legislation to clarify the delegation of authority and to tighten their control over their agent. Second, and more immediate, any complaint may eventually require the imposition of sanctions in order to compel the respondent to comply with a WTO ruling, and the Treaty is clear that only the Council can impose sanctions and must do so by a qualified majority (Bronkers and McNelis 2001). Although the imposition of sanctions is rare, it is a possibility that cannot be ignored. Consequently, it is in the Commission's interests to carry the Council with it.[18] This applies to both the 133 and TBR routes. As a result, the Commission has never initiated a WTO trade dispute without the support of at least a qualified majority of the member governments (Shaffer 2003).[19]

The politics of approving dispute initiation

Finding a qualified majority of member governments to support the initiation of a trade dispute, contrary to some of the concerns in the literature, is actually relatively easy. First, opposition to initiating a trade dispute from other economic actors is rare. Second, the EU's member governments tend to object to a trade policy objective only if their interests are directly negatively affected. These two political dynamics together help to explain why the decision to initiate WTO complaints has been relatively uncontroversial, and, thus, why the EU has been effective in performing its role.

In most trade disputes, the benefits of success are expected to accrue to domestic firms and the costs are expected to fall on the foreign country. Although under the WTO the imposition of sanctions in order to enforce a ruling is a possibility it is both rare and the composition of the sanctions, and thus which domestic firms would be adversely affected, is not known when a complaint is initiated. As a consequence, the initiation of a trade dispute is effectively a non-reciprocal trade policy. Non-reciprocal trade policies have the character of distributive policies, which are characterized by a political dynamic of non-interference; there is no opposition from other firms (Lowi 1964). This explains both the general lack of clash within the EU's role as an advocate of specific interests and between that role and its role as a champion of multilateral rules.

The exceptions to this dynamic emerge in instances where domestic firms benefit from the foreign measure, for example, by having an investment in or by being major suppliers to the protected foreign industry. This was the case with the EU's most internally controversial trade dispute concerning Brazil's export subsidy scheme (Proex). The dispute was initiated by the German aircraft manufacturer Dornier, because its competitor Embraer is a principal beneficiary of the scheme. The prosecution of the dispute was opposed by several French aerospace companies, which collectively held a 20 per cent stake in Embraer, and a number of other European companies that supplied components to Embraer (Goldstein and McGuire 2004; Shaffer 2003). Such clashes within the EU's role as advocate of particular economic interests, however, have been the exception rather than the rule.

The implications for co-operation of the largely distributive character of trade disputes are reinforced by the EU's member governments' general disinclination to interfere with each other's trade interests unless they have strong countervailing interests. There are several possible explanations for this. One is that the member governments identify with each other and are therefore inclined to support each other out of fellow feeling. Those involved in the decision-making process, however, stress more self-interested motivations. In particular, governments' acquiescence seems to be motivated by the iterated nature of their interaction; the next time they might be the *demandeur* of action.[20] This phenomenon is generally referred to as 'diffuse reciprocity' (Keohane 1986) and is common in EU trade policy (Winters 2001). A degree of trust is necessary for diffuse reciprocity to function, and the frequent interaction of the individuals involved helps to build such trust (Johnson 1998), but indications are that trust is the lubricant of co-operation, not its motor. As a consequence of the interaction of the distributive character of dispute initiation and 'diffuse reciprocity', the overwhelming majority of the Commission's decisions to initiate trade disputes have not been controversial.

Exceptions to this internal harmony tend to arise when the EU's, particularly the Commission's, role as the defender of the *acquis* clashes with its role as advocate for particular economic interests. Concern about the implications for EU rules has contributed to the Commission not challenging other governments' export subsidies, labelling requirements or rules protecting geographical indications.[21] The Commission also adjusts how it argues complaints in order to reduce the risk of adverse implications for EU rules,[22] as it did in its complaint against Australia's sanitary and phytosanitary rules.[23] Member governments also sometimes flag potential problems for national rules, as the French government did in a complaint concerning Canada's rules on film distribution (Chatháin 1999). To date the role as defender of the *acquis* has tended to trump the other roles in pursuing WTO complaints.

The challenge of imposing sanctions

Once the decision to initiate a complaint has been taken, the EU's character as an international organization goes into abeyance. The Commission manages the entire interaction with the trading partner and before the WTO, with the member governments kept abreast of developments through the 133 Committee. When it comes to imposing sanctions in order to enforce a successful complaint, however, the EU's character as an international organization reasserts itself with a vengeance.

There are two principal and reinforcing reasons for this. First, as enforcing compliance relies on the imposition of sanctions, it imposes costs, in the form of higher tariffs on imports, on European firms and consumers. As a consequence, the character of the politics involved in the dispute shifts from distributive to redistributive. Thus the role of advocate of particular economic interests encounters an internal contradiction – some economic interests have to suffer in the short run if others are to benefit in the longer run.

Consequently, there are reasons for European firms to oppose sanctions that will hurt them but benefit others. Within the EU these distributional consequences may be amplified by occurring between states. Given the increasing concentration of some industries in some member states, sanctions may affect firms in all or most member states, while the benefits of successful enforcement may fall to firms in only a few member states. As the distributional consequences will not be resolved within an individual member state, member governments whose firms are adversely affected have an incentive to oppose sanctions.

This is particularly significant because of the second reason; the Council becomes the key decision-maker. The Treaty of the European Community makes clear that only the Council can decide to impose sanctions, and that it can do so only by qualified majority. This creates a high threshold for action.

Thus the academic literature's account of the political obstacles to agreeing to impose sanctions, in contrast to that about dispute initiation, is broadly correct, although it overstates the case. There are two reasons why the EU's role performance is more effective than expected. First, the Commission intentionally pursues a strategy designed to mitigate the political opposition to sanctions. This approach also helps to persuade the EU's firms and governments that if they are to enjoy the benefits of the WTO over the long run, they will occasionally need to pay the price entailed by enforcing the rules. This resonates with the EU's role as a champion of multilateral rules. Second, the legalized form of the WTO itself makes the decision within the EU simpler, by taking some difficult aspects of the decision out of its hands.

Boxing clever

The Commission's strategy for overcoming the institutional and political obstacles to imposing sanctions presents sanctions as a last resort that is necessary to ensure the integrity of the multilateral trading system and seeks to identify sanctions that will least hurt European firms and consumers. Thus the role as champion of multilateral trade rules is to the fore while efforts are made to minimize the contradictions within the role of advocate of particular economic interests. The EU has not experienced problems of role performance in the two instances to date in which it has sought to compel compliance through sanctions:[24] steel safeguards and Foreign Sales Corporations (FSC). In both cases the imposition of sanctions, including the specific products targeted, was agreed without serious objections.[25]

The core of the strategy is giving the respondent (the US) a reasonable amount of time to comply *before* the sanctions are imposed. As both European firms and governments value US compliance, they are willing to support the threat of ultimately imposing sanctions if they are persuaded that it is the only way to ensure compliance and thus reinforce the integrity of the multilateral trade regime (UNICE 2004).[26]

Consequently, in both the steel safeguards and FSC cases, the EU did not race to impose sanctions, as the US did in both the bananas and hormone-treated beef complaints. In the safeguard case the Council agreed the sanctions in June 2002 only three months after the US introduced the safeguard measure, but the bulk of the sanctions were not to apply until March 2005 or until five days after the WTO ruled against the US measure (Council 2002). The automatic application of sanctions nearly three years in the future gave time for compliance while making the threat of sanctions credible. The US withdrew its measures just before the EU's sanctions were due to come into effect.

The Commission adopted an even more patient approach with respect to FSC, recognizing that a legislative change was required.[27] Although it repeatedly signalled its intent, the EU did not impose sanctions in the FSC case until 1 March 2004, more than two years after the WTO ruled in January 2002. Even then the sanctions began at a relatively low level and only progressively, albeit automatically, increased. Had they reached their full amount, the sanctions would have been worth $4,000 million a year. In October 2004, however, the US adopted a new law. Although the Commission has some reservations about the changes adopted, the EU has suspended the sanctions, and requested the WTO to assess the new legislation.

Given the very high value of the authorized sanctions, the Commission had to build support for its approach. It consulted extensively with trade associations and member governments and it sought to minimize the adverse impact on European firms and consumers by including in the sanctions list only those products for which the US accounted for less than 20 per cent of EU imports and which the EU also exports (Commission 2002). In addition, giving the US plenty of time to comply not only established that sanctions were being used as a last resort, but also meant that the credibility of the EU's role as an advocate of multilateral trade rules was at stake.[28] As a consequence, even those member governments that had urged caution out of concern for the transatlantic relationship lent their support to the sanctions.[29]

Multilateral legitimacy

The EU's capacity to pursue compliance through the imposition of sanctions is also facilitated by the WTO framework (Bronkers and McNelis 2001: 427).[30] Prior to the creation of the WTO, the EU had agreed sanctions for trade reasons only a few times and these were in response to sanctions imposed on the EU, such as in response to the US sanctions over hormone-treated beef in the early 1990s.[31] The WTO introduced two changes that made it easier for the member governments to agree to impose sanctions. First, the dispute settlement system was made binding. As a consequence, it is unambiguous whether the measure in question is contrary to WTO rules. Second, the WTO has the capacity to authorize the imposition of sanctions in order to enforce compliance, and it establishes the appropriate level of sanctions. This firmly establishes the legitimacy of sanctions as a tool of multilateral rule enforcement. There is also no longer a need to agree what level of sanctions is appropriate.

The governments must still wrestle with the thorny issues of whether they want to use sanctions to enforce compliance and the composition of the sanctions, but the other issues are now out of their hands. As a consequence, while not making the decision to impose sanctions easy for the member governments, the WTO framework does make it simpler than it was.

The EU has been willing and able to impose sanctions, but has sought to do so in such a way as to induce compliance rather than to punish non-compliance. This has meant that the EU has been less quick to reach for the sanctions stick than the US.

Assessing role impact

The extent to which the EU has been able to get other governments to comply is the true test of its role impact. Here, again, the EU would seem to perform on a par with the US. The European Commission (2003) reports that use of the TBR and WTO dispute settlement have tended to lead to changes by respondent governments.

As noted earlier, whether a foreign government complies is affected by many things other that the EU's actions. Tellingly, however, even in the hardest cases, the EU has had an impact. These hardest cases involve the US and require legislative action. They are particularly hard because the large size of the US economy means that it is relatively impervious to sanctions and because its divided system of government makes any legislative change difficult. None the less, the US has replaced the FSC tax break and bills changing the Antidumping Act of 1916 and the Byrd Amendment were making their way through Congress at the time of writing (June 2005).

As the Commission's reservations about the compatibility of the replacement for FSC suggest, however, the EU's victories are rarely complete (Commission 2003). Further, rules are often replaced by ones that are equivalent in effect, even if they are compatible with multilateral obligations.[32] This, however, is not a problem unique to the EU. Witness the limited changes the EU adopted in response to the US complaints against its banana trade regime and ban on hormone-treated beef (Young 2004).

Conclusion

This chapter has argued that the EU is able to use the WTO's dispute settlement system effectively despite the decision-making complications posed by its character as an international organization. Although it does not initiate quite as many complaints as the US, its most obvious comparator, it has actually won more panel judgements and has been at least as capable of imposing sanctions in order to compel compliance with those judgements.

The potentially negative impact of the EU's character as an international organization on its role performance in WTO dispute resolution has been mitigated by the interaction of three key political factors. First, the EU member governments' pragmatic approach to trade policy means that they have been willing to co-operate beyond what is strictly required by the EU's treaties. As a consequence, the EU's role in WTO dispute resolution has not been questioned. Second, the EU's member governments explicitly and implicitly have delegated extensive authority to the Commission. Third, the distributive character of the politics of dispute initiation and the phenomenon of 'diffuse reciprocity' have meant that the member governments only exceptionally object to the initiation of a trade dispute. The interaction of the institutional framework and the politics of dispute initiation mean that the EU performs as if it were a traditional state.

With regard to the imposition of sanctions, however, the EU's character as an international organization is more pronounced because the character of the politics becomes more conflictual and the institutional framework requires that a qualified majority of the governments support the action. None the less, these challenges have not prevented the EU from imposing sanctions. This has been possible because the Commission has pursued sanctions only as a last resort and has done so in such a way that firms and governments are persuaded that doing so is to their benefit in the long run.

As a consequence, the EU has been able to punch its (economic) weight in WTO dispute resolution despite the internal political complexity that stems from it being an international organization.

Notes

I am grateful to the participants of the Uppsala ECPR Joint Sessions of Workshops and the Loughborough Colloquium, particularly Ole Elgström, Ulrich Sedelmeier and Michael Smith, for their comments. The research on which this chapter is based was made possible by a grant from the British Academy (SG-35702). I am also grateful to Edward Duru for research assistance and to the practitioners who took the time to discuss these issues with me.

1 Complaints DS7, 12 and 14 against France's rules on the description of scallops and DS135 over France's ban on asbestos products.
2 Internally the issue of who is the most appropriate actor has been more, although not very, pronounced when the EU and its member states have been on the defensive (Chatháin 1999).
3 DS42 Measures concerning sound recordings (Japan); DS79 Patent protection of pharmaceutical and agricultural products (India); DS114 Patent protection of pharmaceuticals (Canada): DS160 Section 110(5) of the US Copyright Act (US); DS176 Section 211 of the Omnibus Appropriations Act (US); DS186 Section 337 of the Tariff Act of 1930 (US).
4 DS38 Cuban Liberty and Democratic Solidarity Act (US); DS54 Measures affecting the auto sector (Indonesia); DS81 Measures affecting trade and investment in the automotive sector (Brazil); DS142 Measures in the auto sector (Canada); DS146 Measures affecting the auto sector (India).
5 DS117 Measures affecting film distribution (Canada).
6 See http://europa.eu.int/comm/trade/mk_access/index_en.htm.
7 See http://europa.eu.int/comm/trade/mk_access/index_en.htm.
8 See http://europa.eu.int/comm/trade/issues/respectrules/index_en.htm.
9 DS38, DS39, DS88, DS152, DS165, DS200, DS217, DS320, DS321.
10 There is no clear benchmark against which to assess what is a 'normal' level of use of the dispute settlement system (Holmes *et al.* 2003).
11 Based on a table from the Eurochambres report 'Promotion Campaign of the Market Access Database' dated February 2003 included in the information pack for the DTI seminar on 'Resolving Market Access Problems', London, 30 September 2003.
12 DS160 concerning music royalties in the US.
13 Council Regulation 3286/94, amended by Council Regulation 356/95.
14 The TBR's procedures are covered exhaustively in the literature (see, for example, Kuijper 1995; MacLean 1999).
15 Interviews BA1, BA10.
16 Interviews BA22, BA23.
17 Interviews BA1, BA2, BA9, BA12.
18 Interviews BA9, BA12.
19 Interview BA24.
20 Interviews BA2, BA9, BA10.
21 Interviews BA7, BA9, BA17.

22 Interview BA21.
23 Interview BA7.
24 The adoption of Council Regulation 2238/2003 in order to coerce the US to change the Antidumping Act of 1916 was very different as, rather than impose costs on EU firms, it allows them to sue the US plaintiff to recover damages caused by a complaint under the 1916 Act.
25 Interviews BA9, BA22, BA23.
26 Interview BA12.
27 Interview BA9.
28 Interview BA24.
29 Interview BA22.
30 Interview BA23.
31 Interview BA24.
32 Interview BA6.

References

Abbot, K. W., Keohane, R. O., Moravcsik, A., Slaughter, A.-M. and Snidal, D. (2000) 'The Concept of Legalization', *International Organization*, 54 (3): 401–19.

Bronkers, M. and McNelis, N. (2001) 'The EU Trade Barriers Regulation Comes of Age', *Journal of World Trade*, 35 (4): 427–82.

Busch, M. and Reinhardt, E. (2000) 'Bargaining in the Shadow of the Law: Early Settlement in GATT/WTO Disputes', *Fordham International Law Journal* 24 (1–2): 158–72.

Chatháin, C. N. (1999) 'The European Community and the Member States in the Dispute Settlement Understanding of the WTO: United or Divided?', *European Law Journal*, 5 (4): 461–78.

Commission (2002) 'Notice Relating to the WTO Dispute Settlement proceedings concerning the United States tax treatment of Foreign Sales Corporations (FSC): Invitation for comments on the list of products that could be subject to countermeasures', *Official Journal of the European Communities*, C217/2, 13 September.

Commission (2003) 'The Trade Barriers Regulation (TBR)', DG Trade, September.

Conybeare, J. A. C. (1987) *Trade Wars: The Theory and Practice of International Commercial Rivalry*, New York: Columbia University Press.

Council (2002) 'Council Regulation (EC) No. 1031/2002 of 13 June 2002 establishing additional customs duties on imports of certain products originating in the Unites States of America', *Official Journal of the European Communities* L157/8, 15 June.

Davey, W. J. (2001) 'Has the WTO Dispute Settlement System Exceeded its Authority?', *Journal of International Economic Law*, 4 (1): 79–110.

Goldstein, A. E. and McGuire, S. (2004) 'The Political Economy of Strategic Trade Policy and the Brazil–Canada Export Subsidies Saga', *The World Economy*, 27 (4): 541–66.

Goldstein, J. (2000) 'The United States and World Trade: Hegemony by Proxy?', in T. C. Lawton, J. N. Rosenau and A. C. Verdun (eds) *Strange Power: Shaping the Parameters of International Relations and International Political Economy*, Aldershot: Ashgate, 249–72.

Guzman, A. and Simmons, B. A. (2002) 'To Settle or Empanel? An Empirical

Analysis of Litigation and Settlement at the World Trade Organization', *Journal of Legal Studies*, 31: S205–S235.

Holmes, P., Rollo, J. and Young, A. R. (2003) 'Emerging Trends in WTO Dispute Settlement: Back to the GATT?', World Bank Policy Research Working Paper 3133. Washington, DC: World Bank.

Johnson, M. (1998) *European Community Trade Polity and the Article 113 Committee*, London: Royal Institute of International Affairs.

Keohane, R. O. (1986) 'Reciprocity in International Relations', *International Organization*, 40 (1): 1–27.

Kuijper, P. J. (1995) 'The New WTO Dispute Settlement System: The Impact on the European Community', *Journal of World Trade*, 29 (6): 47–71.

Lowi, T. (1964) 'American Business, Public Policy, Case Studies and Political Theory', *World Politics*, 16 (4): 677–715.

MacLean, R. M. (1999) 'The European Community's Trade Barrier Regulation Takes Shape: Is It Living Up to Expectations?', *Journal of World Trade*, 33 (6): 69–96.

Meunier, S. (1998) 'Divided but United: European Trade Policy Integration and the EU–US Agricultural Negotiations in the Uruguay Round', in C. Rhodes (ed.) *The European Union in the World Community*, Boulder, CO: Lynne Rienner, 193–211.

Molyneux, C. T. G. (2001) *Domestic Structures and International Trade: The Unfair Trade Instruments of the United States and the European Union*, Oxford: Hart Publishing.

Pollack, M. A. (2003) *The Engines of European Integration: Delegation, Agency and Agenda Setting in the EU*, Oxford: Oxford University Press.

Schoppa, L. J. (1993) 'Two-level Games and Bargaining Outcomes: Why *gaiatsu* Succeeds in Japan in Some Cases But Not Others', *International Organization*, 47 (3): 353–86.

Shaffer, G. (2003) *Defending Interests: Public–Private Partnerships in WTO Litigation*, Washington, DC: Brookings Institution Press.

Smith, J. M. (2000) 'The Politics of Dispute Settlement Design: Explaining Legalism in Regional Trade Pacts', *International Organization*, 54 (1): 137–80.

UNICE (2004) 'Letter to Pascal Lamy: Foreign Sales Corporations/Extraterritorial Income Exclusion Act (FSC/ETI)', 13 February.

Winters, L. A. (2001) 'European Union Trade Policy: Actually or Just Nominally Liberal?', in H. Wallace (ed.) *Interlocking Dimensions of European Integration*, London: Palgrave, 25–44.

Woolcock, S. (2000) 'European Trade Policy: Global Pressures and Domestic Constraints', in H. Wallace and W. Wallace (eds) *Policy-Making in the European Union*, 4th edn, Oxford: Oxford University Press, 373–99.

Young, A. R. (2002) *Extending European Cooperation: The European Union and the 'New' International Trade Agenda*, Manchester: Manchester University Press.

Young, A. R. (2004) 'The Incidental Fortress: The Single European Market and World Trade', *Journal of Common Market Studies*, 42 (2): 393–414.

Zeng, K. (2002) 'Trade Structure and the Effectiveness of America's "Aggressively Unilateral" Trade Policy', *International Studies Quarterly*, 46: 93–115.

Interview list (interviews were conducted on a not-for-attribution basis).

BA1	British government official, London, 21 May 2003.
BA2	British government official, London, 21 May 2003.
BA6	Trade association representative, Brussels, 15 September 2003.
BA7	Commission official, Brussels, 16 September 2003.
BA9	Commission official, Brussels, 17 September 2003.
BA10	Commission official, Brussels, 17 September 2003.
BA12	Commission official, Brussels, 18 September 2003.
BA16	Trade association representative, telephone, 2 October 2003.
BA21	Commission official, Brussels, 25 May 2004.
BA22	Council Secretariat official, Brussels, 25 March 2004.
BA23	Council Secretariat official, Brussels, 25 March 2004.
BA24	Commission official, Brussels, 26 March 2004.

12 Institutions, ideas and a leadership gap

The EU's role in multilateral competition policy

Chad Damro

The European Union (EU) has established and developed a significant role in international politics in a variety of policy areas. The EU's success may be most apparent in international competition relations.[1] Compared to other policy areas regulated by the EU, the European Commission enjoys considerable – possibly its most extensive – decision-making authority in competition policy.[2] Reflecting this domestic authority, the Commission also plays a significant role in shaping international discussions on competition policy. For example, the EU has consistently advocated the multilateralization of competition policy (Fox 1997).

The EU's role in international competition relations raises a fundamental question. How and why did the EU develop its role in multilateral competition policy? To answer this question, the chapter investigates the institutional development of the EU's competition policy and the possibility that such changes created new ideas, which informed the European Commission's approach to the multilateralization of competition policy.[3]

Despite the inclusion of competition policy as a common policy in the Treaties of Rome in 1957, important elements of this policy area did not come under the authority of the European Commission until the implementation of the Merger Control Regulation (MCR) in 1990. During the intervening period, EU competition policy gradually shifted to the supranational level through a number of internal EU institutional developments. Such historical developments appear to have had an impact on the ideas that inform the Commission's position on international competition policy. Once consolidated internally, the Commission seems to have adopted similar binding and 'integrationist' ideas in its approach to the multilateralization of competition policy. Most recently, the Commission's approach has been witnessed in the current World Trade Organization's (WTO) Doha Round of trade negotiations.

The EU's role in international competition policy cannot be explained without reference to the United States (US), the other most significant international actor in this policy area. The EU's competition policy developed independent of, but influenced by, the institutions and ideas that underpinned antitrust policy in the US. In addition, the US challenged the EU's position on the multilateralization of competition policy prior to the launching of the Doha Round in 2001. The EU's leadership role in this policy area would have been seriously undermined if it could not reach a compromise with the US on the inclusion of competition policy on the WTO's new agenda.[4]

This chapter argues that the Commission's position on the multilateralization of competition policy has been based on a belief in 'binding multilateralism'. This position reflects the historical development of EU competition policy through the gradual changes that led to the Commission's current supranational authority in competition policy. A similar process of gradual regionalization was not experienced by the US. As a result, the different EU and US experiences seem to have generated different ideas, which led to different positions on the multilateralization of competition policy through the WTO.

Despite the Commission's active advocacy for the multilateralization of competition policy, its leadership role in this policy area seems limited. Evidence drawn from the run-up to the Doha Round and the outcome of the WTO's Fifth Ministerial Conference in Cancún raises questions about the Commission's role performance. The Cancún talks collapsed without agreement. Subsequent talks have revealed that, while other previously contentious items may be put back on the table for discussion, competition policy is no longer on the agenda at the WTO. These developments reflect a gap between the Commission's self-perception of and actual performance of its leadership role in the multilateralization of competition policy.

The chapter proceeds in the following manner. First, the chapter describes the institutional development of the EU's competition policy, beginning with the Treaties of Rome and concluding with the 1990 MCR. Second, the chapter discusses the impact that this historical development had on the ideas that inform the EU's approach to international discussions on competition policy. Third, the chapter discusses the different institutions and ideas that inform the US position on this topic. Fourth, the chapter investigates the empirical differences between the EU and US approaches to the multilateralization of competition policy prior to the WTO's Seattle Ministerial Conference. Fifth, the chapter investigates the outcome of the WTO's Cancún Ministerial Conference and addresses the apparent gap between the Commission's self-perception and performance of leadership in this policy area. Finally, the chapter summarizes the findings of the study and offers insights on the future leadership role of the EU in international competition policy.

Institutional development of EU competition policy

The EU's international leadership role in competition policy is, in part, based on institutional foundations. The establishment of those institutional foundations required gradual 'integrationist' pressure by the Commission to expand its authority over this policy. This process of supranationalization reflected the Commission's approach to policy-making and new challenges in competition policy.

The actual development of a European competition policy occurred much later than initially planned. While a multi-sector, Europe-wide competition policy was agreed to be a common policy for the entire EU in 1957, the actual implementation of the policy required gradual and piecemeal statutory advances and court decisions.[5] Indeed, EU competition policy was not truly Europeanized until as late as the implementation of the Merger Control Regulation in 1990.

As a gradual process, the creation of a truly European competition policy was also influenced by US experiences in antitrust policy (Dumez and Jeunemaître 1996).[6] Following World War II, the US actively encouraged the development of antitrust legislation in many European states: the UK promulgated antitrust legislation in 1948, France in 1953 and Germany in 1957. However, these new competition policies were implemented with an understanding by the US that rigorous antitrust enforcement in Europe would be overshadowed by the need to rebuild national economies. This understanding reflected a popular and recurring European approach to rebuilding national economies through government support for cartel-like national champions. It remained unclear exactly how long such a transition period would last. Thus, while US pressure played a large role in the creation of individual national European competition policies, immediate convergence toward a pan-European competition policy remained elusive (Dumez and Jeunemaître 1996: 218–19).

Despite the delayed convergence, the US continued to support the creation of a Europe-wide competition policy. The earliest effort at converging towards a pan-European competition policy can be found in the treaty establishing the European Coal and Steel Community (ECSC) in 1951. In particular, Articles 65 and 66 provide the competition principles for the ECSC: Article 65 of the ECSC prohibited anti-competitive agreements, including cartels; Article 66 of the ECSC prohibited 'concentrations' (i.e. mergers) and 'misuses' of economic power. The ECSC also created a 'supranational' High Authority to oversee the functioning and implementation of the treaty provisions. This High Authority was granted sole responsibility for enforcing Articles 65 and 66.

The next step in creating a pan-European competition policy came with the signing of the Treaty of Rome in 1957, and the creation of the European Economic Communities (EEC). The provisions on competition policy in this treaty reflected the earlier agreements in the ECSC Treaty. The relevant articles cover restrictive agreements (cartels), monopolies and public sector firms, and state aid.

The Treaty created the initial framework for the free movement within the single market of goods, services, capital and persons (i.e. labour). To create this single market, Article 3(f) [3(g) TEU] strove to ensure that 'competition in the Common Market is not distorted'.[7] This basic goal is then elaborated in Articles 85 and 86. Article 85 [81 TEU] follows the basic structure of Article 65 of the ECSC Treaty. Article 86 [82 TEU] addresses monopoly policy by expanding on Article 66 of the ECSC Treaty to prohibit 'any abuse by one or more undertakings of a dominant position' in the single market. These articles placed authority for competition policy in the newly created European Commission.

While competition policy was agreed to be a common policy of the EEC, in practice the creation of a truly common competition policy required additional efforts by the European Commission. At the time, member states still had a patchwork of different competition laws; some (e.g. Belgium) had no competition policy at all. Asserting its authority under the Treaty, the Commission began pushing for a Community structure to implement competition policy as a common policy. The Council of Ministers allowed the Commission considerable discretion to prepare the institutional framework for implementing Articles 85 and 86.

Following negotiations with the Council, the European Parliament and individual national governments, the Commission issued Regulation 17 in 1962.[8] This regulation created the institutional structure for the EEC's competition policy and established significant discretionary authority for the Commission. Despite receiving little academic attention, the importance of Regulation 17 cannot be overstated for the supranationalization of EU competition policy. As Gerber argues, 'Regulation 17 created a competition law system in which the enforcement and policy-making prerogatives were centered in the Commission and the role of national legal systems was marginalized' (1998: 349).

Regulation 17 created a European notification system for proposed mergers, required national authorities to suspend their competition investigations in cases where the Commission began an investigation under the Treaty, and gave significant authority to the EU's Competition Directorate.[9] Under the strictures of Regulation 17, competition decisions taken by the directorate must be sent to the Commission for a final decision.

While the Commission's general supranational authority over competition policy had increased significantly with Regulation 17, the EU's institutional framework still lacked an explicit mechanism to review and control mergers in the single market. As Eleanor Fox, an antitrust expert at New York University, argues, no central law or regulation emerged to check the spread of mergers in the single market because there was a general belief among European decision-makers that such transactions 'would be good for integration' (cited in Davis and Raghavan 2001: A8). Therefore, the Competition Directorate had to look to existing instruments as potential ways to control mergers.[10]

The ECJ appeared to support early Commission efforts to apply existing regulatory instruments to potentially anti-competitive merger activity. For example, in its 1973 Continental Can judgement, the ECJ asserted 'under certain circumstances, a firm holding a dominant position could be regarded as abusing its position when taking over or merging with a competitor' (McGowan and Cini 1999: 179). Thus, the Commission and Court would be able to use the Article 86 [82 TEU] prohibition against abuses of dominance to control merger activity. In addition, in the 1987 Philip Morris case, the Article 85 [81 TEU] prohibition of agreements that prevent, restrict or distort competition was also applied to merger activity.

Capitalizing on the ECJ's apparent support for its position, the Commission issued a draft merger control regulation in the same year as the Continental Can decision (1973). This was followed by three more proposals for merger legislation in 1982 and 1984. All of these proposals failed, largely due to resistance in the Council, especially from France, Germany and the UK (McGowan and Cini 1999: 179). However, external changes were occurring that would eventually facilitate the establishment of the Commission's merger control authority.

The Commission's various proposals for a merger control regulation gained particular impetus during the 1980s from the negotiations over the Single European Act and the approaching completion of the Single European Market (SEM) (Devuyst 2000: 13). During the 1980s, merger activity in the EU was increasing significantly: 'According to Commission data, there were 115 mergers in 1982–83, 208 in 1984–85, 492 in 1988–89 and 622 in 1989–90' (McGowan and Cini 1999: 179). Based on this activity, the Commission developed an argument that overcame the Council's reservations and, in 1990, it implemented Regulation (EEC) No. 4064/89, more commonly known as the Merger Control Regulation (MCR). The MCR greatly expanded the authority of the EU by shifting merger review authority from the individual member states to the Commission.

Within the Union's institutional structure, the Commission is the dominant player in merger review today, exercising supranational powers over mergers with a Community-wide impact. Indeed, McGowan and Cini argue 'in contrast to all other EU policy areas, competition policy is unique, for both the Council of Ministers and the European Parliament find themselves on the sidelines' (1999: 177). Within the Commission itself, merger review became the domain of the Competition Directorate, specifically the Merger Task Force. As McGowan and Wilks (1995) assert, the EU's first supranational policy had finally come into existence.

While the Treaty of Rome launched the idea of competition policy as a common policy, the actual supranationalization of this policy took much longer. With the implementation of the MCR in 1990, the Commission finally acquired its promised authority. The gradual integrationist process confirmed the Commission's view of policy-making and its support for integrationist solutions to new challenges.

EU competition policy: institutions and ideas

The institutional development of the EU's competition policy demonstrates the incremental process through which the Union regionalized and developed this policy area. The gradual approach shifted authority to the supranational European Commission. This gradual erosion of national sovereignty can be seen as informing the Commission's approach to competition issues at the international level.

Given the significant authority acquired by the Commission and the Competition Directorate, these European supranational actors likely viewed competition policy as a domain in which gradual integration via binding legal agreements and the relinquishment of national sovereignty should be the norm. From this vantage point, it was quite natural for the Commission to apply this approach to negotiations on competition policy at the international level. The process of institutional supranationalization in the EU had generated a new idea about how the EU would approach multilateral discussions on competition policy. Rather than seeking to maintain the status quo, the EU adopted a leadership role of promoting the multilateralization of competition policy through the WTO.[11]

Fox has articulated the emergence of a new idea about multilateral solutions within the EU based on its historical experience in competition policy. The EU position on international competition policy can be described as a desire to pursue *binding* multilateral measures through the WTO. According to Fox, this position reflects a 'cosmopolitan' approach, which is familiar to the EU because of its historical experience with economic integration (1997). This approach reflects the EU's desire to eliminate internal discrimination against and barriers to goods or services in order to create the single market. In short, the EU – in particular, the Commission – has exerted considerable effort and spent significant resources over the years attempting to create an environment conducive to the gradual convergence of national regulation. This approach has transformed traditional notions of national sovereignty among the member states of the EU.

The EU's experience with competition policy also reflects a shared interest in benefits for the collective. Fox's cosmopolitanism 'connotes concern for the interests of the entire community without regard to nationality, while recognizing the legitimate role for national and provincial governments to act in the interests of their citizens' (Fox 1997: 2 n. 4). The EU's approach to the multilateralization of competition policy embodies such cosmopolitan aspirations, based on its historical experience and treaty-based mandate to pursue 'an ever closer union'.

This cosmopolitan approach specifically addressed the development of competition policy in the EU. While reducing barriers to trade, the Union also had to ensure free competition in the single market. Fox provides hypothetical examples to demonstrate how these institutional developments reflect an idea of cosmopolitanism:

> after the adoption of the Treaty of Rome, German sugar growers could not cartelize to keep out French and Belgian sugar, and vice versa; nor could the French, the Germans and the Belgians agree with one another that each would keep its home territory to itself. British Telecom could not obstruct the flow of telephone signals through the United Kingdom. [In short,] State action, as well as private action, is subject to limits for the good of the community.
>
> (Fox 1997: 2)

For the EU, the historical and experiential factors do seem to help to explain the Commission's position of binding multilateral cosmopolitanism. The EU may have been particularly amenable to the multilateralization of competition policies based on its own experience with binding, treaty-based harmonization of competition law in the single market (Fox 1997: 4–10). If so, it was quite natural for the EU to view a binding multilateral approach via an international institution – the WTO – as the best means to address the challenges of international competition policy. By addressing the challenges in such a manner, the Commission would pursue its self-perception as a leader in international competition policy.

US competition policy: different institutions and different ideas

Since the 1890 Sherman Act, US antitrust legislation has undergone numerous changes and has expanded to address many different types of commercial activity. While the Sherman Act was originally codified to prohibit monopolies, US 'competition policy' is not now exclusively limited to anti-monopoly policy. US competition policy is now regulating the same types of anti-competitive business behaviour – albeit, occasionally with different economic models – upon which the EU is focused, with the noticeable exception of state aid.[12]

This section will not describe the extensive historical development of the institutions of US competition policy. Rather, it will focus on what might be labelled the US idea of 'non-binding bilateralism'. Based on this idea, the US appears to have developed a very different approach to the multilateralization of competition policy. The US has a very different historical and institutional experience in competition policy, which has not gradually transformed traditional notions of national sovereignty. Quite the opposite, the US approach has been firmly based on traditional notions of national sovereignty.[13]

The US position on international competition policy can be described as a desire to pursue non-binding bilateral measures. According to Fox (1997), this position reflects a 'leave good enough alone' approach in which the US prefers to rely on the established hub-and-spoke system of bilateral competition agreements.[14]

Following on Fox's classifications, the US's position may be loosely viewed as a 'parochialist' approach to the multilateralization of competition policy. Fox argues that such a 'parochialist' approach 'connotes discrimination against and barriers to foreign goods or services' (1997: 2 n 4). The US did not experience the same integrationist developments that are the hallmark of the EU's historical development. Therefore, the US's parochialist approach is potentially inconsistent with the EU's cosmopolitan approach because it engenders a preference for protecting national sovereignty by limiting international co-operation to non-binding measures agreed at the bilateral level. More specifically, this approach conflicts with the EU's desire to pursue changes in international competition policy that would be *binding at the multilateral level*.

In contrast to the EU experience, the US was sceptical of applying a cosmopolitan, 'integrationist' model at the international level. As Fox argues, US resistance to the multilateralization of competition rules should not be surprising because 'Americans are not steeped in the postwar Western European tradition of community building. They have the tools of unilateralism, they fear the compromises of bargaining, and they abjure the "relinquishment" of sovereignty' (1997: 12). When combined with institutional developments that protected national sovereignty, such a characterization of US historical experience likely influenced the US position on the multilateralization of competition policy.

In addition to a different historical experience, the US position was likely motivated by underlying domestic institutional factors, which seem quite different from those found in the EU. Unlike the Commission, US competition authorities (i.e. the Federal Trade Commission, FTC, and the Antitrust Division in the Department of Justice, DOJ) have domestic legal institutions for engaging in a variety of bilateral competition agreements. For example, US competition regulators can enter into binding bilateral executive agreements on competition policy with foreign regulators at their own discretion.[15] In addition, the 1994 International Antitrust Enforcement Assistance Act (IAEAA) authorizes the US competition authorities to enter into antitrust specific agreements that require mutual assistance with foreign competition agencies.[16] Finally, US competition authorities can enter into Mutual Legal Assistance Treaties (MLATs) (Damro 2004a), which provide for exchanges of information in competition and other cases.[17]

These institutional differences influenced the ideas behind the US position of 'leave good enough alone'. The US position on the multilateralization of competition policy should not be surprising because any international agreement to move trade-related competition issues into the WTO's binding Dispute Settlement Mechanism would require treaty ratification – which raises more domestic veto points in the US than would be raised through the pursuit of bilateral executive agreements, IAEAAs and MLATs. As a result, US competition authorities were more likely to support a bilateral system that allowed them more flexibility to engage in co-operation at their considerable discretion. Similarly, and unlike in the EU, competition cases are handled in the US through the domestic court system. Thus, any agreement to subject competition policy to a multilateral dispute settlement mechanism would have bound the US competition regulators to supranational/international judicial decisions.

Given these institutional differences, it is not surprising that the US operated under a different idea of how to approach international discussions of competition policy. In particular, these institutions would have supported a parochialist idea of 'leave good enough alone', in which international competition policy continued to be dealt with on a bilateral basis. Given the institutional advantages enjoyed by the US competition authorities, 'cosmopolitans would have to make a strong case that unilateralism is not enough' (Fox 1997: 12).

The current hub-and-spoke system of bilateral agreements did not challenge the institutions or ideas that served as the foundation of the US competition authorities' approach to international competition policy. The only challenge to this comfortable status quo would be the emergence of an important actor in international competition relations who adopted a more cosmopolitan and integrationist approach to the multilateralization of competition policy. Such an actor emerged in 1999, in the run-up to the WTO's Ministerial Conference in Seattle.

The pre-Seattle multilateralization of competition policy

This section investigates the extent to which the EU and US positions on the multilateralization of competition policy prior to the WTO's Seattle Ministerial reflect the institutions and ideas identified above. During most of the 1990s, the EU and US disagreed whether or not to pursue regulatory efforts in competition policy at the multilateral level. The EU and US ultimately compromised and agreed to put competition policy on the agenda of the Doha Round in 2001. However, the two protagonists staked out the conflicting positions and very publicly disagreed over this issue in 1999.

At an Organization of Co-operation and Economic Development (OECD) conference on Trade and Competition in Paris, 29–30 June 1999, EU Trade Commissioner and Vice-president of the Commission Sir Leon Brittan and US Assistant Attorney General for Antitrust Joel I. Klein delivered contradictory speeches in which they announced their respective positions on the multilateralization of competition policy in the WTO. This EU–US disagreement was particularly significant because it occurred at a time when trade officials were in the delicate process of negotiating the agenda of the WTO's upcoming Third Ministerial Conference to be held in Seattle later in the year. Put very simply, the EU seemed to support the multilateralization of competition policy in the WTO while the US preferred the current system of bilateral agreements.

Speaking for the EU, Sir Leon Brittan declared that WTO trade negotiations preceding the Seattle Ministerial should consider the inclusion of competition policy. The EU position was based on four central requirements for a possible WTO agreement on competition policy:

- *Compatibility of approaches.* A WTO agreement should highlight the compatibility among bilateral, regional and multilateral approaches.
- *Fundamental competition objectives.* A WTO agreement on competition policy should emphasize transparency, non-discrimination, co-operation and convergence.
- *Binding rules.* The binding WTO Dispute Settlement Mechanism (DSM) should be used if a member's legislation and enforcement structure are not in accordance with their WTO commitments or if a pattern of non-enforcement of domestic competition law can be shown.
- *Core principles.* Any WTO agreement should embody the following principles:

    1 Commitment to introduce progressively domestic competition legislation backed up by an effective enforcement structure.
    2 Inclusion of core principles on competition law and its enforcement, based on non-discrimination and transparency.
    3 Provisions for co-operation procedures among competition authorities, including transfer of non-confidential information and non-binding 'positive comity'.
    4 Goals of gradual convergence of approaches to anti-competitive practices that have a significant impact on international trade (Brittan 1999: 3–5).

Brittan's position was most notable for its inclusion of a binding dimension, specifically through the WTO's DSM. According to Brittan, 'A WTO Agreement on competition would have no added value unless it was binding on governments ... I am therefore convinced that the commitments to be included in a multilateral competition agreement should be subject to WTO dispute settlement' (1999: 5). The call for binding measures was in conformity with the EU's cosmopolitan approach to economic integration. While other elements of the position were less controversial, this demand for binding rules would prove a significant point of contention with the US, which lacked any interest in binding, cosmopolitan approaches to international competition policy.

On behalf of the US, Joel I. Klein opposed the inclusion of competition policy in WTO discussions. Klein's argument reflected the US parochialist approach to the multilateralization of competition policy. According to Klein, the incorporation of competition policy in a possible WTO agreement should not be included in the negotiations preceding the Seattle Ministerial because of three central concerns:

- *Utility of bilateral system.* The extensive system of bilateral competition agreements has a commendable record for facilitating co-operation.
- *Lack of experience.* The international community – including the EU and US – has only limited experience in dealing with matters displaying trade–competition linkages. As a result, it is too early to multilateralize competition policy, especially through a trade-oriented organization like the WTO.
- *Politicization of cases.* The incorporation of competition policy issues into the WTO's binding DSM would increase the likelihood of politicizing competition issues (1999: 5–6).[18]

Providing a clear clash with Brittan's position, Klein argued that the international community had not identified the questions, much less the answers, that would be important over the next decade for incorporating competition policy into binding WTO obligations. In short, he declared, 'if we try to run before we have learned to walk, we will stumble and badly injure what we are all tying to promote – sound antitrust enforcement' (1999: 4).

Summarizing his opposition to bringing competition policy into the WTO's binding framework, Klein forcefully stated 'at this point in time, WTO antitrust rules would be useless, pernicious, or both, and would serve only to politicize the long-term future of international antitrust enforcement, including through the intrusion of trade disputes disguised as antitrust problems' (1999: 5). Upon these arguments, the US steadfastly refused to incorporate competition disciplines into WTO negotiations.[19]

It should be added at this point that evidence of an EU–US compromise began appearing as early as Brittan and Klein's public disagreement in 1999. As Klein noted during his speech, the EU did signal willingness to moderate its position regarding the incorporation of the WTO's DSM for competition disagreements: 'The EU and others favoring negotiations . . . have spoken of modifying the extent to which ordinary WTO dispute settlement mechanisms might apply to individual antitrust decisions' (Klein 1999: 5). According to the EU, however, this hint at compromise would limit the application of the DSM to trends of non-enforcement instead of individual competition cases. The fact that the EU still called for inclusion of the DSM when trends of non-enforcement could be shown remained unacceptable to the US.[20]

Cancún and a leadership gap?

Despite their disagreements, the EU and US did finally compromise and agreed to add competition policy to the WTO's Doha Round (Damro 2004a). However, the compromise reflected only minimal concessions on the part of the US. Far from reflecting the EU's position, the Doha negotiations would not consider applying the DSM to this policy area, but would rather only identify core principles for competition policy.

In November 2001 the Fourth Ministerial Conference launched the Doha Round of trade talks. Competition policy figured to be a contentious item as one of the so-called Singapore issues: trade and investment, trade and competition policy, transparency in government procurement, and trade facilitation. These issues are named for the WTO's First Ministerial Conference in Singapore in 1996, during which calls were made for their inclusion in future rounds of trade negotiations.

The Doha Round suffered a setback when the Fifth Ministerial Conference in Cancún failed to reach a consensus in September 2003. According to Kol and Winters (2004), the deadlock on the final day in Cancún was caused by disagreements between the developing countries and other members over agricultural issues. In addition, the collapse was based in part on disagreements over the inclusion of the Singapore issues:

> The topics to be negotiated under each issue were not generally the key ones for developing countries and the clauses proposed by the EU not geared to development objectives. And yet the proposal implied that the Round should devote large amounts of time and effort to them. Developing countries were faced with having to negotiate issues on which they had little experience, little beneficial interest and little information about the other side's intentions or objectives. Given their shortages of negotiating capacity and domestic political capital to spend on these issues, it was hardly surprising that they declined to proceed.
>
> (Kol and Winters 2004: 17)[21]

The striking failure at Cancún raises questions about whether the EU has actually performed as a leader in the multilateralization of competition policy. Put very simply, in order to be a leader, one must have followers.[22] The evidence from Cancún suggests that the Commission has failed in its efforts to rally followers to its position in this policy area. This is not to say that the Union will never realize its leadership aspirations for the multilateralization of competition policy at the WTO, but simply to state that the Commission's self-perception seems to be somewhat erroneous and misguided at this stage.[23] As a result, within the WTO, the Commission has demonstrated a significant gap between its self-perception and the actual performance of its leadership role.

Conclusion

This chapter has analysed the EU's role in multilateral competition policy in order to determine the extent to which it has performed a leadership role. It finds that institutions and ideas help to explain the role of the Union as an advocate for the multilateralization of competition policy. It has been argued that the gradual historical development of the Union's internal domestic institutions for competition policy provides a basis for the European Commission's current self-perception as a leader in this policy area. The historical development also informs the Commission's ideas on the multilateralization of competition policy. Similarly, a brief investigation of the institutions and ideas that underpin US competition policy reveals the sources of the US's conflicting position on the multilateralization of competition policy.

Despite an early, and seemingly intractable, disagreement on the multilateralization of competition policy, the EU and US did ultimately compromise to add competition policy to the WTO's Doha Round. But prior to this compromise, the conflicting positions of these two protagonists can be described as binding multilateral cosmopolitanism for the EU and non-binding bilateral parochialism for the US. The EU's position reflected a desire to add a binding and multilateral dimension to international competition policy by incorporating it into the WTO framework. The US believed the most appropriate approach to international competition policy should remain within the current system of voluntary bilateral agreements.

Historical experience and domestic institutions appear to be important determinants of the conflicting EU and US positions. The EU's position seems to reflect its historical experience with gradual economic integration: pursue the interests of the entire community by integrating national competition policies in order to help create the single market. This historical integrationist experience enjoys little support in the US as a model for multilateralizing competition policy. In addition, the US lacked any interest in pursuing a binding multilateral initiative because its competition regulators already had numerous instruments for entering into competition agreements with foreign authorities (i.e. executive agreements, IAEAAs, MLATs). The Commission had no equivalent domestic instruments for pursuing agreements with foreign competition authorities, which made a multilateral initiative an even more appealing solution.

The extent to which the EU's leadership actually had an impact on multilateral competition policy within the WTO seems fairly insignificant. Ultimately, the EU and US compromised and added competition policy to the agenda of the Doha Round of trade negotiations. However, the US had no interest in making major changes to the current system of bilateral agreements and strongly resisted application of the WTO's binding DSM to competition cases. For its part, the EU was determined that competition policy should be multilateralized through the WTO. As a result, the EU–US compromise that added competition policy to the Doha agenda was very limited: only core principles would be negotiated during Doha and no mention would be made of applying the DSM to this policy area.

Further limiting the Commission's role performance, competition policy was removed from consideration after the collapse of the Cancún Ministerial. After Cancún ended without consensus, the greatest constraint on the EU's role in multilateral competition policy seemed to be the intransigent positions of developing countries. It was not easy for the EU and US to reach a compromise that added competition policy to the Doha Round in the first place. However, it may be even more difficult – following the Cancún collapse – to convince the developing countries that competition issues should be included in a multilateral trade agreement. If the Commission wishes to assert a leadership role in this international policy area, it may now have to moderate even further its original idea of binding multilateralism and adjust its cosmopolitan approach to the multilateralization of competition policy. If it does so, its self-perception of leadership will fall more closely into line with its actual role performance at the WTO.

Notes

1 The EU's competition policy covers a number of different policies, including those to regulate monopolies, cartels, mergers and state aid.
2 For arguments noting the extensive authority of the Commission in competition policy, see Mehta (2003), McGowan and Cini (1999), Gerber (1998), McGowan and Wilks (1995) and Shughart (1990).
3 The primary European actor investigated in this chapter is the European Commission. However, for simplicity, at times, the Commission will simply be referred to as the 'EU'.
4 For useful discussions of the concept of leadership in international negotiations, see Andresen and Agrawala (2002), Malnes (1995) and Young (1991).
5 While the EU did not legally come into existence until the 1992 Maastricht Treaty, for simplicity, this chapter uses only the label 'EU'.
6 While 'antitrust' does not cover all of the component EU policies of competition policy, for simplicity the terms will be used interchangeably.
7 The bracketed TEU citations refer to the numbering system created by the Treaty of European Union.
8 Regulation 17/62, 1962 OJ 204.
9 In 1962 the Competition Directorate was still known as Directorate General IV, or DG IV. To avoid confusion, DG IV will be referred to as the Competition Directorate throughout the current study, regardless of the time period in question.
10 For example, according to McGowan and Cini, 'in its 1966 *Memorandum on the Problems of Concentration in the Common Market*, the Commission asserted that Article 86 [82 TEU] (abuse of a dominant position) might be used to regulate' mergers (1999: 179).
11 For official EU positions on multilateralizing competition rules, see also Mehta (1999), Schaub (1998) and Van Miert (1998). One of the EU's earliest proposals for multilateral competition rules on competition policy came from Sir Leon Brittan (1992).
12 On the possible EU–US disagreement that can arise from the use of different economic models in competition policy, see Evans (2002).
13 See Peritz (1996) and Shughart (1990) on the historical development of US antitrust policy.
14 Devuyst (2000) has argued that the international competition system currently resembles a 'hub-and-spoke system' with the EU and US serving as the hubs from which multiple spoke-like bilateral agreements radiate.

15 This discretionary authority follows from the Case–Zablocki Act (CZA) of 1972. For more on the CZA, see Knaupp (1998) and Hyman (1983).
16 For more on the IAEAA, see Parisi (1999) and ICPAC (2000: Annex 1-C, v–viii).
17 Because they are treaties, the US Senate must ratify MLATs, which it has done since the mid-1970s. Since the mid-1970s the US is a party to 20 MLATs, 'and many more are awaiting ratification' (Klein 1999: 3). According to ICPAC, 'The United States has also entered into 30 MLATs and has signed at least 21 others that are awaiting ratification by the U.S. Senate or equivalent approval from the relevant foreign legislature before entering into force' (2000: Annex 1-C, ix, n 18).
18 Klein argued that the WTO's DSM 'would necessarily involve the WTO in second-guessing prosecutorial decision making in complex evidentiary contexts – a task in which the WTO has no experience and for which it is not suited – and would inevitably politicize international antitrust enforcement in ways that are not likely to improve either the economic rationality or the legal neutrality of antitrust decision making' (1999: 5).
19 For a similar argument that doubts the utility of competition arrangements in the WTO *and* the OECD, see Tarullo (2000).
20 The US aversion to a binding DSM is reflected in its determination to work within the OECD. During the 1990s, while the WTO's working group on the Singapore Issues pursued its mandate, the US proposed a Recommendation Concerning Effective Action against Hard Cord Cartels, which was adopted at the OECD Ministerial in Paris in April 1998. According to Fox, the US preferred this initiative through the OECD because 'the OECD members are "like" (industrialized) nations, and because the OECD has no dispute resolution mechanism' (Fox 2000: 248).
21 See also Kerremans (2004) for a discussion of the failure at Cancún.
22 The author is grateful to Ole Elgström for this perceptive observation.
23 It should, however, be added that the Commission has played a significant role in the multilateralization of competition policy in other forums. For example, see Damro (2004b) and Monti (2002).

References

Andresen, S. and Agrawala, S. (2002) 'Leaders, Pushers and Laggards in the Making of the Climate Regime', *Global Environmental Change*, 12: 41–51.

Brittan, L. (1992) 'A Framework for International Competition', speech at the World Competition Forum, Davos, Switzerland, 3 February.

Brittan, L. (1999) 'The Need for a Multilateral Framework of Competition Rules', speech at OECD Conference on Trade and Competition, Paris, France, 29–30 June.

Cini, M. and McGowan, L. (1998) *Competition Policy in the European Union*, New York: St Martin's Press.

Damro, C. (2004a) 'Multilateral Competition Policy and Transatlantic Compromise', *European Foreign Affairs Review*, 9: 269–87.

Damro, C. (2004b) 'International Competition Policy: Bilateral and Multilateral Efforts at Dispute Prevention', in B. Hocking and S. McGuire (eds) *Trade Politics*, 2nd edn, London: Routledge.

Davis, B. and Raghavan, A. (2001) 'GE–Honeywell Deal gets Caught up in Diverging Histories', *Wall Street Journal*, 3 July, pp. A1, A8.

Devuyst, Y. (2000) 'Toward a Multilateral Competition Policy Regime?', *Global Governance*, 6: 319–38.

Dumez, H. and Jeunemaître A. (1996) 'The Convergence of Competition Policies in Europe: Internal Dynamics and External Imposition', in S. Berger and R. Dore (eds) *National Diversity and Global Capitalism*, London: Routledge.

European Commission (2003) 'Reviving the DDA Negotiations – the EU Perspective', Communication from the Commission to the Council, to the European Parliament, and to the Economic and Social Committee, Brussels, 26 November.

Evans, D. S. (2002) 'The New Trustbusters: Brussels and Washington May Part Ways', *Foreign Affairs*, 81: 14–20.

Fox, E. M. (1997) 'Toward World Antitrust and Market Access', *American Journal of International Law*, 91: 1–25.

Fox, E. M. (2000) 'Competition Law: Linking the World', in G. Bermann, M. Herdegen and P. L. Lindseth (eds) *Transatlantic Regulatory Cooperation: Legal Problems and Political Prospects*, Oxford: Oxford University Press.

Gerber, D. J. (1998) *Law and Competition in Twentieth Century Europe: Protecting Prometheus*, Oxford: Oxford University Press.

Hyman, S. G. (1983) 'Note on Presidential Foreign Policy Power, II: Executive Agreements: Beyond Constitutional Limits?', *Hofstra Law Review*, 11: 805–44.

International Competition Policy Advisory Committee (2000) *Final Report*, Washington, DC: US Government Printing Office.

Kerremans, B. (2004) 'What Went Wrong in Cancún? A Principal–Agent View on the EU's Rationale towards the Doha Development Round', *European Foreign Affairs Review*, 9: 363–93.

Klein, J. I. (1999) 'A Reality Check on Antitrust Rules in the World Trade Organization, and a Practical Way Forward on International Antitrust', speech at OECD Conference on Trade and Competition, Paris, 29–30 June.

Knaupp, B. D. (1998) 'Classifying International Agreements under U.S. Law: The Beijing Platform as a Case Study', *Brigham Young University Law Review*, 1: 239–65.

Kol, J. and Winters, L. A. (2004) 'The EU after Cancún: Can the Leopard Change its Spots?', *European Foreign Affairs Review*, 9: 1–25.

Malnes, R. (1995) '"Leader" and "Entrepreneur" in International Negotiations: A Conceptual Analysis', *European Journal of International Relations*, 1: 87–112.

McGowan, L. and Cini, M. (1999) 'Discretion and Politicization in EU Competition Policy: The Case of Merger Control', *Governance*, 12: 175–200.

McGowan, L. and Wilks, S. (1995) 'The First Supranational Policy in the European Union: Competition Policy', *European Journal of Political Research*, 28: 141–69.

Mehta, K. (1999) 'The Role of Competition in a Globalized Trade Environment', speech at Third WTO Symposium on Competition Policy and the Multilateral Trading System, Geneva, Switzerland, 17 April.

Mehta, K. (2003) 'International Competition Policy Co-operation', in Ernst-Ulrich Petersmann and Mark A. Pollack (eds) *Transatlantic Economic Disputes*, Oxford: Oxford University Press.

Monti, M. (2002) 'A Global Competition policy?', speech at the European Competition Day, Copenhagen, Denmark, 17 September.

Parisi, J. J. (1999) 'Enforcement Co-operation among Antitrust Authorities', *European Competition Law Review*, 20: 133–42.

Peritz, R. J. R. (1996) *Competition Policy in America, 1888–1992: History, Rhetoric, Law*, New York: Oxford University Press.

Schaub, A. (1998) 'International Co-operation in Antitrust Matters: Making the Point in the Wake of the Boeing/MDD Proceedings', EU Competition Directorate's *Competition Policy Newsletter*, February, 2–6.

Shughart, W. F., II (1990) *Antitrust Policy and Interest-Group Politics*, New York: Quorum Books.

Tarullo, D. K. (2000) 'Norms and Institutions in Global Competition Policy', *American Journal of International Law*, 94: 478–504.

Van Miert, K. (1998) 'Globalization of Competition: The Need for Global Governance', speech at Vrije Universiteit Brussel, Brussels, Belgium, 25 March.

Young, O. (1991) 'Political Leadership and Regime Formation: On the Development of Institutions in International Society', *International Organization*, 45: 281–308.

13 The EU's role(s) in European public health

The interdependence of roles within a saturated space of international organizations

Sébastien Guigner

Communicable diseases do not respect national frontiers. Thus, international co-operation in the health sector was one of the first such areas to be developed. When, in 1948, the Constitution of the World Health Organization (WHO) came into force one of its aims was to bring together the various international institutions working on health matters under the United Nations (UN) umbrella. However, this does not mean that the WHO is the only international organization active in this field. If we examine the European geographical and political spaces, the Organization for Economic Co-operation and Development (OECD), the Council of Europe (CoE) and the European Union (EU) are all deeply involved in health issues.

Thus, the EU has not developed in isolation or *in vitro*; it has evolved at the heart of a larger international political system which influences it and that it influences – as highlighted by the multi-level governance metaphor. Yet, rather than using the notion of multi-level governance to explain the institutionalization of the EU's international role in health, this chapter argues that it is useful to depart from international relations (IR) and European studies, and to bring into play concepts developed by the German sociologist Norbert Elias. His central concept, the configuration, is based on a notion of interdependence that can be summed up by the following analogy: 'Like in a chess game, every action done in relative independence corresponds to a move on the social chessboard, which inevitably activates a reaction from another individual ... limiting the freedom of action of the first individual' (Elias 1985: 152–3). Society is thus analysed as an interdependence chain composed of numerous interdependences, where each sort of interdependence constitutes a specific situation called a configuration. Configurations differ according to the length and the complexity of relationship chains. Since one member of a chain can be more dependent on others than others are dependent on them, there can be unbalanced relations but everybody is constrained by others. Unlike the concept of system, the concept of configuration is not determinist; it emphasizes the margin of freedom available to actors. As a consequence configurations are typically unstable.

In the regional health arena, it can be argued that the EU, the WHO, the OECD and the CoE comprise a specific configuration. There are mutual influences between the effective, expected and perceived roles of these different organizations. They cannot independently choose their roles. Indeed, in geographical and sectoral areas where various international organizations are active, an organization must develop advantages or added value compared with the other organizations, in order to become a reflective and decision-making arena chosen by the member states and various actors involved in policy-making.[1]

Due to the specific characteristics of the European configuration of international organizations involved in health, and to the characteristics of the EU, both the EU's internal and external roles, themselves strongly interconnected, have been constrained and limited indirectly by the other international organizations active in this area. However, the EU has developed its internal health activities and undertaken a role in these issues at the international level. The EU has thus structured a presence (Allen and Smith 1990) in the international health area. This presence signifies that the EU has generated objective elements of external presence both within and as an international organization. But the EU has also generated 'subjective aspects embodied in the validation of a collective self by significant others' (Rosamond 2000: 177). EU opinions and policies in matters of health have become credible and authoritative, the EU influences other international organizations' behaviour, and they cannot steer clear of the EU any more. Hence, the EU has developed both actorness and presence in matters of health at the international level (Hill 1994).

To explore this argument, the rest of this chapter is divided into three parts that correspond to three successive configurations of the European space of international organizations intervening in health. However, this is an ideal-typical distinction; it refers to fundamental trends, therefore temporal and sub-sectoral exceptions exist. The first two parts of the chapter are based on Hobbes' and Rousseau's thoughts used in a metaphoric way. The first part examines the period when the EU entered the field of health. This was a period characterized by competition between the organizations studied here and by the subordinate position of the EU: a kind of 'state of nature'. The second part of the chapter explains how and why far-reaching collaborations replaced this state of nature and helped the EU to broaden its legitimacy and to assume an internal and an international role in health. The last part of the chapter appraises the impact of the EU's emergence on the configuration of international organizations involved in health. Via a logic of mimetism, institutionalized collaboration seems to have become a tool for the EU to invade the space occupied by (or to 'phagocytate') coexisting organizations. The EU has become able to act as a leader in exporting norms and now challenges the health activities of other international actors.

The origins of the European space of international organizations dealing with health: the state of nature

Realist international relations scholars base their theory broadly upon an analogy between the state of (human) nature described by Hobbes and the relations between states preserving their competing interests. As a result, Realists see these relations as inherently conflictual and self-interested. The following discussion is based on an extension of this logic. Thus, the relations between international organizations can be characterized in the same way as those between states, with each of them trying to increase or preserve its autonomy and power, as shown by some types of neo-institutionalist analyses. This way of life constituted a specific configuration of the European space of international organizations active in health during the early years of European integration – a configuration in which the EU suffered from comparative disadvantages that limited its credibility and its legitimacy to address health issues and that, in consequence, limited the expansion of its internal and international role in health matters.

A saturated space: overlapping geographies and activities

First of all, competition takes place on a geographical level. The EU, the OECD, the CoE and the WHO act more or less in the same geographical space and, logically, the membership of these institutions is quite similar. The 25 member states of the EU, and the applicant countries, are part of the three other international organizations – with the exception of five states that are not members of the OECD. However, it is important to note that the EU has the smallest geographical and membership coverage (Table 13.1). The OECD includes countries from other continents, and the CoE covers Eastern and Central Europe and parts of Eurasia. As an agency of the UN the WHO, which is based at Geneva, is a global organization, but it is subdivided and organized into regional offices. There is thus a European office based in Copenhagen, which, like the CoE, covers the European continent. Hence, the EU's geographical area constitutes a common zone of activity involving several overlapping organizations.

Geographical overlap would not be very problematic if the activities of these organizations were very different. This is not the case: overlap of competences adds to geographical overlap even if each organization has a distinct broad goal. Thus, though WHO is the only one originally designed to deal specifically with health matters, all the other organizations have developed activities in health issues to pursue their specific

Table 13.1 Membership of international organizations involved in health issues at the European level (date of entry of EU member states)

Country	*EU 25 member states*	*OECD 30 member states*	*CoE 45 member states*	*WHO Europe 52 member states*
Austria	1995	1961	1956	1955
Belgium	1957	1961	1949	1948
Cyprus	2004	–	1961	1960
Czech Republic	2004	1995	1993	1993
Denmark	1973	1961	1949	1948
Estonia	2004	–	1993	1991
Finland	1995	1969	1989	1948
France	1957	1961	1949	1948
Germany	1957	1961	1950	1973
Greece	1986	1961	1949	1948
Hungary	2004	1996	1990	1948
Ireland	1973	1961	1949	1948
Italy	1957	1962	1949	1948
Latvia	2004	–	1995	1991
Lithuania	2004	–	1993	1991
Luxembourg	1957	1961	1949	1948
Malta	2004	–	1965	1964
Netherlands	1957	1961	1949	1948
Poland	2004	1996	1991	1948
Portugal	1986	1961	1976	1948
Slovakia	2004	2000	1993	1993
Slovenia	2004	–	1993	1992
Spain	1986	1961	1977	1955
Sweden	1995	1961	1949	1948
UK	1973	1961	1949	1948

goals. As a consequence of the increasing weight of health spending in national budgets, since the 1980s the OECD has collected and tried to develop comparable data to evaluate and analyse funding, resources and expenditures on health. The Committee of Ministers, which is the CoE's decision-making body, set up the European Health Committee in 1954 to encourage closer European co-operation on the promotion of health, and for example started to work in the blood transfusion area in the 1950s. Moreover, a Partial Agreement in the social and public health field was set up in 1959.[2] From the beginning, the European Community has been involved in health issues, especially in the field of health and safety in the workplace, pharmaceuticals and in the area of health professions. These earliest steps in the health field resulted from a neofunctionalist logic, in which the activities were dealt with as consequences of the construction of the common market (Mossialos *et al.* 2001). The first public health activity not directly linked to the common market can be explained by member states' political will – the programme 'Europe against Cancer' set up in

1987. Nowadays, all these organizations deal more or less with the same health issues.

Comparative disadvantages of the EU vis-à-vis other international organizations

In this environment the Commission – acting as the agent of the EU – has had to prove that it is more effective than other organizations in dealing with these issues, or at least, that its presence in this field is useful. Why delegate power and money to an organization if there is no added value to what is already done elsewhere? The much debated European principle of subsidiarity also applies to international organizations. The problem is that the EU faces several comparative disadvantages that initially condemned it to be a follower and an importer of norms. This was notably due to chronological factors. The EU's intervention in the field of health is the more recent, and thus competing organizations have had time to prove themselves capable of dealing with public health matters. This chronological legitimacy results moreover from the history of membership in these organizations (Table 13.1). States have typically become members of the WHO, the CoE and, in most cases, of the OECD before becoming member states of the EU, where the conditions of entry are more stringent. Governments and experts were already accustomed to working with other organizations when the EU, embodied by the Commission, tried to add itself to this field. So, when the EU began to develop its role in health it could count neither on an empty space nor on a lack of effectiveness of the actors already active in this domain. On the contrary, it was the EU, because of vertical and horizontal inconsistencies, that did not appear a legitimate actor in this field.

First of all, the EU suffers from being an organization with very broad objectives, rather than a functional organization focused towards specific goals. As a consequence, when the Commission first began its activities in the field of public health it had very little expertise in health matters, unlike the WHO. The OECD and the CoE do not have numerous experts either, but as intergovernmental constructs their expertise relies on member states, whereas the EU's expertise is primarily based on Commission officials. The competitions organized to recruit EU personnel favour candidates with general skills, rather than specific health-related expertise, but nevertheless, the Commission has acquired very competent specialists. However, Commission officials involved in health issues note that the weight of the bureaucratic structure and the legislative procedures of the EU often force them to act as administrators more than technical experts:

> I came as a health policy specialist but I have done a massive amount of administrative work, to the detriment of working on health policy.
> (Interview, DG Sanco official, Public Health Directorate, December 2002)

> WHO is differently organized – they are not supposed to do regulation.... It's an easier job, they can point out the problems and they don't have to do something about it ... we are supposed not only to point out the problems but also to solve the problems by better legislation. That is a big difference.... When you start working in the Commission you are supposed to be no longer a public health expert but an administrator with public health skills, and that is different.
>
> (Interview, DG Sanco official, Public Health Directorate, November 2002)

Furthermore, different role conceptions across institutional actors and policy fields within the EU further limit the recognition of the health expertise capacity of the EU, especially that of the Commission. Different dynamics of action at play within the Commission give it a multi-organizational and conflicted nature (Cram 1994). If it is undeniably simplistic to systematically put economic development and health protection up against each other, as the Bovine Spongiform Encephalitis (BSE) crisis showed, the EU as a whole has long privileged economic logic. Moreover, the difficulties in leading concerted and co-ordinated action in the health field are increased by the fragmentation of health interests between different DGs and different locations. Until recently, health services within the Commission were not specialized and did not have the necessary size to be heard and to develop a coherent and robust approach to health issues in the Community, so they had to compromise with the actions of their colleagues from other services (Guigner 2003). The difficulty in convincing the international health field of the Commission's credibility is also compounded by the fact that it appears to be a monolithic entity, because differences in opinion between the DGs are never made public. In any situation where one DG prioritizes economy over health, the entire Commission is associated with an economic identity (Koivusalo 1998).

This ambiguity is increased by the specific strategy adopted by the Commission's health organs in order to become integrated into the surrounding economy-centred environment. Commission officials in charge of health have developed a strategy of 'economicization' of health, which links health and economy in a virtuous circle (Guigner 2004). The first Communication of the Commission concerning public health is explicit:

> An efficient action can prevent premature deaths within the working population.... In short, the productive capacity of the Community can be maximized and at the same time disease related costs can be reduced.
>
> (Commission 1993: 7)

As Héritier (2001: 67) explains, 'by linking an issue with another issue which enjoys wide support, or by re-labelling it, its prospects of being accepted in the political arena may be improved'. According to officials dealing with health within the Commission, this strategy of framing has been useful as a basis for development of their internal autonomy and competences. On the other hand, the 'economicization' of health blurs the health activities of the Commission. Are these primarily motivated by economic or by public health objectives? It is not easy to understand whether the 'economicization' strategy consists of speech (implying conviction), or only rhetoric (the strategic use of speech) (Hay and Rosamond 2002).

In addition, the way the EU works is not well known. Many people involved at the international level in health issues do not even know what the EU is.[3] So specific positions of member states, detrimental for health, can be associated by the international or national health community with an EU position. While the European Commission has the status of a full participant in the OECD – the Commission enjoys all rights of membership, except the right to vote – within the WHO–Geneva framework the European Commission has a very restrictive observer status. The rules applied to the EU are the same as those applied to international organizations and NGOs. The effect is that practical arrangements (like the colour of badges) do not favour the EU's visibility; the EU's interventions are limited in number and can almost never be made at the key points in debate. Furthermore, EU member states are on occasion reluctant to follow lines agreed within the Council or even to keep the Commission informed about informal negotiations. On the other hand the situation is better at the WHO European office owing to the homogeneity of participating countries.

Finally, the public health credibility of the Commission is handicapped by the nature of the EU. As a 'supranational construct' (Mossialos and Permanand 2000: 46), EU decisions have a power of constraint: thus the Commission is under greater pressure from member states that wish to maintain their prerogatives than are the WHO, the CoE or the OECD, as the very restrictive public health article of the Treaty establishing the European Community (TEC) demonstrates. Since the opinions or recommendations of the CoE, the OECD and the WHO have no automatic constraining power, they do not endanger the prerogatives of their member states, and thus these organizations are potentially more capable than the EU of reacting rapidly to new issues and taking decisions. The decision-making process of these organizations is indeed more flexible than the EU's. Furthermore, their decisions can be more ambitious and more targeted than the suggestions made by the European Commission, which has to take into account the reticence of the member states and therefore promote lowest common denominator and imprecise decisions. A good example is provided by the absence of an EU definition of health, in contrast to the very precise and ambitious definition of health formulated by the WHO.

Pacifying the European space of international organizations dealing with health: the social contract

Realist international relations scholars who still rely upon Hobbes's justification of sovereignty consider that the only way to ensure security and continuation of states is to agree on a pact. Thus, the social contract between states, constituting international relations, results from self-interested motives in leaving the state of nature – although it does not involve renunciation of their sovereignty. States thus remain free to co-operate and preserve their autonomy – a conception closer to Rousseau's definition of the social contract, according to which the freedom of individuals is maintained. Once again, it is helpful to use this classical framework to analyse relations between international organizations. Thus, it will be shown in this part of the chapter that the EU has entered into contracts with international organizations to achieve the advantages of security that only a social existence can provide. This has been particularly fruitful for the EU due to its situation of inferiority within this competitive configuration. Collaboration in matters of health with international organizations has as a result increased the legitimacy of EU actions in health matters.

The institutionalization of collaboration

The first tactic used by the Commission to integrate the national and international fields of health was to 'go it alone' (Mountford 1998: 33) and build its authority and legitimacy by unilateral deployment of its policy instruments. This approach led to policy overlaps between the international organizations active in the field, where the policies of the Commission turned out to be less pertinent than those of the other organizations. This strategy came to threaten the very existence of the Commission's public health activities. Indeed, the European Parliament and the member states often attacked the Commission on that point and asked for more collaboration. This preoccupation resulted in the inclusion into successive EU treaties, beginning with the Maastricht Treaty, of an obligation for the Commission to foster co-operation at the international level in the sphere of public health.[4]

In spite of long-standing bilateral relations between the European Commission and the other organizations, co-operation between them really became effective only in the late 1990s (Reiner 1999). Collaboration between the Commission and the WHO was based on exchanges of letters in 1972 and 1982. However, and despite the creation of a WHO embassy to the EU in 1992, until recently the co-operation was limited to sporadic actions. Following the enlargement of EU health competences in the Amsterdam Treaty – mainly due to the BSE crisis – and the appointment of a new WHO General Director, there was a more significant exchange of letters in 2000, identifying common priority areas and outlining practical procedures for co-operation in order to strengthen it. This co-operation is carried out through the participation of Commission officials as observers of decision-making in these organizations (and reciprocally) and through formal and informal meetings. At the political level, since 2001 regular meetings between the Commissioner responsible for health and the WHO Director General have taken place. Meetings of senior officials at a technical level are also regularly organized between the Commission and WHO Geneva or WHO Europe. Moreover, representatives from the WHO office and the Commission's Public Health Directorate have meetings every few months. Contacts also take place, and are perhaps more meaningful, on a daily and personal basis by phone or Internet. In addition, staff exchanges have been set up.

Commission co-operation with the CoE and the OECD is quite similar to its collaboration with the WHO but is less institutionalized. Co-operation with the OECD in the field of public health has been limited to the mutual participation of officials in the health monitoring and health data collection area. The first step in collaboration between the EU and the CoE was based on exchanges of letters in 1987, followed in 1996 by a new exchange of letters. Despite these formal agreements, and the privileged observer status of the Commission in the CoE, the collaboration really became structured only with the joint declaration on co-operation and partnership between the Council of Europe and the European Commission made in April 2001, which set out the general principles of co-operation covering a wide range of activities, including health. In this framework, the Commission, the Council of Europe and the WHO exchanged letters in June 2001 in order to set up trilateral collaboration.

How to increase legitimacy: the strategy of mimetism

This ordering of relations between the Commission and what can now be referred to as partners can also be seen by the use and frequent reuse of WHO's, CoE's and OECD's technical research opinions and data in the preparatory and final work of the Commission. Moreover, in almost all official documents and speeches of the Commission there are very explicit references to the work of these three organizations and to the co-operation that is now in place, as shown by the following examples:

> This proposal for a Directive takes account of the most recent progress . . ., particularly within the World Health Organization and the Council of Europe. . . . These specific provisions take into account international standards (e.g. Council of Europe, World Health Organization . . .). . . . The Commission intends to collaborate closely with the Council of Europe. . . .
>
> (COM (2002) 319 final, 2002/0128 (COD): 15,16 and 17)

> Another example ... is shown in a WHO and World Bank report.... On behalf of the Commission, I would like to turn now to the fact that WHO and the Commission are equally determined to respond positively to challenges in the mental health area.... I personally share the conviction of the World Health Organization, that we ... should closely work together....
>
> (D. Byrne, in Europe Mental Health Conference Brussels, 25 October 2001, SPEECH/01/490)

> ...Directive 2001/83/EC refers to measures to be taken by Member States..., comprising the ... recommendations of the Council of Europe and the World Health Organization (WHO) as regards in particular the selection and testing of blood and plasma donors.
>
> (Directive 2002/98/EC of 27 January 2003: 1)

The concept of epistemic community developed by Peter Haas (1992) can help us to understand the process of cognitive and institutional reconciliation, which is not only a response to the exigencies of collaboration made by the member states. Epistemic communities are networks of professionals sharing a common understanding of a problem and its solution, and that have a strong capacity for expertise and recognized skills in a particular field. As a consequence, they are solicited by decision-makers to provide them with information. Thus the CoE and the OECD can be seen in part as epistemic communities. The CoE would be an epistemic community specifically expert in ethical health issues, whilst the OECD would be an epistemic community specialized in health issues related to economic concerns. WHO in this context would be a sort of meta-epistemic community acknowledged for its role in overall health issues. Inserting itself into other epistemic communities can be considered as a Commission strategy of mimetism.

In the field of biology, mimetism refers to the imitation of a model by an animal in order to ensure the perpetuation of the species. Applied to the policy transfer literature, mimetism is a mode of non-coercive institutional isomorphism (Powell and DiMaggio 1991) generating legitimacy in institutional life by 'imitating organizations which are perceived to be more legitimate or more successful' (Radaelli 1999: 44–5). Thus, mimetism is neither constructivism (Checkel 1999) nor communicative action (Risse-Kappen 1996), but purely rational choice. Indeed, in the logic of mimetism, the importer of norms is not necessarily convinced of their validity. Furthermore, the instrumental use of ideas comes from the importer, not from the exporter. In our case study, by inserting epistemic communities institutionally, and by ostensibly reproducing their ideas, the European Commission leans on models that benefit from scientific legitimacy. Thereby the Commission legitimates its own role in the field of health, which was originally, as shown above, particularly limited in the eyes of the member states, international organizations, experts and NGOs.[5] In this way the Commission can convert its former 'predators' into 'prey' that will, through a virtuous circle, provide the Commission with competences, support, money and expertise.[6]

Why do other organizations co-operate with the Commission? First, member states have typically asked them to collaborate in order not to duplicate activities and to reduce overlaps. There is no binding obligation, as in the EU treaties, but there can be very persuasive budgetary sanctions. Second, having their recommendations and ideas used, and sometimes implemented, by other organizations such as the EU allows them to get their qualities acknowledged and so to increase their own legitimacy; therefore it facilitates the perpetuation of the organization.

The art of co-operation, or how the EU feeds off its competitors

According to Rousseau what makes the social contract legitimate is that everyone has the same status. Therefore everyone gains the equivalent of what they have it has lost and gets more power to keep what they possess. The social contract between the EU and the international organizations working on health issues does not fit into this framework, but corresponds better to the image of international society described by Hedley Bull (1977). International society in this view is a group of independent political communities mutually adjusting their behaviour, sharing a system of values and institutions set up to maintain co-operation. A balance of power between contracting parties ensures order; parties can be unequals as long as all of them recognize their interest in collaboration.

The institutionalization of collaboration between international organizations does not mean that everything is for the best in the best of all possible worlds. Overlaps persist, and can grow, owing to the continuous extension of the public health activities of all the organizations studied here. But resources granted by the member states to these organizations do not necessarily increase at the same time. Consequently co-operation remains motivated by self-interest, and the struggle for life is still a relevant question. Moreover, here the social contract is not a positive sum game. After having initially been a follower, the EU has benefited from comparative advantages that, in combination with the results of the international collaboration, have modified the interdependences of the international organizations involved in health at the European level, and have led to a reconfiguration of this space. To make use of another biological analogy, the EU has 'phagocytated' its opponents, using them to develop itself to their detriment.

Comparative advantages of the EU vis-à-vis other international organizations

Structural advantages

As underlined above, the EU's capacity to compel governments is often an inconvenience, since it can make governments wary of adopting decisions or of giving the EU more competences in this field. However, it is an advantage in dealing with major health crises where strong commitments are necessary. For example, the BSE crisis would have been much more difficult to resolve without the constraining legislative instruments of the EU, which allowed the imposition of embargoes and the development of high-level standards of food safety. In the immediate future, binding competences will be also very useful to regulate blood transfusion and organ donation across Europe. EU tobacco control policy is another example of the utility of a strong legislative capacity. Unlike the EU, other organizations cannot rely on or certify the implementation of their recommendations. This sometimes gives experts and national officials the impression that these organizations are only laboratories of ideas without any practical consequences, and so no real utility. Their utility is vague and indirect, and it often works through logics of learning and diffusion of good practices, which are not as visible as the normative and legislative activity of the EU. For member states the return on their investment is thus not self-evident.

The financial superiority of the EU constitutes a second source of structural advantage. The EU's health budget is much more consequential than that of the OECD, WHO Europe or the CoE. Moreover, the EU enjoys a regular and pluriannual budget thanks to a system of obligatory funding that allows the EU to plan mid-term activities. In contrast, other organizations face irregular and annual budgets that do not permit them to undertake long-term strategy (Beigbeder 1997). Their budgets depend to a large extent on voluntary donations by states and on non-binding commitments, which are often not fulfilled. In reality these organizations operate not only with tight budgets but also with declining ones. In addition to the continuity of its activities, the financial superiority of the EU gives it the capacity to follow up and implement its activities better than the other organizations. Indeed, the European Commission staff dealing with health issues is significantly larger than that of other organizations.

In addition, its financial capacity allows the Commission to finance NGOs, which in turn increases its expertise and implementation resources and reinforces the EU's visibility in health matters. Thus, while taking support from the WHO, the CoE and the OECD, the Commission has also built itself a support network of NGOs and independent experts, which could help it to become emancipated from its tutors in the EU and international health arena. In a similar way to what has been done in other sectors (Mazey 1995), in order to institutionalize its activities the Commission has created what one of our interlocutors called 'positive lobbying' (interview, DG Sanco official, Public Health Directorate, March 2001). By financing NGOs, projects, expert analyses and organizing seminars, the Commission creates and inserts itself into networks of legitimate actors, providing the Commission with support and autonomous expertise. Moreover, this logic of political exchange generates sunk costs: that is to say, groups or individuals devote specific skills, time and money to the EU's health policies and thus make them harder to reverse (Pierson 1996).

Conjunctural advantages

In addition to these structural advantages, the EU has benefited from the broader evolution of public health concerns. First, public health debates have focused for the past ten years on questions associated with health care reform. Since the second half of the 1990s, most European countries have adopted policies on health care reform or are considering it because of the growing cost of care not accompanied by a similar growth of resources. As a result, health care reform has been tackled mainly as an economic issue. Containing costs, sharing costs and controlling resource allocation are now everyday terms in the public health field. Health economics appears now almost as important as medicine in dealing with health issues. This situation is favourable to the EU and the OECD, since they are primarily economic organizations. They possess, or seem to possess, the economic expertise and credibility necessary to study and influence health care reforms, unlike the WHO, which is more oriented towards assistance activities and medical research, and the CoE, which is associated with ethical aspects of health. Perhaps for this reason governments turn more readily to the EU and the OECD to cope with problems of health care reform.

The accent put on health determinants is the second development in health priorities, which works to the advantage of the EU. The idea is that, to reach the highest possible standards of health, action must be undertaken in economic and social fields and not only in the health field. Thus, in the European countries, the main health risks are no longer linked to epidemics (for example) but rather to socio-economic effects of development and to lifestyle. In this setting, the new public health emphasizes health promotion and health prevention rather than care. WHO failed to develop this global approach to health, which was first proposed in the 1970s (Pierru 2004), but relaunched it in the late 1990s, justifying it as a means of reducing the costs of care, thus generating wide support.

Even if this new concern necessitates more public health expertise than economic expertise, the EU has a real advantage compared to all the other international organizations in implementing this strategy. As a regional integration organization, the EU has the potential to deal with the horizontal dimension of this approach because it is involved in almost all relevant sectors of activity. In contrast, the WHO in particular does not have the capacity to interfere directly with any policy other than health. Furthermore, this global approach to health was introduced as a treaty obligation in the TEC, where there is a commitment to integrate health requirements into other European policies. In this framework, the European Commission has set up tools of co-ordination, such as the Interservice Group on Health, aiming at adjusting the EU's economic matrix to health policies, in contrast to its earlier emphasis on the logic of 'economicization'.

Towards a new configuration of the European space of international organizations dealing with health

In conjunction with the above-mentioned elements, particular events and logics have increased the EU's roles in health. Indeed, there are many examples of 'political diseases' (Guigner 2004: 109) showing how the EU's health activities have been enlarged following public health crisis and subsequent political calculations by member state governments, the European Parliament or the European Commission. Politicization of health has thus been the motor of a slow but significant Commission administrative reorganization, leading in 1999 to the creation of a DG almost entirely devoted to the management of health issues: the Directorate General of Health and Consumer Protection (DG Sanco). The Commission's legitimization strategies combined with contingent events have in fact engaged the EU in a virtuous circle, institutionalizing both its internal and its external public health roles. In other words, these roles not only are expanding but there is also a repetition and a stabilization of social norms and policy practices. These two roles support and expand themselves mutually, as shown in Figure 13.1, despite the absence of a specific design for these roles.

This situation has led to the reconfiguration of the European space of international organizations active in health, with a new equilibrium favourable to the EU. Tobacco is probably the most significant example of the EU's new capacity to assume a leadership role in health, both internally and as an international organization. On 21 May 2003 the WHO's 192 member states unanimously adopted the world's first public health legal instrument, the WHO Framework Convention on Tobacco Control (FCTC). The EU was a key player in the development of the treaty, for which the Commission had been mandated by the Council to conduct negotiations in the fields in which the Community had competence. The Commission delegation included among others officials from DG Sanco, the European Anti-fraud Office and the Taxation and Customs Union DG. With regard to Article 300 of the TEC, the EU presidency was active in co-ordinating the member states' positions on questions covered by

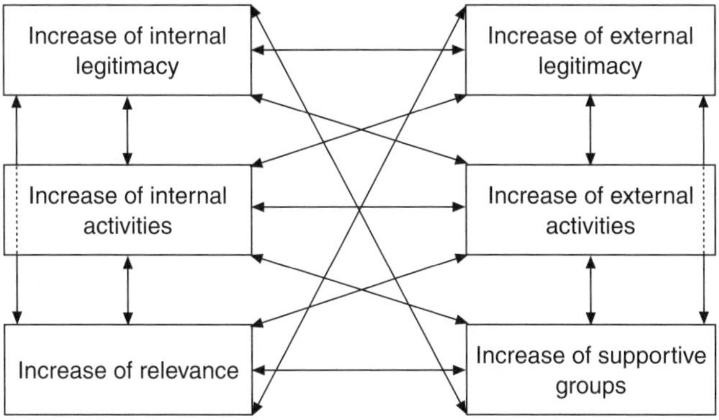

Figure 13.1 The virtuous circle of the EU's internal and external roles.

national sovereignty. It is widely accepted that the EU as a whole (Commission, Presidency and member states) was one of the most significant contributors to the negotiations, and, following the political and personal commitment on tobacco control of the health Commissioner, David Byrne,[7] one of the most demanding.

The EU's strong and united position on tobacco control was supported by NGOs and a large number of delegations, including EU accession states and developing countries. But the EU was not only a leader in the diplomatic negotiating process; it served also as a model for the FCTC's content. Indeed, there are a lot of striking similarities between the EU's pioneering legislation on tobacco control developed since the late 1980s and the requirements of the FCTC.[8] In this case, the proactive role of the EU in health at the international level was possible because there was a consolidated internal activity in this field: this gave the EU a legal basis to intervene in the FCTC negotiating process and to appear as more than a purely economic body. In other words, the EU's credibility benefited from horizontal consistency and vertical consistency.

The EU has thus emancipated itself from its past tutors, and now it threatens to overtake them. The new legitimacy underpinning EU intervention in the health field at national and international levels, along with its comparative advantages, has increased the budgetary crisis for other international organizations. Budgetary crisis is in reality both a cause and a consequence of the reconfiguration of the European order of health organizations. OECD's, WHO's and CoE's budgets have always been tight but they are now declining, notably because EU member states do not want to finance these organizations so generously when they duplicate EU activities that they are obliged to finance. In a very concrete manner, the priority given by the member states to the EU can be seen by their attendance at meetings. According to French health ministry officials, they pay more attention to the EU's work, and where there are parallel meetings in the several organizations studied here, they will prioritize EU meetings.[9] The work with OECD, WHO or CoE appears now almost subsidiary. The EU has thus moved from the position of follower and norm importer, that placed it under pressure to conform to other organizations addressing health issues at the European level (Figure 13.2), to a position of dominator, able to export norms and threatening to swallow up competing international organizations (Figure 13.3).[10]

To reverse this situation, the endangered organizations have tried to enlarge their competences rather than deepening them. In fact, they have tried to reflect member states' health priorities, and thus every organization has developed activities in health care reform. However, this

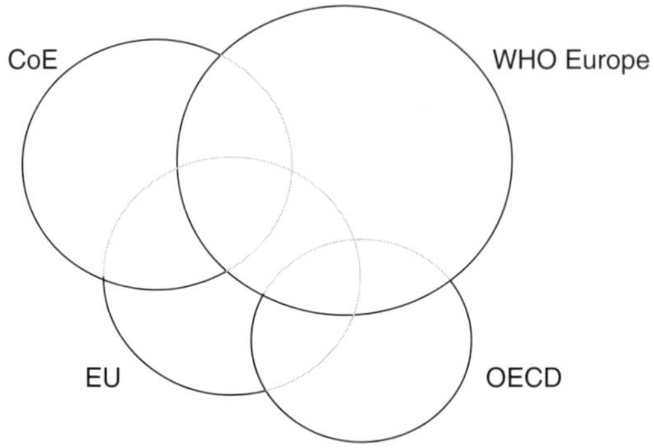

Figure 13.2 The European space of international organizations active in health: first configuration.

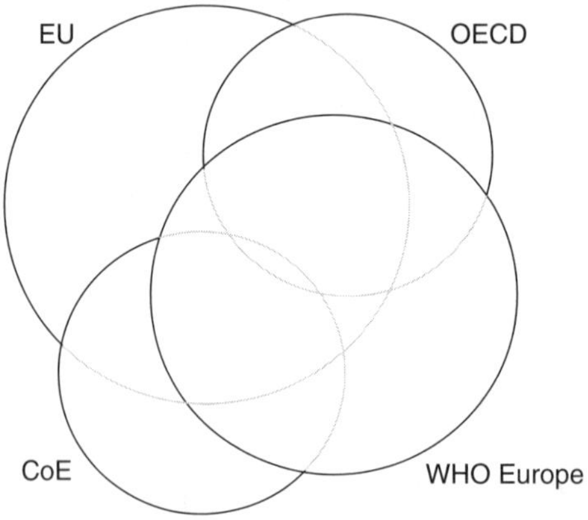

Figure 13.3 The European space of international organizations active in health: second configuration.

strategy does not appear really effective and is probably in reality counter-productive, since it makes overlaps more obvious and brings into question the added value of these international organizations compared with that of the EU. Therefore these organizations, and more specifically their health activities, are at a turning point. The situation of the CoE is the most worrying since almost all its health activities overlap with or duplicate EU health activities. Furthermore, their memberships are very similar, even if the CoE's is still wider. Hence the suppression of its health committee and revision of the partial agreement on health are envisaged in CoE circles. In general, it seems that the CoE remains useful only for those Central and Eastern European countries not yet members of the EU. Like the WHO, the OECD has the advantage of a global membership, which allows it to make broader comparisons than the EU or the CoE. That is probably the element that will allow its health activities to survive, or at least this is the argument that OECD officials advance. WHO will not disappear but WHO Europe needs to adapt its activities with respect to those of the EU. Indeed, if there is no improvement in co-ordination, certain officials of WHO Europe fear that in the long term the European Commission could be used as a regional office of the WHO, in the same way as the Pan American Health Association is for North and South America.

Conclusion

The idea that international relations are not just about states is now well accepted, and relations between the EU and international organizations have been extensively studied. However, in the case analysed in this chapter, the conflict is not about norm diffusion but about survival. There is an ontological interdependence between organizations' roles. If organizations have more or less similar functions and evolve within the same geographical area, there is an impact on the allocation of resources when a new organization enters the field. The second lesson of this chapter is that it is not possible to explain the EU's international role without studying its internal role. The institutionalization processes of these two roles are deeply intertwined. Being legitimate at the external level is a basis for being recognized at the internal level, and vice versa. The third message of this chapter is that the operational role of the EU is linked to the internal and external perception of this role and of others' roles. In short, our case study allows us to state that one cannot understand the EU's international role without looking at the complex configuration (to use Elias's term) in place in a specific area of activity. In a given field of activity, the EU's international role is related to its internal roles, to its perceived roles, to its expected roles and to the roles of the other international actors present in the same field, just as the roles of these latter are linked to those performed by the EU. These networks of interdependences constitute specific configurations that strategies of actors or unexpected events can change, notably in transforming comparative disadvantages into advantages.

Notes

This chapter is notably based upon an internship in the Public Health Directorate of the European Commission and approximately 80 interviews with actors involved in the 'Europe of health'. I would like to express my gratitude to all the people who welcomed me.

1 For convenience the EU will be understood here as an international organization defined as 'a structured group of participants from different countries co-ordinating their activities in order to reach common goals' (Smouts 1995: 12). However, this does not mean that we take a stand on the controversy on the nature of the EU.
2 A CoE Partial Agreement is a convention between states that want to work on specific themes not dealt with by the committees emanating from the Committee of Ministers.
3 For example, a Commission official involved in relations with WHO told us that a representative of Pakistan at WHO Geneva asked, seriously, when the EU would include Pakistan.
4 Article 129.3 of the Maastricht Treaty, Article 152.3 of the Amsterdam Treaty and Article III.179.3 of the draft Treaty Establishing a Constitution for Europe.
5 Thus, it is not unusual to see posters published by the WHO in the corridors of the Public Health Directorate of the European Commission.
6 Mimetism is not limited to copying international organizations. The EU imitates good examples wherever they can be found. For example, the European Centre for Disease Prevention and Control is explicitly modelled on the renowned US Centers for Disease Control and Prevention.
7 See the declaration made by D. Byrne at the WHO Conference for a Tobacco-free Europe, Warsaw, 19 February 2002, SPEECH/02/74.
8 For example on issues of packaging and labelling of tobacco products Article 11 of the FCTC is directly analogous to the Articles 5, 6 and 7 of Directive 2001/37/CE of 5 June 2001 concerning the manufacture, presentation and sale of tobacco products.
9 For example this comment of a French health ministry official: 'It is clear that we give priority to the EU [where] norms are very strict and coercive' (interview, December 2003).
10 These figures are based on Wallace's (2000: 74) policy-making location diagram. Our illustrations aim at showing both the international organizations' scope of activities and the overlaps between these actions.

References

Allen, D. and Smith, M. (1990) 'Western Europe's Presence in the Contemporary International Arena', *Review of International Studies*, 16 (1): 19–39.

Beigbeder, Y. (1997) *L'Organisation mondiale de la santé*, Paris: Presses Universitaires de France.

Bull, H. (1977) *The Anarchical Society: A Study of Order in World Politics*, London: Macmillan.

Checkel, J. (1999) 'Social Construction and Integration', *Journal of European Public Policy*, 6 (4): 545–60.

Commission européenne, Direction générale de l'emploi et des affaires sociales (1993) 'L'Europe pour la sécurité et la santé sur le lieu de travail', *Europe sociale*, vol. 3, Luxembourg: OPOCE.

Cram, L. (1994) 'The European Commission as a Multi-organization: Social Policy and IT Policy in the EU', *Journal of European Public Policy*, 1 (2): 195–217.

Elias, N. (1985) *La Société de cour*, Paris: Flammarion (1st edn 1969).

Guigner, S. (2003) 'L'Odyssée de l'administration européenne de la santé: une administration en quête de leadership', *Politique européenne*, 11: 31–55.

Guigner, S. (2004) 'Institutionalizing Public Health in the European Commission: The Thrills and Spills of Politicization', in A. Smith (ed.) *Politics and the European Commission: Actors, Interdependence, Legitimacy*, London: Routledge, 96–115.

Haas, P. (1992) 'Introduction: Epistemic Communities and International Coordination', *International Organization*, 46: 1–35.

Hay, C. and Rosamond, B. (2002) 'Globalization, European Integration and the Discursive of Construction of Economic Imperatives', *Journal of European Public Policy*, 9 (2): 147–67.

Héritier, A. (2001) 'Overt and Covert Institutionalization in Europe', in A. Stone Sweet, W. Sandholtz and N. Fligstein (eds) *The Institutionalization of Europe*, Oxford: Oxford University Press, 56–70.

Hill, C. (1994) 'The Capabilities–Expectations Gap, or Conceptualising Europe's International role', in S. Bulmer and A. Scott (eds) *Economic and Political Integration in Europe: Internal Dynamics and Global Context*, Oxford: Blackwell: 103–26.

Koivusalo, M. (1998) 'Les organisations internationales et les politiques de santé', *Revue française des affaires sociales*, 3 (4): 57–75.

Mazey, S. (1995) 'The Development of EU Equality Policies: Bureaucratic Expansion on Behalf of Women?', *Public Administration*, 73 (4): 591–609.

Mossialos, E. and Permanand, G. (2000) *Public Health in the European Union: Making it Relevant*, Discussion paper 17, London: LSE Health.

Mossialos, E. *et al.* (2001) *The Influence of EU Law on the Social Character of Health care Systems in the European Union*, report submitted to the Belgian Presidency of the European Union.

Mountford, L. (1998) *European Union Health Policy on the Eve of the Millennium*, Public Health and Consumer series SACO 102 EN, Luxembourg: European Parliament, Directorate General of Research.

Pierru, F. (2004) 'Un classement révélateur: les voies de l'économicisation de la doctrine de l'Organisation Mondiale de la santé', in P. Hassenteufel and S. Hennion-Moreau (eds) *Concurrence et protection sociale en Europe*, Rennes: Presses Universitaires de Rennes: 265–90.

Pierson, P. (1996) 'The Path to European Integration: A Historical Institutionalist Analysis', *Comparative Political Studies*, 29 (2): 123–63.

Powell, W. and DiMaggio, P. (1991) *The New Institutionalism in Organizational Analysis*, Chicago: University of Chicago Press.

Radaelli, C. M. (1999) *Technocracy in the European Union*, Harlow: Addison Wesley Longman.

Reiner, L. (1999) 'WHO and the EU: United will they Stand?', *Eurohealth*, 4 (6): 2–4.

Risse-Kappen, T. (1996) 'Exploring the Nature of the Beast: International Relations Theory and Comparative Policy Analysis Meet the European Union', *Journal of Common Market Studies*, 34 (1): 53–80.

Rosamond, B. (2000) *Theories of European Integration*, Basingstoke: Palgrave.

Smouts, M.-C. (1995) *Les Organisations internationales*, Paris: Armand Colin.

Wallace, H. (2000) 'Analysing and Explaining Policies', in H. Wallace and W. Wallace (eds) *Policy-Making in the European Union*, 4th edn, Oxford: Oxford University Press: 65–84.

Conclusion

Ole Elgström and Michael Smith

In this final chapter we return to the basic themes of this volume and to the discussion on how role theory may contribute to an expanded understanding of the EU as an actor in international relations. We relate the theoretical and empirical contributions of the various chapters to each other and place their findings in the context of role theory's attention to role conceptions, the origins and institutionalization of roles, role performance and role impact. At the end of the chapter, we return briefly to the three themes raised in the Introduction: the EU as a source of puzzles in international relations, role theory as an approach to understanding the EU's international activities, and issues of IR method.

Role conceptions

The contributions to this volume have paid much more attention to the role conceptions and self-images promoted by the EU itself than to structurally driven expectations of other actors.

Developments internal to the Union have resulted in a large number of policy documents where the values and principles underlying EU foreign policy have been detailed and presented to the surrounding world – but also to EU public opinion, perhaps in an effort to foster a common European identity. Many of the contributors critically scrutinize the self-proclaimed role conceptions that can be drawn from these policy statements. Sjursen (Chapter 5) and Whitman (Chapter 6) thus investigate the civilian power role conception of the EU, with Whitman concluding that it still has substantial theoretical and empirical purchase despite the development of a European Security and Defence Policy. Sjursen on the other hand problematizes the civilian/normative role by developing two alternative conceptions of it: EU foreign policy as value-based or rights-based, reflecting a more communitarian and a liberal conception of norms, respectively.

Manners (Chapter 4) examines the constitutive parts of the normative role conception of the Union, claiming that the EU to a certain extent is normatively cultured by Kantian cosmopolitan ethics and Habermasian discourse ethics. The normative role also, according to Manners, includes a tendency to emphasize longer-term conciliation in international disputes, and the need to address the structural causes of conflicts, rather than short-term intervention. Jørgensen (Chapter 2) analyses yet another self-proclaimed role, that of champion of multilateralism. While the role conception of the Union clearly is that of a true believer in multilateralism, the author questions whether this self-image really reflects EU foreign policy practices. He finds significant variation in EU multilateralism across time and policies, and clear evidence that the EU is engaged in unilateral and bilateral strategies as well. He therefore characterizes EU practices in terms of a differentiated approach, with pragmatic choices of means and ends.

Finally, some chapters (those by Damro, Guigner and Kerremans) discuss and evaluate the EU's role as a leader in different types of multilateral negotiation. They all describe how the EU, represented by the Commission, has aspired to such a role in their respective policy fields (competition, health, trade), but while Guigner (Chapter 13) and Kerremans (Chapter 10) find evidence of proactive leadership, Damro (Chapter 12) discovers a gap between the EU's self-conception and its role performance. We shall return to this issue later in the Conclusion.

Different authors emphasize different roles. This is probably partly due to the specific policy field or issue area each respective scholar is looking at. Those who study the EU's relations to its near neighbourhood (Sedelmeier, Panebianco) tend to stress its roles as stabilizer and as norm promoter. Those who focus on EU declaratory foreign policy towards the less developed countries (K. Smith) put the searchlight on the export of norms and models. Those who research trade or competition policy focus on the role as a champion of multilateral rules and international regulation, but also as a defender of particular economic interests. This suggests that role-sets, to use Aggestam's term (Chapter 1), vary with issue area, in terms of substance, but also in terms of how developed and robust (cf. Sedelmeier) they are. The roles pursued in security policy are, for example, probably less developed, less specific and less widely shared than those to be found in commercial policy. Why this is the case is a question for future research: it may partly be the result of the degree to which internal divisions exist within the EU or other reasons emanating from the EU itself, partly to variations in structural conditions and in expectations from other actors.

Role origins and institutionalization

The preoccupation with the EU's own role conceptions in this volume is reflected also in the suggested origins of the roles that are analysed. Most authors stress what Aggestam (Chapter 1) calls the intentional sources of roles. Manners refers to the 'normative constitution' of the Union, Lucarelli discusses the *telos* of the European integration process as a source of foreign-policy values, and Sjursen ventures that roles may change because of communicative processes within the EU machinery. One main message of Sedelmeier's chapter is that collective policy practice may result in the formation and institutionalization of norms which may then spread from one policy area to another. Kerremans argues that roles may be partly attributed to the complex internal EU multi-level political system, and driven by rational considerations of institutional constraints and possibilities, while Damro points to the part played by institutional path-dependence in explaining the origin of EU roles. According to Damro, the EU transfers solutions that have been successful in its internal integration process to its external relations: for example, a strong internal EU competition policy is mirrored in a preference for binding regulation on the international stage.

What all have in common, despite their differences in attributing the origins of EU roles to either ideational or institutional considerations, is their focus on the internal sources of EU roles. Agency is prioritized at the expense of structure or interaction (cf. Aggestam in this volume). Other interpretations are certainly possible. Adrian Hyde-Price (2006) has, for example, offered a structural realist explanation of the evolution of the EU ESDP. He argues that the development of the ESDP is a function of systemic changes in the structural distribution of power, which has created a unipolar world and a multipolar Europe. Although not speaking in terms of roles, his account can still be translated into such terms: EU roles in the security policy field are then seen as preordained by the existing power balance, leaving little room for agency. Hyde-Price (2006: 233) is careful to stress, however, that structural theory is not determinist: the theory 'does not suggest that states are like prisoners trapped in an iron cage of structural forces'. But neither are they totally free to decide what roles they are to perform on the international arena. Structural forces 'shape and shove' state behaviour but do not determine it.

More concretely, it could be argued, for example, that the fall of the Soviet empire left little choice for the EU but to engage in the role of stabilizer if it wanted to protect its own security and welfare. And the decision of the US government under George W. Bush to pursue a primarily unilateralist strategy, thereby abdicating its leadership role in many multilateral settings, created a leadership gap where expectations that the EU would assume such a role became extremely strong.

In our view, future research should pay much more attention to the complex and dynamic interplay of structural forces, including structurally driven expectations, and intentional sources of roles. Furthermore, empirical studies are needed that describe how roles are chiselled out and shaped over time as a result of interaction in multilateral fora. We believe that role theory has special potential to capture the intricate interplay between agency and structural forces, allowing also social processes of learning and communication that may shape roles and role performance.

Role performance and impact

Another prominent theme in this volume is a critical comparison of role conceptions with role performance. Many contributors contrast the EU's proclaimed self-conceptions with what it actually does in world politics. Jørgensen finds that the performance of the EU role as a multilateralist is 'variable', as the Union is engaged in unilateral and bilateral strategies as well as in multilateral ones. Panebianco explores and evaluates the performance and impact of the EU as a promoter of human rights and democracy through regional co-operation with its Mediterranean partners. The conclusion is that the impact has been meagre. The explanation offered is multi-faceted: first, adherence to the Barcelona Declaration is basically voluntary and the EU has been loath to introduce sanctions on its partners; second, in the absence of membership prospects, too few incentives – for example, in terms of financial resources – have been offered to induce compliance; third, different EU institutions have sent contradictory signals; fourth, the civil society-oriented approach of the Commission has been unsuccessful, in the absence of government support in the Mediterranean states for such grass-roots actors.

Taking up a similar theme, Karen Smith analyses deficiencies in EU role performance when enacting the role of a proactive cosmopolitan – a promoter of liberal values and norms – in its relations with geographically distant Third World countries. She detects a high degree of inconsistency in EU role performance, and a tendency to formulate lowest-common-denominator policies, and attributes these shortcomings to the incapacity among member states to agree on far-reaching sanctions that might damage their political or commercial interests. Chad Damro is also critical of EU role performance. Evidence from the WTO negotiations in Cancún, not least the limited impact that the EU seems to have had on the negotiation outcome, suggests that a gap exists between the Union's role conception as a leader in multilateral competition policy and its actual role performance.

These contributions to the volume may indicate that we could talk about a 'conception–performance gap' in addition to the 'capability–expectations gap' introduced by Chris Hill (1993, 1998). Not only is there a discrepancy between what other actors expect from the Union, considering its size, resources and presence, and what they actually perceive they receive from the Union, but there is also in many policy areas a large distance between the roles the EU proclaims it will perform and actual role performance as perceived by outsiders. EU external policy is often seen to be inconsistent – both across policy domains or institutional contexts ('horizontal inconsistency') and when comparing declaratory and operational aspects of roles ('vertical inconsistency'). Self-declared leadership roles are often marred by perceived 'double standards' or role ambiguity. In the light of role theory, this is neither odd nor unexpected. In many concrete international negotiations, outsiders' expectations of leadership, implying proactive efforts to move negotiations forward and concomitant concessions regarding its self-interests, are confronted with 'domestic' expectations that the EU should play the role of defender of EU values or interests. To take WTO negotiations on trade as an example, others' expectations that the EU should engage in a leadership role meet with demands from internal actors that the Union should promote human rights and environmental concerns but also that it should protect the interests of EU producers. Such diverse role expectations, leading to *role conflict* (cf. Aggestam in this volume) are not easy to handle. The result is either change, given any actor's desire for cognitive consistency, or an uneasy balancing between competing demands resulting in continuing perceived inconsistency.

It should be emphasized, however, that EU does not experience such problems in all areas (geographical or issue-based). As pointed out by Sedelmeier (Chapter 7), the degree of inconsistency varies with the *robustness* of EU roles; when these are specific and based on shared values they are more consistent (and therefore more effective) than when they are vague and based on common values only. EU policy towards Eastern and Central Europe is one example of a relatively robust policy. And Panebianco (Chapter 8) contrasts the EU's inconsistent policies towards its southern Mediterranean neighbours with its more resolute and robust strategy towards Turkey (informed by an accession perspective).

Despite the attention given to role performance, the chapters in this volume have relatively little to say about role impact. Our knowledge about the EU's ability to achieve desired effects, in terms of (among other factors) effectiveness (goal realization), efficiency (gains versus costs) and legitimacy, is scarce. The authors' inclination to stress inconsistencies and incoherence in EU policy can of course be interpreted as signs of ineffectiveness. But we still have little knowledge about the wider implications of EU role behaviour. How is the impact of EU external policy perceived by its negotiating partners and by its policy targets in various policy areas and in different geographical arenas? Does the Union have a long-term 'civilizing' impact on the world arena because of its peculiarities as an international actor? Is the EU seen as an agent of international structural change (cf. Keukeleire 2003), as a guardian of the multilateral order or merely as acting as a 'traditional' Great Power with an emphasis on self-interests? This theme is linked to evaluations of both short- and long-term consequences of EU role-taking. Are responses to and feedback on EU role performance leading to adaptation or to reinforcement? Is the result role multiplication and diversification, or role specialization, where the EU increasingly takes on a limited number of selected tasks in the international system? Once again, a call for more research is warranted.

The EU, role theory and international relations

At the beginning of this volume we raised three themes as the basis of our exploration of role theory and the EU's international activities. First, we argued that the EU presents a number of puzzles about the nature of international 'actorness', and specifically in terms of the goals and values it pursues, the configuration of political instruments it deploys, and the implications of its distinctive institutional construction. Second, we argued that role theory could provide a way into an understanding of these puzzles, and a source of propositions that could lead to further empirical and conceptual development. Third, we suggested that this kind of exploration by a diverse group of scholars focusing on certain key questions could inform broader debates about theory and policy, about ontological and epistemological differences and about levels of analysis. On the basis of the overview provided in this Conclusion, we can say the following about each of these themes:

- First, that each of the contributions in its own way has illuminated key aspects of the distinctiveness of the EU as an international actor. Without rehearsing any of the detailed findings reviewed above, we can say that the contributions to the volume raise significant new questions about and provide insights into the goals and values of the EU's in the international arena, the ways in which the EU's international activities are shaped by its available instruments, and the impact on those activities of the EU's institutional make-up. We have gained a fuller understanding of the variability of these elements, and of the ways in which they enter into specific relationships or policy domains.
- Second, that role theory does provide a fruitful way of juxtaposing and on occasion integrating the study of EU international activities, because of its focus on key questions about role conceptions, role origins and institutionalization, and role performance and impact. As noted above, the volume takes us further in some of these areas than in others, and one task of future research should be to focus on the 'gaps' we have identified, in particular those relating to role impact, as well as on the key relationships we have uncovered, such as those between expectations and performance.
- Finally, we feel that the ways in which the diverse contributors to this volume have addressed the questions we posed, adjusted and adapted their perspectives and recognized the value in the focus on role theory provides substantial justification for our belief that such an analytical focus would throw light on the contributions to be made by competing or complementary approaches. The question of role provides an opportunity for different ontological and epistemological positions to be juxtaposed and explored, and for areas of mutual rein-

forcement to be identified. In the same way it can enable us to explore important questions about theory and policy (and also about what might be termed 'policy-maker theory' as expressed through understandings and intentions in relation to role conceptions and expectations), and about the significance of levels of analysis (for example the relationship between the internal generation of role conceptions and expectations and their pursuit in a number of institutional and political arenas).

References

Hyde-Price, A. (2006) '"Normative" Power Europe: A Realist Critique', *Journal of European Public Policy*, 13 (2): 217–34.

Keukeleire, S. (2003) 'The European Union as a Diplomatic Actor: Internal, Traditional and Structural Diplomacy', *Diplomacy and Statecraft*, 14 (3): 31–56.

Index